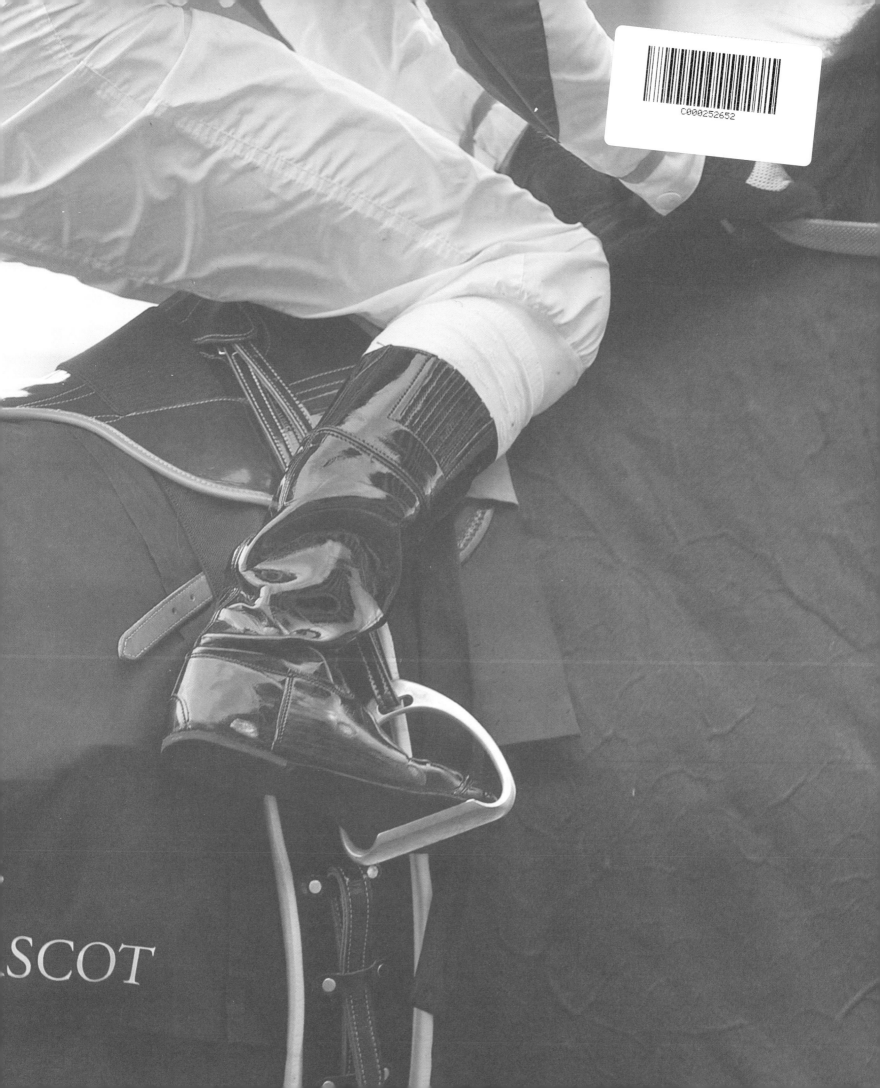

SCOT

FASHION
AT
ROYAL ASCOT

FASHION
AT
ROYAL ASCOT

THREE CENTURIES OF THOROUGHBRED STYLE

JAMES SHERWOOD

Forewords by
The Duke of Devonshire and Amanda Wakeley

WITH 439 ILLUSTRATIONS, 368 IN COLOUR

Thames & Hudson

PAGE 2
HM Queen Elizabeth II arrives
in the Parade Ring at Royal Ascot
in 2010.

PAGE 3
The Queen's colours are always
scrutinized and copied by the
ladies of the Royal Enclosure;
2010 was the year to think pink.

PAGES 4–5
Two gentlemen (possibly lords?)
leaping on the trackside Royal
Enclosure lawn.

PAGE 6
In 1932, a lady simply wasn't
dressed if she wasn't swathed in
furs. Here, an elegant Royal Ascot
racegoer sports an arctic fox-fur
'chubby' stole, as popularized by
glamour goddess Joan Crawford
in the definitive fashion film of
the year, *Letty Lynton*.

PAGE 7
An aerial view of the second day
of racing at Royal Ascot 2007
with a lady holding on to her
audacious scarlet 'flying saucer'
hat. Her peep-toe polka-dot
platform shoes with cork wedge
soles are a classic style patented
by 'shoemaker of dreams' Salvatore
Ferragamo in 1937. Despite
sometimes hazardous conditions
during the Royal Procession, the
Queen has never lost a hat at Ascot.

PAGE 8
A view from the Grandstand of the
dividing fence between the elegant
Royal Enclosure lawn, where formal
day dress and morning coats
are mandatory, and the densely
populated Grandstand Admissions
Lawn, where lounge suits, shirts
and ties are encouraged.

For Suzi Perry and Katy Thomas
My leading ladies at Royal Ascot

First published in the United Kingdom in 2011 by Thames & Hudson Ltd,
181A High Holborn, London WC1V 7QX

Copyright © 2011 James Sherwood

Jacket and book design: Peter Dawson, www.gradedesign.com

British Library Cataloguing-in-Publication Data

A catalogue record for this book is available from the British Library

ISBN 978-0-500-51596-9

Printed and bound by EBS – Editoriale Bortolazzi Stei s.r.l., Verona, Italy

The opinion and comments expressed in this book are those of the author.

To find out about all our publications, please visit
www.thamesandhudson.com. There you can subscribe to
our e-newsletter, browse or download our current catalogue,
and buy any titles that are in print.

ACKNOWLEDGMENTS

In addition to all the marvellous ladies and gentlemen named and photographed
in this book, the author would particularly like to thank HG the Duke of
Devonshire, Her Majesty's Representative at Royal Ascot, and Amanda Wakeley
for writing two superb forewords for *Fashion at Royal Ascot*. Thank you to
Deborah, Dowager Duchess of Devonshire, for permitting me to reprint
a photograph from her private collection, to Jasper Conran for the costume
sketches for his production of *My Fair Lady*, Don Rouse and the Hardy Amies
Archive for sketches of the Queen, and Stephen Jones and Philip Treacy for
allowing me access to their photographic archives. Thank you also to Kerry
Taylor Auctions for the exquisite fashion still life shots that enhance this book
immeasurably.

At Ascot, my sincerest thanks to the Trustees, fashion maestro Gary England
and marketing manager Emily Pearce. At Thames & Hudson, my gratitude as
always to publisher Lucas Dietrich for trusting that *Fashion at Royal Ascot* would
be a winner and to art director Peter Dawson, editor Jennie Condell, production
controller Jane Cutter and Adélia Sabatini for working like Trojans to produce
this book at full gallop. My readers are Keith Levett, Helen Ball, Jane Hurring,
James Shepherd, Patricia Carruthers, Rosy Runciman, Stephen Pulvirent and
Mrs T (Mrs Dominic Thomas). My Saint Martins mentor, Bobby Hillson, cast her
discerning gimlet eye over the layouts and made her usual rapier-sharp, accurate
critiques. Finally, thanks to the art and book dealers of Cecil Court: Tracie Brett,
David Drummond, Natalie Galustian and Storeys.

www.james-sherwood.com

CONTENTS

FOREWORD

THE DUKE OF DEVONSHIRE KCVO, CBE, DL
HER MAJESTY'S REPRESENTATIVE AT ASCOT

It is my great pleasure to be writing the foreword to our first official retrospective of Royal Ascot fashions through the ages in this, our tercentenary year.

Through the reigns of twelve monarchs, Royal Ascot has been synonymous with world-class racing, tradition, heritage, pageantry, society and, of course, fashion.

Ascot racecourse was founded in 1711 by Queen Anne in a small clearing of Windsor Forest known as Ascot Heath. On the eve of the historic first meeting on 11 August, Jonathan Swift wrote of Miss Forrester, a maid of honour to Queen Anne, whose unorthodox dress choice was commented on by the monarch. Royal Ascot as we know it and the formal dress code that applies today were still some way away, but perhaps this anecdote serves to illustrate that the tone for Ascot's unique association with dress etiquette was set from the very beginning.

Ascot's history has been defined by the stars that have graced the track, from early icons of the turf like Eclipse and Gimcrack through to legends of the modern era, such as seven-times Royal Ascot winner Brown Jack and, latterly, quadruple Gold Cup winner Yeats. Alongside the sporting action, the history of fashion has been played out on Ascot's famous lawns, punctuated by defining Royal Meetings, many traced within the pages of this book, and probably none better known than the 'Black Ascot' of 1910.

Whilst the Royal Enclosure and its dress code remain fundamental to the identity of Royal Ascot, long gone are the days of classes divided, as the Royal Meeting in the twenty-first century attracts people from all walks of life and from all over the world, united in the love of racing and the excitement of dressing to impress. One of the most noticeable and pleasing aspects of modern Royal Ascot is to see how much care and pride people in all our enclosures take in what they wear to a day at this unique racecourse. Royal Ascot is unequivocally the most famous race meeting and the most stylish fashion event in the world of sport.

I step down from my role as Her Majesty's Representative after the 2011 Royal Meeting with fourteen years of very happy memories and I wish my successor, Johnny Weatherby, all the very best in a role that it has been an honour and privilege to perform.

OPPOSITE
Peregrine Cavendish, His Grace the 12th Duke of Devonshire and Her Majesty's Representative at Ascot between 1997 and 2011. He is photographed with the Royal Ascot Greencoats, whose forest-green velvet livery tailored by Denman & Goddard echoes the livery of the royal Yeoman Prickers (huntsmen) employed by the Master of the Buckhounds in Queen Anne's reign.

FOREWORD

AMANDA WAKELEY OBE

I don't think there is anything more alluring than a woman wearing the right hat with elegance and poise, and Royal Ascot is undoubtedly the fashion moment for great British millinery. You cannot think of Royal Ascot without thinking of fashion. It is terrific fun; it showcases contemporary elegance and it enhances the atmosphere of the Royal Meeting. I have shown my collection at Royal Ascot twice in recent years and it is wonderful to be included in such a prestigious occasion.

I attended my first Royal Meeting in my twenties and, because of my passion for fashion, I made a point of researching the dos and don'ts for the Royal Enclosure. In those days, the rules of engagement were definitely stricter: no trouser suits, no open-toe shoes and you had to wear tights or stockings. Those rules have relaxed slightly and I don't consider that a bad thing.

However, there is something quite charming in the fact that the Royal Enclosure is still fairly strict with codes of dress. You don't have to apply for Royal Enclosure badges if you want to bend the rules. I like that the rules are laid down by the court and that this quintessentially British occasion has not allowed standards to slip. For ladies, the real challenge is very much a balancing act between the dress or suit and the hat. Stephen Jones or Philip Treacy might not agree, but certain dresses do work better with hats than others.

I love the fact that Ascot can really celebrate millinery as well as beautifully cut dresses and suits. For me, if you are celebrating millinery you need to keep the rest simple: cleaner and more understated. It is either all about the dress, in which case you opt for sharp, simple millinery, or it's all about the fantastic hat, and then you need a very minimal silhouette.

Everyone makes a huge effort in their own way, but I would stress that dressing for Ascot is not costume. You should be wearing a sublime dress or suit that you would wear in normal life. It should be about beautiful, contemporary, glamorous clothing. There have been comments about celebrities attending Royal Ascot, but I do think that when they get it right – the hair, the make-up, the hat, the dress – beautifully dressed stars up the game. Elegantly attired people can only be positive for Ascot, as this handsome book proves, skilfully walking us through three hundred rather thrilling years of social and sartorial history.

OPPOSITE
Miss Amanda Wakeley, a keen racegoer and fashion leader at Royal Ascot, who has shown her collection in several Royal Ascot fashion shows.

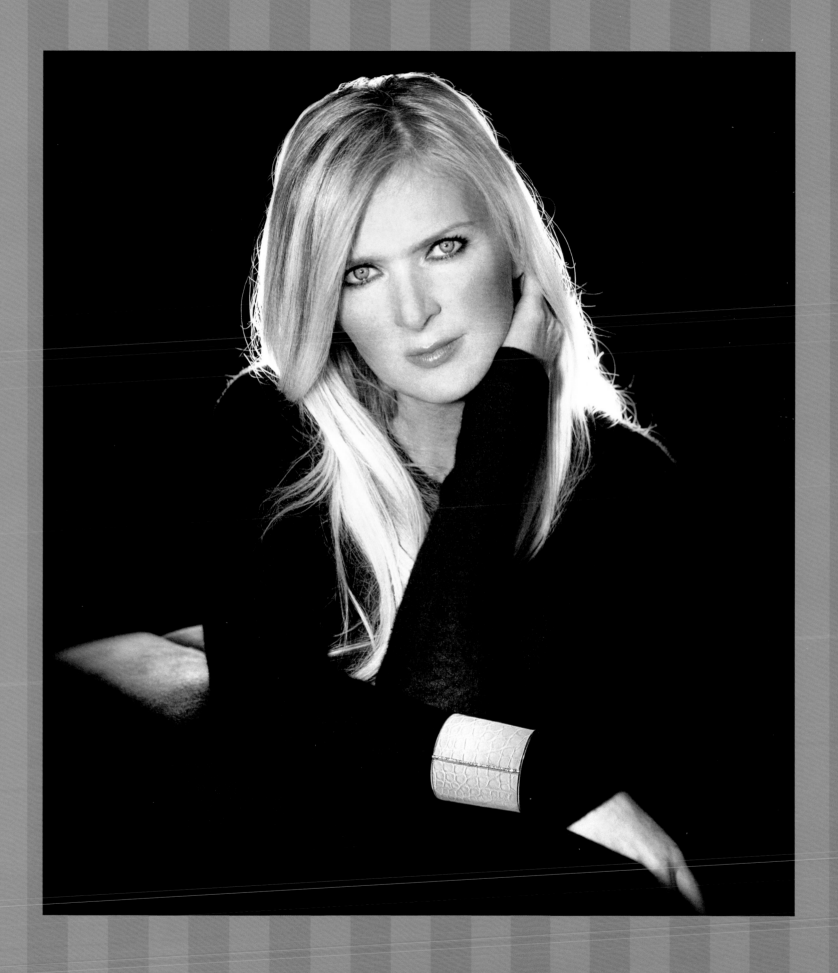

INTRODUCTION

IN 2011, ASCOT, THE WORLD'S MOST FAMOUS RACECOURSE, FOUNDED BY QUEEN ANNE, CELEBRATES ITS TERCENTENARY. In those three hundred years, the world's most influential, fashionable and, perhaps, hedonistic ladies and gentlemen have gathered annually for Royal Ascot in the Royal Enclosure as guests of the monarch to observe superlative flat racing and, of course, each other.

Royal Ascot is unique in the world of the turf in that fashion plays an equal part in the week's proceedings, alongside the thoroughbreds that race for their owners and trainers. Ascot is the only race meeting where codes of dress and manners are led by the monarch. For the past sixty years, the monarch in question has been HM Queen Elizabeth II, who is perhaps equal to her great-grandfather, King Edward VII, in her love for horses and knowledge of flat racing.

Traditionally, those wishing for Royal Enclosure badges must be recommended by social lions who have attended Ascot for decades, if not for generations, though current rules dictate that a member of four years' standing may nominate. These golden tickets may only be acquired by writing to Her Majesty's Representative at the Ascot Authority:

presently the 12th Duke of Devonshire, Peregrine 'Stoker' Cavendish. A previous King's Representative was purported to divide Enclosure requests into three separate files: 'certainly', 'perhaps' and 'certainly not'.

Even in the early decades of the twentieth century, acceptance or, more to the point, exile from the Royal Enclosure was a social marker that could make or destroy a reputation. When the infamous five-times divorcee Idina, Countess of Errol, bagged her third husband, the Earl of Errol, in 1923, they were told in no uncertain terms that the couple would not be welcome at Royal Ascot ever again. Idina, who was lampooned by Nancy Mitford as 'the Bolter' in her novel *Love in a Cold Climate*, fled to Kenya with the Earl, who was shot dead in 1941.

Changes in attitude as to what is socially acceptable resulted in that rule being considerably relaxed during the course of the twentieth century, but the dress code remains. Royal Ascot is one of the last occasions in the British social calendar where,

The Queen and the Duke of Edinburgh arrive at Royal Ascot 2010 in the distinctive landau (carriage) with its basket-weave panelling. Her Majesty wears the Cullinan V brooch: a heart-shaped 18.8 carat diamond given by the government of South Africa to Queen Mary in 1910. It is the fifth-largest stone of a nine-diamond suite cleaved from the largest diamond ever mined (3,106 carats). Cullinan I and II are set in the Royal Sceptre and the Imperial State Crown respectively. Cullinan III and IV were set by Queen Mary as a brooch known to the royal family as 'Granny's chips'.

Black silk plush or grey felt toppers with black mourning band (introduced at the second 'Black Ascot' of 1910) must be worn at all times in the Royal Enclosure, except when a chap is indoors or when doffed to acknowledge a member of the royal family.

in the Royal Enclosure, formal day dress is required for ladies and morning dress for men. There is no finer sight in modern England than Car Park No. 1 at Royal Ascot on a bright June morning, when members arrive dressed in their best for a day's racing. The sunlight dances on antique black silk top hats as plush as a vinyl record and on the important diamond brooches that ladies deem acceptable to wear for day dress in homage to Her Majesty The Queen.

The Queen is above fashion. Until the death of her mother Queen Elizabeth The Queen Mother, and her glamorous sister Princess Margaret, the Queen demurred from leading or even liking fashion. But since her Golden Jubilee in 2002, when every day's racing from Tuesday to Saturday was deemed royal (hence the dress codes applied even on the weekend people's day), Her Majesty's style has flourished. Aided and abetted by her personal assistant and curator of dress and jewels, Angela Kelly, the Queen is now the leading lady of fashion at the Royal.

Much has been made of the decline in dress codes that has occurred in tandem with the accelerating pace demanded by modern life. Can one really be expected to attend a race meeting in immaculate morning dress regardless of the weather, when Ascot traditionally experiences four seasons of weather in just one week? One needs time or, better still, the services of a valet to negotiate stiff detachable stud collars and perfectly dimpled ties held in place with a single pearl pin. The answer, of course, is: yes, one must. If standards are set, ladies and gentlemen rise to the occasion.

Royal Ascot is by its very nature an elitist occasion, if by 'elite' one means well dressed, well groomed and very well behaved. Naturally, there are exceptions, where guests in their gaudy disguises think anything goes – from bets to inhibitions – and it usually does. However, the lion's share of racegoers know that they are guests of the Queen, and she leads by example. The newspapers will always focus on the exhibitionists who think a satin cocktail frock and a tuft of chicken feathers will pass for formal day dress. They relish the folk who dress up like carnival floats, balancing anything from a lobster to a football on their heads, thinking they are being terribly amusing rather than simply terrible.

In a world slavishly obsessed by third-rate celebrity and youth, it is pleasing, to say the least, that at Royal Ascot a lady in her eighties is the glass of fashion. Ascot is a classless event, but also one that has the highest level of class.

OPPOSITE
A lady studies the form in the Royal Ascot race card wearing a delightful French lavender shot silk dress. In the Royal Enclosure, shoulders must be partially covered by a strap at least one inch thick.

CHAPTER I

QUEEN ANNE TO KING GEORGE IV
The Birth, Fall and Rise of Royal Ascot
1711–1837

'This Queen of England's Augustan Age demonstrated
her love of racing while Ascot was yet a common,
unprinted by the hoof of racehorses. Those pleasant
meadows where loyal multitudes now acclaim the
royal procession were an exclusive rendez-vous for
highwaymen.'

COPE'S ROYAL CAVALCADE OF THE TURF, EDITED BY ALFRED COPE (1953)

THE BIRTH OF ASCOT, THAT MOST GLAMOROUS OF GREAT BRITISH RACECOURSES, coincided with the twilight of the Stuart royal dynasty. By 1711 Queen Anne, the last of her bloodline, was forty-six, morbidly obese, widowed for three years and childless after eighteen miscarriages. Within three years, she would be dead and buried in, as legend has it, a square coffin, so fat had she become; she was hardly the most auspicious founder for what would become the only race meeting in the world as celebrated for fashion as for fillies.

And yet the clichés about Queen Anne do not do justice to a woman so passionate about the turf. She established the first race meeting on Ascot Common on Saturday, 11 August 1711. Earlier that year, *Gulliver's Travels* author Jonathan Swift had observed the Queen riding to hound at Ascot, recorded in his *Journal to Stella*: 'The Queen was abroad today in order to hunt; but, finding it disposed to rain she took to her coach; she hunts in a chaise with one horse, which she drives herself, and drives furiously, like Jehu, and is a mighty hunter, like Nimrod.' Was it this particular ride that inspired Queen Anne to found the first horse race at Ascot?

Queen Anne was genetically disposed to love horses. Her uncle, King Charles II, consolidated the royal stud at Hampton Court Palace, founded the Newmarket races (the Rowley Mile course is named after Charles, or 'Old Rowley' as he was known, after his favourite racehorse) and built a palace there with a connecting passage to the residence of his mistress, Nell Gwynn. An inveterate gambler like her uncle, Queen Anne was equally aware that monarchy was strengthened by spectacle: not only on state occasions, but also in public ceremony, such as at a race meeting, where she could see and be seen by all classes of her kingdom.

'Resplendent in full regalia, [she] could rise to the occasion,' writes Maureen Waller in *Sovereign Ladies: The Six Reigning Queens of England* (2006). Not that the inaugural race meeting at Ascot immediately established the traditional symphony of royalty, high fashion and horse racing that would come to characterize it over a century later, in the reign of Queen Victoria. Although Alfred Cope describes the event thus: 'The Queen, with a brilliant suite, drove over from Windsor Castle to Ascot Common on the 11th of August … [and] proceeded along the Common with her long train of courtiers and other attendants,' the event itself was as rackety as Queen Anne's skills in a horse-drawn chaise. In addition to the races, cockfighting, gambling tents and gluttony entertained the crowd.

ANNE.

Anna R

As for attire, early eighteenth-century fashion was ostensibly led by the Versailles court of the ageing Louis XIV, who on his death in 1715 had reigned for seventy-two years. With Queen Anne on the English throne and Madame de Maintenon presiding at Versailles, fashion desperately needed a leader. For aristocratic ladies, court dress varied little, be it for a morning levee or court ball, the only difference being the weight of fabric worn for outdoor activities such as a day at the races.

Men still dressed like the Queen's uncle, King Charles II, wearing full-skirted court coats in heavy brocades with deep, frilled cuffs and lace jabots. Breeches and long waistcoats were the form, as were shoes with high heels, huge buckles and – in a very early precursor of Christian Louboutin's signature stilettos today – red soles. Generous curled, full-bottomed wigs also echoed the appearance of the late King.

For women, perhaps in homage to Queen Anne's fuller figure, the 'sack dress', otherwise known as the loose silk 'Watteau dress' after its appearance in the paintings

ABOVE
A fine pair of brocaded silk shoes with watered silk ribbon laces, c. 1714–20. Social rank was denoted by the shoe. King Louis XIV decreed that only those in royal favour could wear a red heel, a tradition later taken up by Christian Louboutin, whose signature stiletto soles are crafted in red leather.

OPPOSITE, LEFT
Fashion was led by the French court and remained relatively unchanged for a century. Gentlemen would have worn variations on the embroidered French silk tailcoat and breeches such as this young man's striped velvet ensemble, cut in the 1780s.

RIGHT

On the death of Louis XIV in 1715, women's dress became looser. The English court adopted the 'sack' or 'Watteau' dress, with its distinctive train falling from the back of the neckline in box pleats, in the year after Queen Anne's death in 1714. The style endured until well into the 1760s, as seen in this *robe à la française* of Chinese lampas satin, *c.* 1760.

of Antoine Watteau, cloaked at the back and balanced almost off-the-shoulder to reveal a magnificent, creamy décolletage, was de rigueur. 'The characteristic eighteenth-century sleeve ended just above or just below the elbow and was wide enough for the chemise-sleeve to emerge from it, with its ruffles of lace,' according to James Laver's *Costume & Fashion* (1969).

An interesting anomaly introduced to the English court by Queen Anne's stepmother, Mary of Modena – a true beauty despite being a feckless creature – were masculine-cut, gold-embroidered or brocade riding coats and breeches, worn with a lace jabot and flowing balloon sleeves for ease of movement when riding astride. It was a style that had first been set by the sapphic Queen Christina of Sweden in the previous century. The fashion for royal ladies to dress *en travesti* when riding seemed particularly well suited to the lifestyles of the more controversial royal consorts. Mary of Modena had gone into exile with her husband, ex-King James II, in 1689. As late as 1771, Queen Marie Antoinette of France was painted by Elizabeth Vigée Le Brun riding astride in a 'mannish riding habit'. 'For her expeditions on horseback, she abandoned long, flowing skirts of the side-saddle rider for the slim breeches – and the straddled mount – of a man', writes Caroline Weber in *Queen of Fashion: What Marie Antoinette Wore to the Revolution* (2006). She scandalized Versailles.

To be painted in men's riding clothes was a political action – particularly for a childless Dauphine – that ultimately afforded Marie Antoinette little sympathy, seeming to confirm the rumours of romantic liaisons with her ladies-in-waiting, the pretty Princesse de Lamballe and Madame de Polignac. The rumours haunted the Queen until 1789, when she was forcibly removed from Versailles and imprisoned in Paris, and the Princesse de Lamballe was torn limb from limb by an angry mob, with her severed head paraded on a spike beneath the Queen's prison window.

Queen Anne's death in 1714 was more gentle and prosaic: as she lay dying, she was informed that one of the royal horses was galloping to victory at York. This scenario was curiously echoed nearly 200 years later, when King Edward VII's final breath acknowledged congratulations for his horse Witch of the Air's win at the 1910 Derby.

The early Hanoverian kings, George I and George II, were not friends of the turf. German-born George I (whose mother was a granddaughter of King James I) could barely speak English and never graced Ascot races with his presence. His successor did attend in 1730, but took no pleasure in this most British of pastimes. It was George II's son, the soldier, compulsive gambler and roisterer William Augustus, Duke of

Queen of European fashion, Marie Antoinette of France, painted by Elisabeth Vigée Le Brun in a portrait titled *Marie Antoinette à la Rose* (1783). Le Brun had scandalized society earlier that year by painting the Queen '*en deshabille*' in one of her chemises, signifying her hatred of the stiff, formal court dress of the *ancien régime*. The portrait led to accusations that the Queen lacked both dignity and moral compass. Thus *Marie Antoinette à la Rose* depicts the Queen in an extravagant lace-trimmed blue-grey silk *robe à la française* with her hair powdered, curled and dressed high from the forehead with a feathered court bonnet.

Cumberland (also known as 'Sweet William', 'the Butcher of Culloden' or 'Stinking Billy' depending on who you spoke to), who championed Ascot during his father's reign.

The Duke was one of the early members of the Jockey Club (founded around 1750) and lived at Cumberland Lodge in Windsor Great Park in his capacity as ranger. He led London society back to Ascot, so that in 1752 the Duke of Bedford received a letter from his friend Mr Rigby declaring that during Ascot week 'I could find no soul to dine or sup with' in London because all the fashionable world was at Ascot.

It is slightly misleading to say that men's Ascot fashion was led by beaux. Bath's self-appointed Master of Ceremonies, Richard 'Beau' Nash, dictated etiquette and dress from the early eighteenth century until his death in 1762. However, Nash was what we would now consider a patched, powdered, bewigged fop; rather different from the severe, correct and minimally chic style established by George 'Beau' Brummell at the end of the eighteenth century.

Marie Antoinette, played by Kirsten Dunst in the 2006 Sofia Coppola film of the same name, awaits her lover Count Axel Fersen in her small private château – Le Petit Trianon – in the grounds of Versailles, wearing only her underskirts and the white ostrich feathers popularized in England by the Queen's friend, Georgiana, Duchess of Devonshire.

OVERLEAF, LEFT

Top left: David Morier's *An Equestrian Portrait of King George III, Wearing the Order of the Garter* (1769). The King is wearing formal court dress as he would in the Royal Procession at Ascot, or when he would ride out accompanying Queen Charlotte in the carriages.

Top right: Flaunting, extravagant heir to the throne George, Prince of Wales – or 'Prinny', as he was known – drawn by John Raphael Smith after Thomas Gainsborough (1783). London's sartorial dictator George 'Beau' Brummell was in the ascendant and the Prince was copying his radical new look of exquisitely cut wool coat, fine lawn cravat, skin-tight riding breeches and boots polished to a vinyl sheen.

Below left: John Doyle's pencil sketch of King George IV in the Royal Procession at Ascot in 1825 masks his multiple chins with a tall velvet stand-collared greatcoat.

Below right: William Augustus, Duke of Cumberland, was an inveterate gambler and a passionate man of the turf. Jean-Baptiste van Loo's portrait (*c.* 1745) depicts him in a scarlet cour coat with heavy gold work embellishment, tricorn hat, ermine-trimmed mantle and swagger stick, and sporting the frilled lace cuffs that were popular in mid-eighteenth-century aristocratic dress.

Of Nash, *Vanity Fair* author William Makepeace Thackeray wrote in *The Four Georges* (1869): 'I should like to have seen the Folly [Nash]. It was a splendid embroidered, beruffled, snuff-boxed, red-heeled, impertinent Folly, and knows how to make itself respected.' Though Nash regulated gambling in the pump room at Bath, it was his ilk as well as the hearties such as the Duke of Cumberland who flocked to mid-Georgian Ascot.

There is no more pertinent mid-eighteenth century artwork than Thomas Gainsborough's famous *Mr and Mrs Andrews* (1750) to demonstrate the contrast between what is expected of males and females in a rural context such as Ascot. While Mr Andrews wears the informal attire of a country gent, Mrs Andrews wears the wide paniered day dress with beribboned lace cuffs and a pert straw hat fashionable in the day. Her heels are high and she carries a decorative lace handkerchief that is more ornament than use.

When King George III ascended the throne in 1860, none could predict he would preside over a sixty-year reign that encompassed revolution in France, independence in America and a valiant attempt to conquer the western world by Emperor Napoleon. For aficionados of the turf, his reign will be remembered for the founding of all five Classic races on the horse racing calendar today: the St Leger, the Oaks, the Derby, the Two Thousand Guineas and the One Thousand Guineas.

The glass of fashion at Ascot in the reign of George III was political hostess, compulsive gambler and friend of 'Prinny', Georgiana, Duchess of Devonshire. Inspired by her friend Queen Marie Antoinette, the Duchess introduced fashions in head apparel to Ascot that have resonance today.

'Whatever she wore became instantly fashionable,' writes Amanda Foreman in *Georgiana, Duchess of Devonshire* (1998). 'Women's hair was already arranged high above the head, but Georgiana took the fashion a step further by creating the three-foot hair tower. She stuck pads of horsehair to her own hair using scented pomade and decorated the top with miniature ornaments. Sometimes she carried a ship in full sail, or an exotic arrangement of stuffed birds and waxed fruit, or even a pastoral tableau with little wooden trees and sheep.'

The Duchess's decorated hair towers are no different in intent, if not elegance of execution, from the ladies who make their own hats today for Royal Ascot, decorated with social scenes pertinent to contemporary culture such as dartboards, billiard tables and footballs; or indeed from the infamous Mrs Shilling wearing such wonders as an Eiffel Tower or giraffe's head hat fashioned by her son, David. There are perhaps only

a few milliners who can match the quality and craft of the Duchess's hair ornaments: Philip Treacy, as witnessed by the black galleon hat he crafted for the late fashion editor Isabella Blow, or Stephen Jones's creations for John Galliano's Christian Dior collections.

The Duchess of Devonshire was a fashion adventuress, introducing the muslin chemise tied at the waist by a ribbon, à la Marie Antoinette playing milkmaids at her toy farm in the grounds of Versailles; and the four-foot-long drooping ostrich feather that eventually morphed into white plumes, traditionally worn by ladies at court and, particularly, debutantes being presented to the monarch.

Queen Charlotte, by contrast, was more conventional and championed the crinoline and high powdered wig of *ancien régime* Versailles. Despite attending Ascot with Queen Charlotte and the royal family, George III showed little more interest in racing than his royal namesakes. His 'personal appearances' at Ascot were calculated to bring him closer physically and metaphorically to his people. According to the *Sporting Magazine* of 1794, 'The royals displayed their accustomed benignity and mingled with that degree of affability amongst all ranks and descriptions.'

Despite the construction of the first permanent stand in 1793, Ascot was still as bawdy as it had been in the era of Queen Anne, with marquees erected to house banqueting, gambling, cockfighting and prizefighting. The atmosphere was more P. T. Barnum circus than the regal high-water mark of the season it would later become. This atmosphere of bawdiness and excess was encouraged by 'Prinny', the future King George IV, whose love for the turf bordered on obsession and for whom the title 'the sport of kings' was coined. It was he who stocked the royal stud at Hampton Court to be the finest in Europe, with the very best jockeys.

By 1808, the 'madness' that would intermittently confine King George III to a straitjacket for the last decade of his reign was manifesting itself. In the same year, a new royal pavilion near the home turn at Ascot was erected. Only those in the royal family, court and royal household were invited to enter. By 1810 'Prinny' had assumed the title of Regent and, according to *Ascot: The History* by Sean Magee with Sally Aird (2002), even Queen Charlotte had to ask her autocratic and egomaniacal son's permission to enter. This was in effect the infancy of what was to become known as the Royal Enclosure.

In 1813, an Act of Enclosure placed Windsor Great Park (and, by definition, Ascot Heath) into the ownership of the Crown Estate. A year later, Ascot played host to a glittering party of royal guests, including Tsar Alexander I of Russia and King Frederick William III of Prussia, as well as Queen Charlotte. There is no record of the

Regent's sartorial Svengali, George 'Beau' Brummell, attending Ascot in Ian Kelly's biography *Beau Brummell: The Ultimate Dandy* (2005). But the man who wrote the rule book for contemporary formal men's attire was a proficient horseman and, one could surmise, would scarcely miss an opportunity such as Ascot to show off both his sartorial superiority and his hold over the Prince Regent, which was soon to be loosened by ignominy, arrogance and debt. The Beau is recorded riding in Rotten Row in London's Hyde Park and dropping such affected epithets as that his riding boots were 'blackened using the finest champagne' (a tradition revived by revered French shoe designer Olga Berluti in the twenty-first century with her infamous Swann Club).

Tempting though it might be to imagine Regency Ascot as populated by exquisitely understated disciples of Beau Brummell, it was more likely dominated by excesses of fashion, as satirized by caricaturists Cruikshank and Gillray. By 1816 Brummell had fled his debts to France, and the Regent – closely followed by the court – reverted to the decadent, overblown court dress of pre-Revolutionary Versailles.

When George IV acceded to the throne in 1820, he immediately set about forming the blueprint for Royal Ascot as we know it today. In 1822, he commissioned celebrated architect John Nash to build a new Royal Stand in the Neoclassical style for the royal family. In 1825, George IV inaugurated the royal carriage procession up the Straight Mile with four carriages and twenty servants in scarlet liveries on horseback. The King's guest of honour in that year was the Duke of Wellington, hero of the Battle of Waterloo, who rode with the King in the first carriage. Queen Elizabeth II continues this tradition, inviting guests such as the Aga Khan, Sheikh Mohammed and senior royals such the Prince of Wales and Duchess of Cornwall to ride in the first carriage.

The death of George IV in 1830 saw a relaxation of the pomp and ceremony at Ascot. New King William IV was observed turning his back on horses at full gallop and his wife, Queen Adelaide, caused great offence by knitting during a race. Journalist and sportswriter Pierce Egan observed in his *Book of Sports and Mirror of Life* (1836) that 'it is at Ascot, delightful Ascot races, where the public have the opportunity of beholding his Majesty and of hearing his remarks without the least reserve'.

'Ascot', Egan continues, 'may be deemed the rallying point for all the nobility and gentry, for miles round Windsor, to pay homage to their beloved monarch. It is also truly interesting to view the King at his ease, divested of the paraphernalia and etiquette of the court, habited like a private gentleman.' Observing Queen Elizabeth II at Royal Ascot more than 180 years later, Egan's comments are equally pertinent.

Top: The Royal Stand at Ascot in the latter years of King William IV's reign (mid-1830s), when the poker bonnet popularized by a young Queen Victoria was in its infancy.

Below left: Gentlemen's riding habit of 1836, sketched on Ascot Common with Windsor Castle in the background. Top hats had become taller in the manner of the stovepipe adopted by Prince Albert, and coats were more waisted with extravagantly cut skirts. Trousers had replaced breeches when a gentleman was not in the saddle.

Below right: The equestrian world inspired late Georgian ladies' fashion. The crinoline had been soundly deflated, as the diaphanous muslin or cotton Empire-line tea dress printed or embroidered with flower sprig motifs took fashion to a more innocent Arcadian and pastoral landscape, compared with the overblown extravagance of *ancien régime* court dress.

THE ROYAL STAND.

Gentlemens Fashions for July, 1834.
Riding Dresses.

Mrs Thornton.

FOUR SEASONS, FIVE DAYS

'In some of the tents women fainted. Four collapsed together in one small tent. Word sped that a man had been killed by lightning in Tattersalls. The real terror showed then. Men went pale. Women gazed on the storm with fascinated horror, deadly white.'

THE *DAILY HERALD* REPORTS ON THE ROYAL ASCOT STORM OF 1930

OPPOSITE AND OVERLEAF
As these photographs and prints from the Royal Ascot Archive demonstrate, the weather is as unpredictable as the racing. George James Cawthorne wrote of the 1887 Queen Victoria Golden Jubilee Ascot in *Royal Ascot: Its History & Its Associations* (1902): 'The race was run in a deluge of rain. … For upwards of an hour the stands presented the appearance of a forest of umbrellas, but the clouds then broke, and the remainder of the sport was carried through in brilliant sunshine.'

As Deborah, Dowager Duchess of Devonshire, writes in her 2010 autobiography *Wait for Me*, 'The invitation [to Windsor Castle] was for five nights and four days' racing. The weather is always a gamble and had to be taken into consideration, but somehow four daytime outfits for the races and five best evening dresses were gathered up.' Though most ladies these days do not have to negotiate five full-length evening dresses and family tiara for Ascot, all must abide by the rule that the weather at the Royal Meeting can, and does, encompass four seasons of British weather in five days. Torrential rain often strikes and the crowd is inevitably disappointed when the Queen is first sighted in the Royal Procession wearing her Burberry rain cape and holding her signature domed 'birdcage' see-through Fulton umbrella, trimmed by royal appointment in the colour of the Queen's dress that day.

Fortunately, Ascot is seldom rained off, and has not been lashed in recent years as it was in the notorious downpour of 1930. As Sean Magee writes in *Ascot: The History*, 'After two races on Wednesday 18 June a more appropriate mode of transport at Ascot would have been Noah's Ark, as the course was ravaged by a storm of Biblical intensity.' In *Five Times Winner* (1968), champion jockey Doug Smith describes the aftermath of this fatal storm: 'The frigid stare of terror, incongruous in painted eyes, melted. Women pinned up their frocks in the manner of charwomen and trooped out. It was almost impossible to find their motor-cars. Once-smart men and women jostled, ran, searched. …Their clothes? They were past caring for them.'

Lightning struck again in 1954 on Gold Cup day. 'As it cut a swathe through the crowd on the Heath side a woman fell dying. Forty-nine others lay injured among the 100 or more knocked flat or hurled in the air,' recalls *Ascot: The History*. 'When the last of the injured had been taken away a twisted and charred umbrella remained. It is believed to have been carried by the woman who died on her way to Windsor hospital.' The woman was Mrs Barbara Batt, who was pregnant with her first child.

Mercifully, rain is the exception rather than the rule; rarely does a season pass without at least one day when the Royal Meeting is bathed in English summer sun. Seen in this light, the thoroughbreds in the parade ring and the smart set promenading in the Royal Enclosure both look their very best.

MARVELLOUS MILLINERY I: THE GLORIOUS HATTERS WHO CROWN ROYAL ASCOT

OPPOSITE
Black-and-white striped organza hat by Philip Treacy, photographed at Ascot 2009 by Philippe Kerlo.

OVERLEAF
There is a fundamental difference between audacious hats by Britain's great milliners and fancy dress worn to attract tabloid attention. In 2009, Disneyland Paris asked Stephen Jones to make an Ascot hat reminiscent of Minnie Mouse ears. Clever Mr Jones created a flying feathered fantasy as modelled by Jasmine Guinness (bottom left) that is more Alfred Hitchcock than Walt Disney. See page 219 for a list of milliners whose work is shown.

'Royal Ascot gives me the opportunity to create and style some of the most amazing hats to suit each and every one of my clients. It's an honour to have them worn at the greatest race meeting in the world.'

PHILIP TREACY (2008)

'Traditional hats are worn as part of an immovable social uniform, whilst the British Social season provides a saviour to couture millinery,' wrote Emma Damon in Amy de la Haye's *The Cutting Edge: 50 Years of British Fashion* (1996). Damon quite rightly makes the point that Ladies' Day at Ascot is the most important daytime event in the social calendar, and quotes royal milliner Frederick Fox in his theory that 'hat wearing has survived only due to royal patronage and the institution of race meetings'.

As master milliner Philip Treacy says, Royal Ascot might even be seen as British millinery's answer to an AGM, but royal patronage and a day at the races are not the sole reasons for which millinery is once again at the top of the agenda for British fashion. London produces the most marvellous milliners: Freddie Fox, Philip Somerville, Stephen Jones, Philip Treacy, Rachel Trevor-Morgan and Cozmo Jenks, to mention only the most established. Stephen Jones worked magic in his collaboration with John Galliano, the former creative director of Christian Dior couture, for fifteen years, and has created hats for international designers as diverse as Jean-Paul Gaultier, Thierry Mugler, Vivienne Westwood, Jasper Conran and Comme des Garçons.

But without the clients and the occasion, millinery would indeed have died. Tastemakers such as Madonna, Lady Gaga, Grace Jones, the late Isabella Blow and Daphne Guinness are all inspirations to the ladies who attend Royal Ascot, and have gone some way towards assassinating the inconsequential fascinator in favour of sculptural, magnificent millinery that takes poise, guts and style to carry off as the crowning glory of formal day dress.

CHAPTER 2

QUEEN VICTORIA TO KING EDWARD VII
Empire Ascot and the Belle Époque
1837–1910

'I found Ascot Week very tiring. After a long afternoon spent greeting acquaintances in the Royal Enclosure there were evening rides in Windsor Forest, which meant changing from diaphanous organdies into a habit. Fortunes were yearly spent on dresses selected as appropriate to a graduated scale of elegance which reached its climax on Thursday; for fashion decreed that one should reserve one's most sumptuous toilette for Gold Cup day.'

ETTIE, LADY DESBOROUGH, ON EDWARDIAN ASCOT, AS QUOTED IN HER AUTOBIOGRAPHY
THE GLITTER & THE GOLD (1953)

THE BRITISH MONARCHY'S POPULARITY HAD REACHED A NADIR WITH
THE DEATH OF KING GEORGE IV. Though relatively innocuous, his brother
William IV's brief reign was overshadowed by the not-too-distant memory of the worst
excesses of his spendthrift, decadent predecessor and equally dissipated siblings. But the
crowds who continued to flock to Ascot already had their hope for the future invested
in the young heir to the throne, Princess Victoria, who first attended Ascot in 1832,
aged thirteen; the same year a drunken sailor called Dennis Collins threw a stone at
her uncle William IV that scored a direct hit to his head.

In 1834, Princess Victoria, accompanied by her mother, the manipulative Duchess
of Kent, rode with the King and Queen in the first carriage as it processed towards
Ascot. In her diary, the Princess recorded: 'I was very much amused indeed at the races.'
William IV set the precedent for only attending opening Tuesday and Thursday (the day
of the big races) rather than the full four days in June, which Victoria was to emulate.

Though diminutive and on the plain side, it would be unfair to think of Princess
Victoria as a younger version of the dour, reclusive widow she became in the latter
half of her reign. The Queen led Ascot fashion and set a tone of high-spirited fun at the
races in her youth, even shattering a window in the Royal Box one year as she cheered
home a winner. In 1838, her first year at Ascot as monarch, she was accompanied by
her Prime Minister Lord Melbourne, on whom she had something of a crush; she
wrote that he 'never left the stand, and stood near me near the window in the beginning.
I was so happy that he should be seen with me on such public occasions. He does not
care the least about the races but yet was amused and pleased. I stayed [for] five races.'

As *Cope's Royal Cavalcade of the Turf* records, 'Little Vic' was 'dressed in a pink
silk slip, over which was a lace dress or frock; she wore a white drawn gauze bonnet,
trimmed with pink ribands [sic], and ornamented with artificial roses both inside and
out. She repeatedly during the day conversed with great liveliness with those around
her, and surveyed the races through a double opera glass; and if we are not misinformed,
occasionally entered into the spirit of the scene and indulged in a few bets.'

The gaudiness of late Hanoverian fashion was exorcised practically overnight at
the prompting of the new young Queen. Following her example, the lace headdresses
and ludicrously elaborate curled hair of her Aunt Adelaide were replaced by a demure
'poker bonnet' that shielded a lady's face (ergo her modesty) from all but those
standing directly in front of her.

PRECEDING PAGES, LEFT
Sandy Powell's Oscar-winning
costumes for 2009 film *Young Victoria*
perfectly capture the submissive,
demure and dainty fashions
introduced by Queen Victoria
when she came to the throne in
1837. Here actress Emily Blunt
wears Powell's interpretation of
Queen Victoria's wedding dress.
The large sapphire brooch was
given to the Queen by Prince
Albert on the day before their
wedding in 1840.

ABOVE
Mrs Gertrude Shilling, the 'Ascot
Mascot', wears a super-sized
interpretation of the Victorian poker
bonnet by her son, milliner David
Shilling. Mrs Shilling's maximum
millinery was a highlight of the Royal
Meeting and bets were placed as to
whether her hats would actually fit
between the Royal Enclosure gates
each year.

OPPOSITE
Stephen Jones and Dame Vivienne
Westwood reinterpret mid-Victorian
fashion for the icon image of the
2011 Ascot tercentenary advertising
campaign. Jones's poker bonnet soars
sky-high, while the crinoline
with puff sleeves is supported by
tulle underskirts rather than the
crinoline cage popularized by
couturier Charles Frederick Worth.

Ladylike cashmere and paisley shawls became the fashion, as did vast, bell-shaped skirts supported by layers of petticoats that were designed to make a woman look as neat, petite and fragile as a porcelain doll. The sheer volume of women's skirts kept men at arm's length, while exaggerated puffed sleeves replaced by neater fitted ones sitting demurely on the wrist suggested submissiveness. Led by Prince Albert, men's tailoring became funereally monotone, with the tall silk top hat accentuating a gentleman's stature in comparison to the dainty lady on his arm.

In 1840, Prince Albert first accompanied his new wife and cousin the Queen in the leading carriage. *The Times* of 1842 reported that 'the great attraction to the course this day was not so much the racing, though it must be admitted there was no want of that, but the presence of Her Majesty and her illustrious Consort. The recent dastardly attempt of the wretched assassin [who tried but failed to shoot the pregnant Queen on a carriage ride] … had awakened a spirit of loyalty which everybody was anxious to testify on all occasions of the appearance of Her Majesty and Prince Albert in public.' Assassination attempts may have been responsible for the enclosure of the lawn in front

ABOVE

Sheet music for Charles Merion's ditty 'The Great Racing Song' written for Victorian music hall star Miss Annie Adams to perform, *c.* 1875. The scene is a picnic on Ascot Common with the lady in her carriage wearing a very similar humbug stripe gown to the Charles Frederick Worth (pictured, left), with sheer fabric added to cover embonpoint to neck and billowing white balloon sleeves added for modesty.

LEFT

A peachy pink-and-white striped moire gown, *c.* 1865, designed by king of the crinoline Charles Frederick Worth. Worth's gowns were cut to make it appear that a lady was quite literally walking on air. The silhouette is nostalgic for eighteenth-century court dress as worn at Versailles, but it is lighter, with fewer petticoats beneath.

A young Queen Victoria and Prince Albert in the Royal Stand at Ascot, *c.* 1840. In the years before the crinoline cage, multiple layers of petticoats were added to give full skirts sufficient shape.

of the Royal Stand in 1845: the true beginning of the Royal Enclosure that today still holds such cachet for all those fortunate enough to secure a badge. Queen Victoria and Prince Albert continued to attend two days of racing at Ascot in June throughout the 1850s, the decade in which fashion first equalled, if not took precedence over, horse racing. The reasons for this were threefold.

In 1856, aniline (synthetic) dyes were patented that allowed for fabrics to carry brilliant colours, such as magenta, scarlet, sapphire-blue and ink-black, which had only been achievable with natural dyes at great expense of time and money. In the same year, American manufacturer W. S. Thompson patented a caged frame that liberated women from weighty crinoline petticoats and allowed skirts to billow like hot-air balloons.

Though modern women may find little liberating about a skirt the size of a barrage balloon and a waist so tightly laced and corseted as to render a lady in a constant state of faintness, the caged crinoline of the 1850s made dresses of the era

S. M. L'IMPÉRATRICE EUGÉNIE

as light and pliable as a kitten's tail in comparison with their layered, lumpen predecessors.

Then, in 1858, Englishman Charles Frederick Worth opened his eponymous couture house in Paris and established himself as the king of the new crinoline silhouette. Pioneer Worth was the first designer to elevate himself above the role of dressmaker and dictate fashion to his customers, who – like Royal Enclosure badge holders – had to be recommended to the house by an illustrious client.

No client was more illustrious than the Empress Eugénie, consort of Emperor Napoleon III of France, whose Second Empire regime had risen to power in a coup in 1851. Worth was the court dressmaker to the Empress, who, though not as classically beautiful as the goddess-like but neurotic Empress Elisabeth of Austria, had elegance and poise that perfectly modelled Worth's crinolines. The evidence is captured in court paintings by Franz Xavier Winterhalter of crinoline queens the Empress Eugénie, Empress Elisabeth and England's Queen Victoria, who commanded her court dressmaker Elizabeth Gieve to imitate the scale, grandeur and romanticism of Worth's signature style.

Winterhalter never painted Queen Victoria as dressed for Ascot, but his dreamlike (and idealized) portraits of the British royal ladies do go some way towards reflecting the prettiness and glamour of the royal race meeting in the 1850s. It is indeed tragic for Ascot, not to mention the Queen, that in 1861 Prince Albert died, plunging Victoria and her court into a mourning from which she never recovered. Queen Victoria abandoned Ascot for the next forty years, never to return.

Though the Edwardian era historically began in 1901 with the death of the Queen, it began in fashion as early as 1863, when the twenty-one-year-old Prince of Wales, also known as Bertie, first attended Ascot on behalf of his widowed mother, who had retreated into the shadows of her castle at Balmoral and Osborne House on the Isle of Wight. The Prince had married Princess Alexandra of Denmark (sister to the Empress Dagmar of Russia) three months previously and she made her fashion debut by her husband's side at the 1863 Ascot.

OPPOSITE

Queen Victoria, painted to her commission in 1842 by Franz Xavier Winterhalter, wears a diamond-and-sapphire tiara (worn unconventionally low on the head) designed by Prince Albert and set by Garrard, and now in the collection of the Earl and Countess of Harewood. The Queen wears an ivory duchess satin off-the-shoulder gown trimmed with lace, and a matching Honiton lace shawl, made fashionable at the English court by Her Majesty.

ABOVE

Eugénie, Empress of France, consort of Emperor Napoleon III, befriended Queen Victoria on reciprocal royal visits to Paris and London in the 1850s. The elegant Spaniard introduced Charles Frederick Worth to the fashionable courts of Europe.

R. Caton Woodville.

15

Princess Alexandra was a rather gay, some said childlike young lady, who – in sharp contrast to the short, stocky Queen – had a statuesque figure that admirably showed off the late-Victorian fashions, many of which she introduced to high society. Of her first Ascot, *The Times* reported: 'The Princess, who now wears half-mourning, took her place at the window of the Royal Stand and, with a little book of the races in her hand, gave herself up to the enjoyment of the scene with the most vivid interest.'

By the end of the 1860s, at the instigation of Worth, the crinoline had flattened at the front and become more exaggerated at the rear, rising into a pronounced bustle replete with bows, frills and furbelows that fell into an extravagant train. As the century progressed, the bodice became longer and more tightly laced over the corset to produce the S-bend silhouette so beloved of Princess Alexandra.

OPPOSITE

A tinted etching from the *Illustrated London News* by R. Caton Woodville (1885) shows Victorian noblemen and women riding (and showing off their Savile Row-tailored riding habits) in London's Rotten Row, a tradition dating back to the Regency and the era of Beau Brummell.

RIGHT

A lady's riding habit, *c.* 1890, by William Scott, Dublin. Unlike eighteenth-century aristocratic ladies, the Victorians did not ride astride and were judged by their posture while riding side-saddle.

OVERLEAF

In Ascot's Royal Enclosure in the 1880s, ladies followed the style of Princess Alexandra. The stolid lines of the crinoline had been replaced by S-bend bustle-backed formal day dresses that showed off a lady's décolletage, waspish waist and sinuous hips, and betrayed just a flash of ankle as flounced skirts rose and fell. The vogue in millinery was for exotic feathers, artificial flowers and wisps of veiling. For chaps, the black silk plush top hat ruled and the frock coat had not yet been replaced by morning tails.

An explosion in the volume of the sleeve balanced the lean line of the torso. Being a woman of delicate constitution (she was partially deaf and thus vulnerable and shy in society), Princess Alexandra reflected her fragility in a love for delicate fabrics, such as lace, which dominated fashion, particularly in the ubiquitous high-necked blouses worn for day attire. Her gowns were trimmed with real and silk flowers and her accessories were those of a porcelain doll: lace-trimmed parasols, embroidered kid gloves, ostrich-feather boas, painted fans and hats trimmed with other exotic feathers.

Queen Victoria was not amused by Alexandra's self-appointed role as a fashion plate (a precedent, perhaps, for the late Diana, Princess of Wales), and she was positively disapproving of her son Bertie attending all four days of Ascot. In a letter of 1870, she admonished him to 'confine your visits to the Races to the two days, Tuesday and Thursday, and not go on Wednesday and Friday, to which William IV never went, [and] nor did we'.

The Prince of Wales had spent his early life relatively isolated, excluded from any political significance or influence, and was the subject of his parents' relentless disapproval. As Sean Magee eloquently puts it in *Ascot: The History*, 'The principal pursuits that sustained him through four decades of kicking his heels in the green room of monarchy were travel, women and the Turf.' As a result, by 1906, when he was enthroned as Edward VII, *The British Turf and the Men Who Have Made It* said of the King: 'It is impossible to overestimate the good service that our Monarch has rendered to the King of Sports during the thirty-five years that his colours have adorned both flat and steeplechase courses.'

Perhaps more than his own gambling activities, it was Bertie's support for Ascot as an institution that sets him apart as the greatest royal patron of Ascot prior to our present Queen. He reinstated the royal carriage procession in the 1870s and was swift to introduce his sons and heirs, Princes Albert Victor and George (the future King George V), to Ascot in 1877. It was under his watch that the promenade – a tradition dating back to the 1820s, in which fashionable ladies and gentlemen would walk the turf in between races to show off their finest – was effectively ended. It was a good decision for runners and riders in both the racing and fashion stakes. The promenade moved to the paddock, leaving the racetrack in finer condition for racing.

The death of Queen Victoria in 1901 occasioned the first Black Ascot, when the entire Royal Enclosure went into full court mourning. It also inaugurated a new era for the Enclosure: the King relaxed the rules of admission, but the newly appointed King's

OPPOSITE
The Critical Moment: A Scene on Cup Day at Ascot, drawn from life by Paul Renouard for *The Graphic* on 22 June 1895.

ABOVE
Illustrated London News fashion plate from the second Black Ascot of 1910, when the Enclosure went into full mourning for the death of King Edward VII. Notice the dress in the foreground trimmed with white lilies, signifying mourning. The second Black Ascot provided inspiration for Cecil Beaton's *My Fair Lady*.

Representative, Viscount Churchill (appointed in 1901 on the abolition of the Royal Buckhounds, whose Master previously controlled the race meeting), instigated draconian new rules. The Viscount initiated the system of admission whereby only people eligible to attend court were permissible as Royal Enclosure members. He would sort applicants into piles of letters under the subsections 'certainly', 'perhaps' and 'certainly not'.

'Certainly not' included divorcees, who were branded as undesirables; but at the King's insistence the Enclosure was opened out to incorporate his social circle: previously unacceptable American millionaires, Jews, actresses and pretty (first) wives of men of all social standings were included. By the time he became King, Bertie's mistress, the actress Lillie Langtry, had become Lady de Bathe. However, propriety still forced a lady to race under a male name; in Mrs Langtry's case it was Mr Jersey, a reference to her stage moniker the 'Jersey Lily', named after the island of the celebrated beauty's birth.

To quote Virginia Cowles's 1956 book *Edward VII and His Circle*, the Edwardian reign was 'larger than life. There was an avalanche of balls and dinners and country house parties. More money was spent on clothes, more food consumed, more horses were raced, more infidelities were committed, more birds were shot, more yachts were commissioned, more late hours were kept, than ever before.'

At the epicentre of this social whirl was the winsome aesthete and aristocrat Ettie, Lady Desborough, whose Ascot house party invitations were more sought after than the King's invitations to Windsor Castle. Lady Desborough vied with American heiress Consuelo Vanderbilt, Duchess of Marlborough, as the greatest beauty of Edwardian England. By classical standards, the Duchess wins as the beauty and fashion plate of her day. But photographs do not capture the near-magical spell that Lady Desborough cast over her many beaux.

'[Lady Desborough] kept a full house at Taplow Court for Ascot week,' writes Richard Davenport-Hines in *Ettie: The Intimate Life and Dauntless Spirit of Lady Desborough* (2008). He quotes her 1894 Ascot diary: 'It was a wild racket at Taplow during Ascot week. We are twenty-four in the house, most of them more or less insane – we went on the river last night till two in the morning.' Admirer Sir Edgar Vincent wrote after one Ascot party, 'You have never been more brilliant and I have never been more completely under your wand. It really is a privilege to have lived in the same century as you.'

If Lady Desborough eclipsed Queen Alexandra and the Duchess of Marlborough as a brilliant society hostess, few were in doubt that Edward VII led sartorially and

socially. His grandson, the Duke of Windsor, wrote in *A Family Album* (1960): 'My grandfather unquestionably had wider influence on masculine fashions than any member of the royal family since George IV. He was a good friend to the tailors of Savile Row, consolidating the position of London as the international sartorial shrine for men, as already Paris was for women.' As the German Prince von Bülow said of Edward VII, 'In the country in which unquestionably the gentlemen dressed their best, he was the best dressed gentleman.'

It may be inconceivable for men today to wear anything other than morning tails in the Royal Enclosure. But in the Edwardian era, the King wore a formal single-breasted black frock coat because the cutaway was unforgiving on his rotund waist. Where the King led, the Enclosure followed. Another of the King's innovations was to leave the lowest button on the Ascot waistcoat undone. His weight gain was the accepted motive for this fashion foible, though the Duke of Windsor's verdict in *A Family Album*

Ettie, Lady Desborough, fashion plate, society leader and darling of the artistic and aristocratic set she christened 'The Souls', hosted lavish parties for Ascot week at Taplow Court that rivalled Windsor Castle for luxury and excess. Lady Desborough was considered one of the most statuesque of Edwardian ladies and counted Balfour, Asquith, Churchill, Kitchener, Kipling and Siegfried Sassoon among her conquests. She is photographed here in 1909 with Lord Desborough and their daughter Imogen.

ABOVE

The Royal Enclosure at Ascot in the mid-1910s clearly demonstrates the oriental influence on fashions of the day. The lady at the far left wears an exotic *robe à la japonaise*, modelled on a classic kimono cut.

OVERLEAF

The death of King Edward VII plunged society into deepest black and, arguably, gave Royal Ascot one of the chicest seasons in its history. At the far left are Mrs Boyd-Rochfort and Major Cox; the two gentlemen standing in the centre are Lord Ilchester (left) and Lord Londonderry (right); and Lady Fingall wears a feathered hat, centre right.

was: 'I rather suspect he many have in the first place left it undone by mistake.' But, over and above such royal peculiars in men's attire, Edward VII is perhaps most beloved at Ascot for paying as much attention to the public areas as to the Royal Enclosure. In 1901 the King ordered all the old stands be razed to the ground, while insisting that the new Royal Stand, Royal Enclosure Stand and Jockey Club Stand should not be improved to the detriment of the views from the common enclosures, the Iron Stand and the Grandstand. The King also commanded the construction of the Five Shilling Stand, the precursor to the present Silver Ring. So, although a Wesleyan Methodist Conference speech condemned the King as 'a second George IV' for his addiction to gambling and horse racing, he was also an honourable man of the turf, friend to Ascot and successful monarch. As he declared when Prince of Wales in 1863, at his first Ascot, 'To be neither elated by success nor discouraged by reverses has always been considered the first attribute of a good sportsman.'

THE FORM: TOP HATS AND MORNING TAILS

'The Grey Top Hat: This has become popular since it became socially acceptable to hire morning dress. As a black silk hat is so delicate to handle, you are not encouraged to hire it. It is, however, incorrect to wear a grey topper on any occasion in the winter. It is never incorrect to wear a black silk with morning dress, even at a wedding. It is, of course, totally incorrect to wear a grey topper at a funeral.'

ABC OF MEN'S FASHION BY HARDY AMIES (1964)

OPPOSITE
An elegant crocodile led by chaps in morning tails makes its way up the long walk from Ascot station to the racecourse in June 1930. Within hours, Royal Ascot was lashed with a storm of an intensity not seen on record before or since.

OVERLEAF
Photographs from the Royal Ascot Archive admirably display the magnificence of the top hat. If one is fortunate enough to own a vintage black silk plush top hat, one will also know some of the eccentric tips for retaining its sheen. A military wife once accosted the author at Royal Ascot with a damp sponge laced with glycerine to polish up his topper. But hatters recommend brushing it with a velvet pincushion saturated with witch hazel, always going with the grain of the fur.

The ladies in the Enclosure often complain that chaps have it easy when dressing for the Royal Meeting, but formal men's dress is a minefield of terribly subtle signifiers of U and non-U. As royal couturier and Savile Row arbiter of men's style, Hardy Amies made many inflammatory pronouncements about the rules of men's formal dress and he was seldom wrong. A rare exception was his *ABC* entry for Ascot, in which Amies said that 'if you are going to any of the enclosures or the boxes at the Royal Ascot Meeting, you will probably be very unhappy if you do not join the Moss Bros brigade'.

Moss Bros may be the official sponsor of men's attire at Royal Ascot but a hired (grey three-piece) morning suit in the Enclosure stands out and does not fit in. The mark of a Royal Ascot male is perfectly tailored black bespoke morning tails (a one-button cutaway coat) made on Savile Row, accompanied by grey pinstripe or puppy-tooth trousers and plain wool or linen waistcoat. Contrary to Amies' advice, white shirts are frowned upon in the Enclosure. The form is a very pale base colour or stripe, preferably with white collar and cuffs.

Fashion does inform formal day dress at Royal Ascot, but subtly so. Puppy-tooth trousers have become the fashion since Prince Michael of Kent revived the tradition initiated by the Duke of Windsor when Prince of Wales. The grey three-piece has once again been popularized by the present Prince of Wales. The Windsor style of mismatching shirt, tie, waistcoat and pocket square is adopted by the smarter chaps in the Enclosure, and in royal buttonholes the red carnation, yellow rose and cornflower are popular. Though Amies' grey toppers are acceptable, it is universally acknowledged that the reconditioned black silk top hat from St James's Street hatter James Lock & Co. is the smartest choice for Ascot.

L.A.R. La Princesse Marie-José de Belgique et le Prince Umberto d'Italie

MY FAIR LADY: THE FASHION FILM OF THE CENTURY

'The difference between a lady and a flower girl is not how she behaves, but how she is treated.'

ELIZA DOOLITTLE TO PROFESSOR HIGGINS IN *MY FAIR LADY* (1964)

'To design fifty new costumes for Ascot or the Ball is no problem,' writes Cecil Beaton in his 1963 diary, 'but at this point in the operations it often takes considerable time to devise just the right costume for a principal in a certain scene.' Nothing before or since has surpassed the stylized Edwardian splendour evoked by Cecil Beaton's costume for principal Audrey Hepburn as Eliza Doolittle in *My Fair Lady*'s Ascot scene.

'Hundreds of yards of fabric were unfolded for the Ascot scene – many of them imported from heaven-knows-where,' reported the official Warner Brothers programme. 'The Ascot is in black and white and grey, with a few square inches of alabaster flesh showing among the ladies. The 130 men in grey morning coats, top hats, Ascot (what else?) ties and spats, carry binoculars and swing canes. The event takes place in front of huge latticed pavilions with striped canvas tops, ornamented with enormous baskets of lavender hydrangeas, in the middle of 2500 square yards of lush green carpeting.

'The central figure of the Ascot scene is, of course, Audrey Hepburn, in her first flush of instant glamour. Her gown is the costliest, her hat the flashiest, her bearing the most regal and that single red flower the reddest.' Of *My Fair Lady*, Hepburn herself would say, 'It was enchanting, a once-in-a-lifetime experience.'

ABOVE
Left to right: Wilfred Hyde-White, Rex Harrison, Audrey Hepburn, Jeremy Brett and Gladys Cooper in the Ascot scene from *My Fair Lady*. This famous frame sees flower-girl-posing-as-society-girl Eliza holler at the passing horses in a broad cockney the immortal line, 'Come on, Dover, move your bloomin' arse.'

OPPOSITE
In his *Cecil Beaton: The Authorized Biography* (1985), Hugo Vickers reports that when Beaton saw Hepburn in her Ascot costume for the first time, 'Cecil yelled with laughter, a reaction that surprised him, but he was pleased that the dress was "funny, elegant and just right for the scene".'

ALL THE QUEEN'S MEN: THE LADIES AND GENTLEMEN WHO SERVE HER MAJESTY

'I look forward to welcoming you at Ascot Racecourse to enjoy racing, the landscape and the jollity of a day out, all of which I believe Queen Anne would have appreciated. We owe her and her successors a great debt for their patronage: none more than Her Present Majesty.'

HER MAJESTY'S REPRESENTATIVE, THE DUKE OF DEVONSHIRE, WHEN MARQUIS OF HARTINGTON (2002)

OPPOSITE AND OVERLEAF
Though the Greencoats serve at Royal Ascot ostensibly to attend and protect the Queen, the crowd has also traditionally policed behaviour. As George James Cawthorne wrote of Georgian Ascot, 'The crowd protected one another and got a good deal of fun out of the capture of thieves … [one] was paraded several times in front of the stands with a halter round his neck, while all the crowd hooted.'

As the figurehead of Royal Ascot, Queen Elizabeth II could technically count all of the gentlemen who attend the Royal Meeting as 'the Queen's men'. But there is a strict protocol. The Duke of Devonshire, Her Majesty's Representative at Ascot until 2011, has led the field, holding the keys to the Ascot Authority Box. It is he who has formally greeted the Queen's arrival in the Parade Ring before escorting the royal party to the Royal Box. It is to Her Majesty's Representative at the Ascot Authority that nominees for the Royal Enclosure must apply.

The Ascot Authority is made up of the three Trustees who control the annual calendar of race meetings and events held at Ascot. Those closest to the Queen during the Royal Procession are her two postillions, who ride the Windsor Greys that lead her landau, and two riders in black top hats and red frock coats who ride behind the Queen and the Duke of Edinburgh in the carriages. Her Majesty is then saluted by the Ascot Greencoats: a corps of ex-servicemen who guard the territory between the Parade Ring and the entrance to the lift to the Royal Box, who are as popular a sight with the crowds at Ascot as BBC commentators Willie Carson and Clare Balding.

Often most intriguing are the guests the Queen invites to her annual Ascot house parties at Windsor Castle, or to attend her in the Paddock or Parade Ring. They are, to a man, ladies and gentlemen of the turf, such as Andrew Balding and John Warren, Lord Vestey, the Earl of Derby, Sheikh Mohammed, Lord Lloyd-Webber and actor Martin Clunes. But there is one uniting rule for all of the Queen's men at Royal Ascot: when the royal party passes by, all gentlemen must doff their top hats and bow from the neck.

CHAPTER 3

KING GEORGE V
From Empire to Jazz Age Ascot
1910–1936

'Why have women come racing in such vastly greater numbers in recent years? They may be excused for thinking the meeting is run for them and not primarily for the horses and their owners.'

'HOTSPUR' OF THE *DAILY TELEGRAPH* (1934) AS QUOTED IN *ASCOT: THE HISTORY* BY SEAN MAGEE WITH SALLY AIRD (2002)

IF KING GEORGE V'S REPUTATION RESTED ENTIRELY IN HIS ELDEST SON AND HEIR'S HANDS, his reign as custodian of Royal Ascot would be considered as undistinguished as that of George II. As the Duke of Windsor wrote twenty-four years after his father's death in *A Family Album* (1960), 'After my Grandfather died, the character of the court ... reverted to a way of life if not, it's true, as Queen Victoria's time, but quieter, more sedate and more essentially British than the Edwardian age.' The Duke further twists the knife by adding, 'My father set few if any fashions.'

Yet no monarch, excepting our present Queen, has been as conscientious of the dignity of monarchy as a 'family firm' and the importance of leading by example at Royal Ascot. The rules of entry and engagement for the Royal Enclosure were tightened under the beady eye of George V and his consort, Queen Mary. As early as 1895, the Master of the Buckhounds, Lord Ribblesdale, reported that 'an individual with a Kodak was at loose in the Enclosure photographing the royal party and when last seen was actively engaged upon a group of Duchesses.' It transpired that the rogue snapper was a diplomat and relative of an ex-crowned head, so he was reprimanded then invited to lunch by the Master. By 1911, it was reported that photography was 'a plague' at Royal Ascot, with the added pestilence of moving picture cameras to combat. In 1919, the King decreed that cameras be banned in the Enclosure. Though the BBC fashion crew very publicly flouts this rule in the twenty-first century, Her Majesty still insists protocol is upheld. Cameramen must wear morning coats; in 2009 the Queen communicated her disapproval of a BBC cameraman wearing a baseball cap with his morning coat in the Parade Ring.

It is not without irony that the rigidity of dress codes led by Queen Mary in the 1910s coincided with some of the most magical, innovative advances in fashion. In 1910, Sergei Diaghilev's Ballets Russes exploded onto the London stage and 'Sultan of fashion' Paul Poiret's oriental costumes for Scheherazade sent society into a frenzy of *Arabian Nights*-inspired attire. Poiret banished the bustle and tightly laced corset in favour of the 'hobble' skirt, so named because this tight, tubular line constricted the ankle. His was a world of plush, madly patterned velvet opera coats trimmed with Russian sable, exquisitely beaded and embroidered draped dresses, and exotic turbans trimmed with jewels and aigrettes: a fountain of feather trim usually culled from the egret bird.

ROYAL ASCOT: THE ENCLOSURE BEFORE THE RACE FOR THE CUP

Lucile, Lady Duff Gordon, had opened Mayfair fashion house Maison Lucile in 1894, but in the 1910s her star was at its peak; she designed for her own aristocratic circle as well as for actresses such as Sarah Bernhardt and Lily Elsie. Her tea gowns were ostensibly polite, but were touched with orientalism and little scandalous details, such as skirts that revealed slightly more calf than Queen Mary would approve of. In contrast to the high-necked blouses that the Queen wore all her life, by 1913 designers such as Poiret, Lucile, Redfern and Charles Creed had introduced the V-neck on what some wags christened a 'pneumonia blouse'.

Venetian designer Mariano Fortuny went a step further with his gathered-silk tubular 'Delphos' shift dresses, inspired by the seductiveness of the classical Grecian drape dress. Though first designed in 1907, the Delphos became the fashion in the 1910s, its freedom of movement demonstrated admirably by the mother of modern dance, Isadora Duncan. Parisian couturier Jeanne Paquin, meanwhile, took inspiration from Ballets Russes costume designers Iribe and Bakst for brilliantly coloured kimono-cut short, draped opera cloaks in wild floral silks, and the lampshade look of above-the-knee belted tunics over a clashing coloured hobble skirt, fringed or fur-trimmed.

While the beau monde at Ascot danced on the precipice of decency, the storm clouds of the First World War were gathering over the Royal Meeting and the Derby. In full view of the King and Queen, suffragette Emily Davison threw herself in front of the King's horse Amner at the Derby, and died of her wounds four days later.

Suffragette Emily Davison was trampled to death under the King's horse at the Epsom Derby in 1913. A return ticket was found in her pocket, suggesting that her protest was spur of the moment. The incident was caught on camera by Pathé News.

ABOVE

A rare Lucile jade-green velvet
gown with ivory chiffon and lace
bodice piped with velvet and edged
in satin, labelled 'Lucile Ltd, 23
Hanover Square'. Lucile, Lady Duff
Gordon, was one of London's first
star society dressmakers and led
the charge with Paul Poiret-
inspired silhouettes, such as this
from the early 1910s.

RIGHT

A Scheherazade costume designed
by Léon Bakst in 1910 for the
Ballets Russes. Bakst and
impresario Sergei Diaghilev
inadvertently unleashed a wave
of oriental-inspired fashions on
London society. He would later
employ Gabrielle 'Coco' Chanel
to design costumes for his 1924
ballet *Le train bleu*.

Etched by W. Heydeman

OPPOSITE
An etching by W. Heydemann
of Queen Alexandra, stamped
in gold Royal Proof, depicts a
romanticized, soft-focus image of
this definitive Edwardian beauty,
who never wavered from a style she
found in the 1880s. The Dowager
Queen was a popular figure in
the Royal Procession at Ascot.
The snake's head bracelet she
wears in this portrait is still in
the Royal Collection, but remains
unworn; it is said that Queen
Elizabeth II and her late sister,
the Princess Margaret, disliked
insect- and reptile-motif jewels.

BELOW
This 1914 oil painting of the Royal
Enclosure lawn at the finishing post
illustrates precisely why the season
was christened the 'Parasol Ascot'.

Miss Davison's protest had little impact on the fashionable set at Royal Ascot, however. In 1914, the social pages reported that 'this was emphatically a Parasol Ascot … to look down upon the sunshades from an upper tier in one of the stands was like gazing down on a gorgeous flower garden.' Nine days after the Royal Meeting, Archduke Ferdinand of Austria and his Duchess were shot dead by an anarchist in Sarajevo. On 4 August, Britain declared war on Germany, with George V leading his country in a fight to the death with his cousins Kaiser Wilhelm II and Tsar Nicholas II of Russia.

Thus the First World War, or 'the end of civilization', began. One of the lesser casualties was the abandonment of Ascot between 1915 and 1918. *The Times* opined: 'We are convinced that any attempt to hold the great popular racing festivals, such as Epsom and Ascot, will make a desperately bad impression upon our neighbours.' Colonel Henry Knollys, private secretary to British Queen Maud of Norway, wrote: 'Is it unreasonable to hope that in 1915 the upper classes of men and women will forbear from assembling in their tens of thousands, say, at Ascot, peacocking in their plumes and prattling their puerilities, eating plentifully and drinking still more so, semi-intoxicated with the splendour and spangle of the gaudy scene?' There was no more racing until 1919.

The elation demonstrated by the victorious British when the Armistice was signed in November 1918 initiated a seismic fashion shift. A new line called the 'barrel', with mid-calf skirts and flattened embonpoints, and a vogue for shorter, shingled hair were fashion's first steps towards the boyish 'flapper' look that dominated the 1920s. Within weeks of the Armistice, housing agents in Berkshire were receiving enquiries about letting the grander houses and estates for Ascot week. In honour of Royal Ascot's revival, the King decreed that the carriage procession would take place on all four days of the meeting.

The thrones of Russia, Austria and Germany had all fallen, so it was not without calculation that King George and Queen Mary rode out in the carriages at the 1919 Ascot dressed ostensibly as Edwardians: he in a black frock coat and black silk top hat, she in floor-length brocade with a feathered, veiled toque more suited to 1901. Court protocol at the royal family's Windsor Castle Ascot house parties was as strict as eighteenth-century Versailles, even if dress was infinitely less ostentatious. But when the King and Queen retired at eleven o'clock sharp, the young Princes, Edward (known as David to the family), and George, Duke of Kent, entertained the young in the Green Drawing Room with cocktails and dancing to the gramophone.

Edward, Prince of Wales, and his brother George had all the glamour, spark and rebelliousness of the present young royal 'Boujis set', the Princes William and Harry. It was they who set the tone for Jazz Age Ascot, when every eligible gal in the Royal Enclosure longed to 'dance with a man who danced with a girl who danced with the Prince of Wales', as the popular song of the day had it. By 1923, skirts had risen an inch or two above the line of decency (the knee), hair was bobbed, beads were twirled, lips were rouged, eyebrows were pencilled and breasts were suppressed to boyishness as flat as Norfolk.

This rebelliousness against the older generation who had led so many bright young men to slaughter in the trenches was championed by the Prince of Wales, who rejected the frock coat in favour of a grey three-piece morning coat, the grey topper that he popularized and a signature red carnation boutonnière (still worn by the present royal males), as tailored by his Savile Row tailor, Scholte. The Prince recalls in *A Family Album*: 'Anyway, here I was at Ascot, looking my smartest, I liked to think, in my grey morning coat. Unfortunately, I had forgotten something: The Court was in mourning for some distant relative. On reaching the racecourse, I thus earned rebuke from my father, who pointed out that in the circumstances a black morning coat was required.'

A *Punch* magazine satirical cartoon titled 'Manners and Modes at Ascot', depicting the gaping sartorial chasm between the young flapper generation and the old guard.

A 1920s Chanel couture printed silk drop-waisted flapper dress trimmed with tone-on-tone ruffled fringe, with matching stole to cover the shoulders, as the Royal Enclosure Dress Code dictates.

OVERLEAF, LEFT

A fashionable couple attend Royal Ascot in 1925. The lady is dressed in the latest rage: a chiffon drop-waisted, flat-chested knee-length formal day dress tied on the hips by an extravagant sash. The chap is copying style leader Edward, Prince of Wales, who was wont to wear a stiff wing collar with his bow tie (as opposed to the more conventional flat collar shape) and a morning coat trimmed with black grosgrain. He is wearing spats to protect his none-too polished Oxfords.

OVERLEAF, RIGHT

A young couple who own a vintage fashion boutique on London's Portobello Road Market attend Royal Ascot in 2010 echoing the *Brideshead Revisited* style of 1920s aristocrats. Neither would be allowed admission to the Royal Enclosure: he for not wearing formal morning dress and she for wearing what is essentially a beaded cocktail shift designed by Amanda Wakeley with lattice-work beaded skullcap. Both, however, look delectable and entirely appropriate for the public grandstands or, indeed, Goodwood, Epsom or Newmarket.

The Prince broke protocol again by actually visiting his tailor Scholte on Savile Row, who cut the black morning coat then toiled overnight to complete the garment in time for the carriage procession the next day. This was one of the few occasions when the Prince obeyed his King.

The 2nd Duke of Westminster introduced an even more profound sartorial rule-breaker to Ascot society. In 1923, the Duke met fashion revolutionary Gabrielle 'Coco' Chanel in Monte Carlo. As Justine Picardie writes in her biography *Coco Chanel: The Legend and the Life* (2010), 'It was as impossible for Chanel as it was for anyone to ignore Westminster's wealth and power,' and she subsequently became his mistress.

For students of style today, the only comparison in recent fashion history to the profound 'shock of the new' that Chanel brought to the 1910s and 1920s is anarchic Japanese designer Rei Kawakubo's Comme des Garçons label, which was unleashed on Paris in 1981. Chanel exorcized the luxury fabrics, frills and furbelows of the Edwardian demi-monde from fashion, relishing the irony of dressing the moneyed upper classes in Paris and London in severe little black dresses cut from workaday jersey cloth, matelot tunics and masculine slouch pants, with faux-jewelled cuffs and multiple strands of fake pearls. The aesthetic was perverse *pauvre chic*.

Chanel's contrary approach to fashion was all the more ironic considering she was at the height of her powers between the General Strike of 1926 and the Wall Street Crash of 1929. The strike prompted His Majesty's Representative Sir Frederick Ponsonby to call for the Royal Enclosure registration fee to be reduced for young aristocrats. As he said disdainfully, 'There is also the consideration that we may be letting in all the Mosensteins [Jews] and leaving out the gentlemen of England'; an unfortunate comment, considering Adolf Hitler had penned *Mein Kampf* the year before.

While Berlin danced to the divine decadence of Weimar cabaret, at Ascot skirts were at their shortest. The flapper set, including compulsive womanizer Edward, Prince of Wales, and his mistresses, would eschew Windsor Castle to dance the Charleston and sip Martinis at the Savoy, the Café de Paris and the Embassy Club, often accompanied by his bisexual brother, George, and golden youth of the West End theatre Noël Coward.

In the last year of the decade, an unwell George V absented himself from Ascot and the Prince of Wales was spared the carriage procession. Had Queen Mary attended, she may have been pleased to see that ladies' skirts had commenced their descent, first dipping at the back, then with the addition of sheer chiffon panels and, by 1929, plummeting like the bankrupt stockbrokers on Wall Street to rest at the ankle.

LEFT
Queen Mary's formal gown, tailored in the early 1930s, that could easily have been worn in the first decade of the twentieth century without comment. The Royal Dress Collection at Kensington Palace has detailed maps of Queen Mary's dresses showing strategic places to position her diamond chokers, multiple strands of pearls, diamond fringe necklaces, stomachers, brooches and orders. Her pigeon-breasted dresses were little more than blank canvases on which to display her formidable jewelry collection, which was bolstered in no small part by jewels sold to her by Russian royal exiles.

OPPOSITE
A state portrait of Queen Mary, that magnificent galleon of a lady, fully festooned with diamond trellis tiara, choker, diamond fringe necklace and pearl-trimmed sleeves.

The ankle-length diaphanous bias-cut dress – at its most extreme as worn backless and cut in white satin by Hollywood platinum blonde Jean Harlow on screen in *The Public Enemy* (1931) – was a more demure, pretty and modest proposition at Royal Ascot. The line was slim and straight, but was balanced with fluted sleeves cut to resemble folds of millefeuille and wide-brimmed, flower-trimmed picture hats worn at an angle. White was the predominant colour, as dictated by Paris 'Mesdames' Jeanne Lanvin, Madeleine Vionnet and Alix Grès, whose experiments with the clinging bias cut were inspired by the drapes of ancient Greek statues.

With women dominating the fashion world, it was little surprise to hear that chaps in the racing fraternity thought the fairer sex were also trying to dominate Ascot. In 1934, Sidney Galtrey, 'Hotspur' of the *Daily Telegraph*, wrote: 'Why have women come racing in such vastly greater numbers in recent years? They may be excused for thinking the meeting is run for them and not primarily for the horses and their owners.'

Despite the Jazz Age liberalization of women's costume, the ladies in Ascot's Royal Enclosure were still restricted by draconian rules supported by the King. It was an unwritten rule that ladies were forbidden to approach a bookmaker (hence the foundation of the Tote in 1931). Ladies were also forbidden to smoke in the Enclosure. This did not prevent Teutonic Hollywood goddess Marlene Dietrich chain-smoking on location at Ascot in 1936 when filming a scene for *Knight Without Armour* (1937) dressed in nothing more than black silk lounging pyjamas and a floor-length black fox-fur coat.

If there was a joker in the pack of Ascot's favourite couturiers, it was Italian-in-Paris Elsa Schiaparelli. 'Schiap' was to fashion what Salvador Dalí was to art. She was not only inspired by, but also collaborated with, the eccentric ringmaster of the Surrealist movement on *trompe l'oeil* follies such as the Shoe Hat; the Desk Suit, complete with drawer pockets and button doorknobs; the Tears Dress, whereby a chiffon bias-cut white organdie gown was printed to look as if torn to shreds; and the now infamous Lobster Dress.

It is with no little irony that an early adopter of Schiaparelli's mischievous couture was Mrs Ernest Simpson, the woman who would seduce the Prince of Wales in 1934 and initiate a constitutional crisis for the British monarchy as profound as the madness of King George III. Though Wallis Simpson wore Captain Edward Molyneux for her sole appearance on the arm of the Prince of Wales at Ascot in 1935, she did possess a white silk Lobster Dress with the lobster hand-painted by Dalí.

In 1936, King George V died. *Cope's Royal Cavalcade of the Turf* concluded: 'King George was never able to achieve the scintillating brilliance of his father [Edward VII] as an owner but his heart was always very near the sport.' Full court mourning precluded any royal presence at Ascot that year, and a still unmarried Edward VIII was proclaimed King with twice-divorced Mrs Simpson, albeit in the shadows, at his side.

In the same year, Deborah Mitford, now Dowager Duchess of Devonshire, attended Ascot with a gaggle of debutantes, and reports from the Royal Enclosure in her autobiography *Wait For Me!: Memoirs of the Youngest Mitford Sister* (2010): 'I persuaded Madame Rita – who displayed her hats on sticks with padded tops in her cheerful showroom on the first floor of a house in Berkeley Square – to make a copy in spotted muslin of a "fore and aft", the traditional tweed cap worn by deer stalkers, the ear flaps tied with a white satin ribbon on top of my head. It was ridiculous, but lots of Ascot hats are ridiculous.'

The Duchess continues, 'It was the racing I loved more than the social side, but both were all they were cracked up to be. We rattled down from London in one of the many special trains that took you to the racecourse. The sight of a crowd of overdressed women and top-hatted, tail-coated men assembled on one of our dirty old stations is somehow incongruous, like women in evening dresses and men in black tie leaving for Glyndebourne in the middle of the afternoon.'

Despite his many glamorous appearances at Ascot, first in a black morning coat trimmed with grosgrain, tailored (like those of his three brothers) by King George V's Hanover Street tailor Davies & Son, then latterly in his Scholte grey three-piece and grey top hat, the Prince of Wales was not interested in flat racing. His passion was for steeplechasing but, after a hunter collapsed and died beneath him, George V prompted Parliament to table a question about the wisdom of the heir to the throne riding cross-country like a highwayman being pursued by the local squire.

When he acceded to the throne, one of Edward VIII's first proclamations, as pronounced by Lord Derby, was that 'His Majesty would maintain the Royal racing stables and the Sandringham Stud'; but he never returned to Ascot after that sole appearance with Mrs Simpson in 1935. On 11 December 1936, 'Prince Edward' formally abdicated the throne to his brother Arthur (who would be styled King George VI) so that he could marry 'the woman I love', Mrs Simpson.

1935. *The Prince of Wales at Ascot Races.*

The 1935 Royal Ascot was the only occasion when Edward, Prince of Wales attended the Royal Meeting with his mistress, Mrs Simpson. The Prince is sporting the grey top hat and grey three-piece morning coat that he made fashionable in the mid-1920s.

The Hon. Deborah Mitford
attends her first Royal Ascot in
1936 wearing a characteristically
contrary mad hat based on the
shape of a hunting deerstalker.
She casually throws an ocelot
fur coat over her country tweed
skirt suit, thus epitomizing the
irreverent English aristocratic style.

A 1937 photograph by Ref Sayers,
taken on the crossing between
Ascot station and the Royal
Enclosure entrance, shows a lady
wearing the full-length Edwardian
revival graphic rose-print skirt,
nipped-in peplum coat with
overblown rose corsage and natty
little hat worn at a jaunty angle.

EVERY EARL AND DUKE AND PEER IS HERE: THE ROYAL ENCLOSURE

'Side by side with the beautifully dressed members of the aristocracy, the diplomatic world and Society there have always been, right from the first Ascot of all in 1711, outbursts of ebullient eccentricity of dress …'

ROYAL ASCOT: A HISTORY OF ROYAL ASCOT FROM ITS FOUNDING BY QUEEN ANNE TO THE PRESENT TIME BY DOROTHY LAIRD (1976)

OPPOSITE AND OVERLEAF
In 1822, King George IV founded a small enclosure around the new Royal Stand guarded by policemen and gatemen. This was primarily for safety, as the profligate King was so unpopular. Today, as seen in photographs from the Royal Ascot Archive, the Enclosure is a jollier, less elitist but no less exclusive affair.

Being named in Debrett's Peerage has not been a prerequisite for entry to the Royal Enclosure since the Edwardian era, when favourites from the stage, the colonial rich and even trade were invited by King Edward VII. Today, Royal Ascot is more democratic than it has ever been. Nevertheless, the Enclosures retain a magic woven by what some consider to be draconian dress codes and the presence of the Queen.

'Even when I was old enough to attend, it still meant something then to get a badge to the Enclosure, and the atmosphere was special,' recalls milliner David Shilling. 'The various members of the royal family strolled freely amongst us; it was like a well-ordered private party where every five minutes you met up with someone you knew or wanted to know, with so many distractions, not just for the eyes, but for all the senses.'

Yes, the Enclosure is something of a fashion parade; you will still see pieces from the Spring/Summer Paris couture collections and new-season dresses by great British designers Bruce Oldfield, Amanda Wakeley, Jasper Conran, Vivienne Westwood, Alexander McQueen,

Burberry and Alice Temperley. But the best-dressed ladies are inevitably those of the old families, the owners and trainers and the veterans of Royal Ascot who dress appropriately, quietly and practically. When Cecil Beaton was researching Edwardian fashion for *My Fair Lady*, he asked Lady Diana Cooper what her mother, the Duchess of Rutland, would have worn to Ascot. She wrote: 'Certainly cream. A straw hat trimmed, of course, by herself, with little bits of bird's breast and/or ribbon in dirty pink, wide-ish brimmed and fairly shallow because of the Grecian back-handle, and the Sarah B[ernhardt] fringe in front. I don't suppose she ever set foot in a milliner's shop … the whole rag-bag camouflaged over by a démodé, once-good, three-quarter length coat of beige, lace or brocade, inherited from sister Marjorie, perhaps. Good suede gloves (beige and long). Very high heeled shoes she hoped didn't show. Parasol of course.' The 'parasol of course' balanced by the hand-me-down coat from sister Marjorie says it all about the insouciant aristocratic style of formal – rather than fashionable – dress in the Royal Enclosure that still holds true today.

THE PICNIC SET IN CAR PARK NO. 1

'[After the Second World War] the refreshment pavilion and the lesser buffets suffered severely from the prevailing austerity. Even so, there were strawberries and ice-cream for half a crown and champagne for sixty shillings a bottle, while on the course a peach could be bought from a tray for five shillings.'

ASCOT: THE HISTORY BY SEAN MAGEE WITH SALLY AIRD (2002)

OPPOSITE AND OVERLEAF
The distinguished tradition of picnicking in style in Car Park No. 1 is still carried on with gusto by guests of the Royal Enclosure.

Tradition at Royal Ascot dictates that Car Park No. 1, reserved for members of the Royal Enclosure with its own entrance directly on to the Enclosure Lawn, will begin to fill at 11.30 a.m. with museum-quality vintage cars. Drivers will unpack Fortnum & Mason picnic hampers, trestle tables, white linen tablecloths and family silver to prepare lavish picnics that will outdo fellow racegoers who have parked in the same spot for decades. Certain members of the Enclosure will pay the subscription for their Car Park No. 1 allocation even if they are not attending that year, rather than lose a prestigious family spot.

Picnics gained popularity after the Second World War, when food rationing and austerity prevented the official restaurants and buffets at Royal Ascot from serving the lavish food that the aristocracy – with their full game larders and vegetable gardens – had managed to maintain privately without recourse to a ration book. But it wasn't until 1964 that Car Park No. 1 and its picnic set were immortalized on film in *The Yellow Rolls-Royce*. The film opens with writer Terence Rattigan's alternative vision of

the Ascot scene in *My Fair Lady* (coincidentally, also released in 1964). The Rolls-Royce Phantom II Barca Sedanca de Ville 9JS is acquired by the Marquis of Frinton (Rex Harrison) as a gift for his Marchioness (Jeanne Moreau).

The couple are filmed departing for Ascot, parking in No. 1 next to similarly glamorous carriages, then preparing to watch the Gold Cup, in which the Marquis has a horse running. As the Gold Cup starts, the Marquis is told his wife is having an affair. Abandoning the race, the Marquis is filmed navigating the elegant No. 1 Car Park as he nears the yellow Rolls-Royce. The blinds are down; he lifts them and discovers the Marchioness in a passionate embrace just as it is announced over the tannoy that his horse has won the Gold Cup.

It would be rather presumptuous to think that such raciness still occurs in No. 1, though most contemporary luxury cars do now have smoked windows, so how would one know? Only those who have an allocation in the famous Car Park No. 1 at the Royal Meeting are in a position to find out.

BY APPOINTMENT

Ascot 1937

The Grey Topper	40 -
The Morning Coat	6½ Gns.
The Grey Waistcoat	30/-
The Cashmere Trousers	63/-
The White Shirt	15/6
The Linen Collars *(dozen)*	11/6
The Large Shape Tie	8/6
The White Linen Handkerchiefs *(dozen)*	21/-
The Silver Grey Gloves	16/6
The Umbrella (with Pigskin-covered handle)	55/-

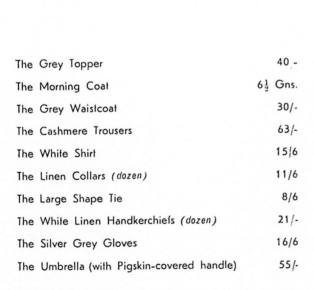

CHAPTER 4

KING EDWARD VIII TO KING GEORGE VI
Austere Royal Ascot
1936–1952

'Some people genuinely thought it deplorable that
racing should continue to exist at such a time [as the
Second World War]; let it never be forgotten then,
that in England's most critical days the King remained
in London not only to share the perils of his people
but to share – and defend – their pleasures also.'

COPE'S ROYAL CAVALCADE OF THE TURF, EDITED BY ALFRED COPE (1953)

WITH THE COURT IN MOURNING FOR THE DEATH OF KING GEORGE V, THE ROYAL FAMILY DID NOT ATTEND ASCOT IN 1936. If it had, the presence of the Mrs Simpson set would have divided the Royal Enclosure into two hostile camps: the old establishment traditionalists led by Dowager Queen Mary, horrified by the new King's dalliance with a twice-divorced American, and the 'new court' of rackety socialites such as Lady Emerald Cunard, Lord Berners, Sir Alfred 'Duff' and Lady Diana Cooper, Sir Philip Sassoon, Lady Sybil Colefax and Prince George, Duke of Kent, and his Duchess, Princess Marina of Greece.

On the eve of Ascot week 1936, American-born Conservative politician and diarist Sir Henry 'Chips' Channon gave a dinner party for the King and Mrs Simpson in the famous blue-and-silver dining room of his Belgrave Square townhouse, modelled on the rococo Amalienburg hunting lodge in Munich. As Charles Jennings writes in *Them and Us: The American Invasion of British High Society* (2007), 'It was a triumph for him and his set; and a terrible confirmation to the rest of the Court that the King had fallen irretrievably into the hands of the second-rate, the superficial, the unreliable.'

The louche 'new court' was populated by characters whom the late King's Representative Viscount Churchill would have placed firmly on his 'certainly not' list for the Royal Enclosure. As a divorcee, Mrs Simpson would not have been welcome without the patronage of the King. Similarly, society disapproved of the bisexual coterie

PRECEDING PAGES, LEFT
A Gieves Ltd promotion for full morning dress, including a rather excessive order for twelve linen collars and white linen handkerchieves.

OPPOSITE
Sir Henry 'Chips' Channon's rococo dining room in Belgrave Square. Edward, Prince of Wales, and Mrs Simpson were regular dinner guests alongside Lady Cunard, Lady Colefax and Sir Philip Sassoon, who thought they would constitute the new court under King Edward VIII. It was not to be; and the townhouse was later bombed, utterly destroying the beauty of Channon's Bavarian fantasy.

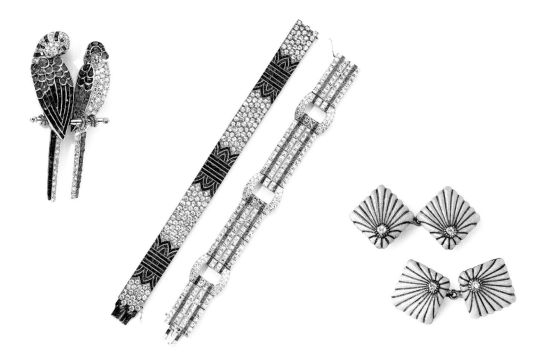

The Art Deco era was a golden age for fine jewelry, and the Duchess of Windsor led the field in commissioning spectacular pieces from Van Cleef & Arpels and Cartier for her and her Duke. The fashion at Ascot in the 1930s was for an intricate diamond and ruby or emerald-set bracelet, an amusing gem-set brooch and, for the chaps, diamond-set cufflinks, such as this antique Fabergé set from the Wartski collection.

LEFT
The social calendar inspired many of the world's great luxury goods houses to create bespoke pieces for their moneyed clients. This extremely rare Hermès race bag was hand painted in 1930 and contains an in-built race card and pencil to place one's bets.

OPPOSITE
In the 1930s the three royal princes led fashion, and none more so than the dashing Edward, Prince of Wales. Practically from adolescence, all of King George V's boys patronized his tailor Davies & Son, but Edward broke with tradition and crossed the floor to Savile Row maestro Scholte. It was Scholte who tailored the Prince's black morning tails with black grosgrain trim. Top, left to right: the Prince of Wales, the Duke of Gloucester and the Duke of York (later King George VI). Below: a portrait of King George VI, left, and the three princes, right.

that included George, Duke of Kent, Lord Berners, Noël Coward and Chips Channon, who was famed for cutting his cocktails with Benzedrine. Americans, such as social butterfly Lady Cunard, were frowned upon as nouveau riche; Cunard was mooted as Queen Wallis's Lady of the Bedchamber should Mrs Simpson carry off her King. Sir Philip Sassoon, the Jewish heir to a fortune made in opium, gold and silks, was equally thought of as 'not quite our sort'.

In a 1936 letter to her Aunt Bessie, Mrs Simpson wrote: 'I prefer the English mode of life, the dignity and the wide outlook – but I prefer the US pep and sense of humour – and detest their bourgeois morals.' When the King signed the instrument of abdication in December 1936 and went into near-permanent exile overseas, novelist Evelyn Waugh caustically commented in a letter that 'there can seldom have been an event that caused so much general delight and so little pain'. The Mrs Simpson set was roundly shunned as the more disciplined, traditional court surrounding King George VI began to close ranks. Chips Channon was humiliated at the Palace of Westminster when Lady Astor said in a stage whisper, 'People who have been licking Mrs Simpson's boots ought to be shot.'

King George VI's solemnity, dignity and courage would have a profound effect on the nation and on Royal Ascot. 'Many voices – not all irresponsible – were raised in declaring that the British monarchy had outlived its usefulness,' writes Alfred Cope in *Cope's Royal Cavalcade of the Turf*. 'When he died in February 1952, the crown stood

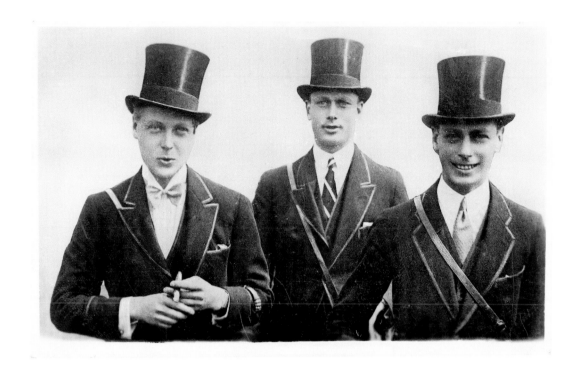

The Duke of Windsor, ex-King Edward VIII, marries Mrs Simpson in 1937 at the Château de Candé in France, photographed by Cecil Beaton. The Duchess is wearing a formal day dress cut by Mainbocher. The wedding was boycotted by the Duke's family.

BELOW

A champagne-and-gold silk gown designed by Schiaparelli *c.* 1937 and possibly ordered to be worn at the coronation of King George VI.

secure as never before, buttressed by the life of a man whose splendid character and utter selflessness shone out, white and clear, a beacon of hope to his peoples throughout the long agony of war torn years.' Royal Ascot enjoyed a renaissance in 1937 with the new King and his Queen (later Queen Elizabeth The Queen Mother) riding out in the carriage procession, as tradition dictated, with Dowager Queen Mary in attendance.

The Mrs Simpson set had always mocked the Queen's sense of style, or lack thereof, nicknaming her 'Cookie' because they considered her short, solid figure and round face that of a Mrs Bridges. The Queen got her own back by naming one of her corgis 'Dookie' as a parody of Mrs Simpson's American accent. But it was the Queen who led fashion at Royal Ascot in 1937; in January of that year, she invited British couturier Norman Hartnell to Buckingham Palace to craft a new image for her in stark contrast to the whip-smart Disney witch aesthetic of Mrs Simpson.

Hartnell instantly dismissed the angular, architectural lines of Mrs Simpson's preferred Parisian couturiers such as Schiaparelli, Mainbocher and Englishman-in-Paris Captain Edward Molyneux. Inspired by Winterhalter's portraits of Queen Victoria and her court in Buckingham Palace, Hartnell crafted a wardrobe of pretty, delicate, crinoline-style tiered white evening dresses for the Queen that emphasized her purity, majesty and lightness in demeanour, as photographed by society snapper Cecil Beaton in 1939. Beaton's reminiscences in *Self-Portrait with Friends: The Selected Diaries of Cecil Beaton*, edited by Richard Buckle (1979), reveal a mischievous side to the Queen, who ran Adolf

OVERLEAF

King George VI and Queen Elizabeth arrive at Ascot on Royal Hunt Day in 1938. The Queen, looking rather pleased with herself, wears a gown by Norman Hartnell and a white fox-fur stole.

The Jockeys' Dressing Room at Ascot (1923) by Sir John Lavery. The jockey in the foreground wearing pink and imperial yellow striped silks is in the livery of the Earl of Rosebery. A bolt of this pure silk survives in the Henry Poole & Co. archive jockey silks book.

Hitler a close second in her mastery of sartorial messaging: 'The Queen made tentative suggestions: "And I thought, perhaps, another evening dress of – tulle? And a – tiara?"' Whilst in the gardens of the palace photographing the Queen, who wore a champagne-coloured floor-length tea gown and held a parasol more reminiscent of the Victorian era, Beaton was asked, 'Will my parasol obliterate the palace?' and replied, 'It is a very big palace, Ma'am.' Beaton lovingly describes all of the Queen's Hartnell outfits for the sitting: 'a ruby-encrusted crinoline of gold and silver' and 'spangled tulle like a fairy doll', with three rows of enormous pearls, a tiara and a two-strand diamond rivière necklace. 'Are three rows of pearls too much?' Beaton asked in a faux-naive fashion.

Just as Queen Elizabeth gave British fashion a terrific fillip with her nostalgic wardrobe, so the King paid close attention to the traditions of Ascot and the welfare of trainers and jockeys employed by the Royal Stud. He was conscious that Royal Ascot was as much an occasion for the 'common folk' as for the court laughing and chaffing in

The last of the four carriages in the Royal Procession at Ascot swings into the old Parade Ring, observed by the fashionable crowd. The gentleman seated on the left, facing the camera, is George, Duke of Kent, the fourth son of King George V.

the Royal Enclosure. *Ascot: A History* records the King's Representative writing to register his concern that 'greater comfort might be achieved by limiting the number of vouchers for admission, though this would cause widespread disappointment'. The King's response was to make the Royal Enclosure and the public areas larger.

In 1938, basking in the goodwill of his people, King George VI decreed that he and the Queen would ride out in the Royal Procession on all four days of the Royal Meeting. Previously it had been restricted to Tuesday and Thursday. A young Deborah Mitford attended Ascot again that year and waxed lyrical about the sight. 'I was as fascinated by the carriage horses in the King and Queen's procession – the famous Windsor Greys and Cleveland Bays – as I was by the thoroughbreds,' she writes as Dowager Duchess of Devonshire in *Wait for Me!*. 'There was something moving about the King and Queen's carriage appearing at the racecourse as a tiny dot a mile away and getting slowly bigger as it drew nearer; it was thrilling to see the skill of the postillions as they swung the carriage round to enter the paddock, judging to perfection the width of the entrance, and to hear the cheer of the crowd and the band playing the National Anthem. When the King had a winner, it was hats off all round.'

The Dowager Duchess also offers an insight into the royal house parties at Windsor during Ascot week. She and Andrew, the late Duke of Devonshire, were first invited in 1948. 'During those bleak post war years, these visits were the most cheering days I can remember, four daytime outfits for the races and five best evening dresses,' she writes. 'To be driven in a carriage as part of the procession down the racecourse at Ascot was a fascinating experience. As well as the obvious fun it is [to see] the jockey's eye view of the course and the intoxicating smell of horse and harness – it had an unexpected side.' The Duchess then reveals that comments from the crowd were audible in the carriages, one in particular: 'Doesn't she look awful in that hat.'

The Duchess commented that sitting next to the King at dinner was 'a rather difficult, frightening experience'. The longevity of the Queen Mother and the private nature of King George VI had until the 2011 film *The King's Speech* cast a shadow over his reputation. His chronic shyness, difficulties in public speaking and, in latter years, terminal illness often resulted in outbursts of temper and fist-banging. Suffice to say, Colin Firth's Golden Globe and Oscar-winning portrayal of George VI has gone a long way towards rehabilitating the essentially kind, decent and dignified King's reputation.

On 3 September 1939, Britain and France declared war on Germany. All racing was cancelled forthwith for three months; Royal Ascot was abandoned for the duration of the Second World War, with the Grandstand being given over as temporary barracks for the King's men. Nevertheless, the King and Queen continued to attend race meetings elsewhere. For security reasons their movements were not recorded in the Court Circular. When the Derby was relocated from Epsom to Newmarket, the royal family made a surprise appearance but, instead of his requisite grey morning coat and top hat, the King wore the uniform of the RAF.

Like the abdication crisis, the Second World War was to have a profound effect on the ladies and gentlemen who would ordinarily meet annually in the Royal Enclosure. Not a few members of the English aristocracy had great sympathy for Herr Hitler and his aversion to Jews, and not least the Mitford clan. The Duchess of Devonshire's mother, Lady Redesdale, and sisters Unity and Diana knew Hitler socially. Unity Mitford moved to Germany to be closer to her Führer and later shot herself in the head when the Nazi regime fell. Diana, Lady Mosley – who signed her letters to Unity with

ABOVE
'Madcap Millinery at the 1939 Ascot' from *The Sphere*, subtitled: 'The striking, the bizarre and the incomprehensible viewed in Paddock and Enclosure'. The 'mainsail'-shaped hat in the bottom right-hand corner has been reinvented in the twenty-first century by the great royal milliner Philip Treacy.

OPPOSITE
Diana Mitford, Lady Mosley, strikes an Aryan goddess pose in 1930 with her sons Bryan and Desmond Guinness from her first marriage to the Hon. Bryan Guinness. Her spotted, frilled organdie day dress remained the fashion for the decade. Lady Mosley and her second husband, Sir Oswald Mosley, leader of the British Union of Fascists, were both interred as highly dangerous nationals for the duration of the Second World War.

'Heil Hitler!' — had taken as her second husband the leader of the British Union of Fascists, Sir Oswald Mosley. Both were imprisoned for the duration of the war and were identified as 'very dangerous people' by Lady Mosley's sister, the Hon. Nancy Mitford.

Somewhat surprisingly, the war did not stymie the Paris fashion industry. Despite the occupation, the couturiers continued to trade, with designer Lucien Lelong reporting rather imperiously to Nazi high command that 'it does not lie within the power of any nation to take away from Paris the creative genius of fashion'. While British fashion appropriately bowed to the pressure of clothing coupons and 'make do and mend', Paris enjoyed a boom in haute couture, with houses such as Jacques Faith, Nina Ricci, Marcel Rochas and Maggy Rouff launching long careers during the occupation.

When the Allies won the war in May 1945, Paris fashion designers like Coco Chanel, who had allegedly collaborated with the Nazis during the occupation, were forced into exile. Though England was still in the grip of clothing rationing, a new generation of British fashion designers emerged from the ashes of the Blitz. Norman Hartnell resumed his duties as image-maker-in-chief for Queen Elizabeth and the Princesses Elizabeth and Margaret Rose, and in 1946 Hardy Amies opened his couture house at No. 14 Savile Row, anticipating Christian Dior's 'New Look' — a romantic, sumptuous and feminine reappraisal of nostalgic fashion — by two seasons with his circular-cut skirts that used yards of fabric, and neatly tailored little peplum jackets.

The austerity of the war years clearly demanded that fashion give European nations a reason to be cheerful. Women used to war work in overalls and headscarves, with a touch of scarlet lipstick to remind themselves of glamour long past, were yearning for a little escapism and romance. Fashion obliged. When Christian Dior presented his first haute couture collection to Paris in 1947, he made fashion history. 'Elitist and deliberately ignoring the practicalities of life, Christian Dior's designs were in no way intended as consumer products for the masses. But what they did provide was spectacle for an entire society,' writes François Baudot in *A Century of Fashion* (1999).

In 1946, the first post-war Ascot was reported by *The Times* as 'restored to the calendar of social events, but like much else in our new peacetime, its grandeur is greatly diminished': so much so that morning tails and formal day dress were given over to lounge suits and service uniform. 'Neither the Royal Enclosure nor the paddock had any startling note of fashion to catch the eye,' *The Times* noted.

The New Look in Paris prompted some disaffected members of society to heckle ladies wearing the new 'let them eat cake' silhouette in the streets and even sling mud

at those who had the capital to patronize the haute couture houses. England, as always, was more sanguine, and celebrated the touch of glamour that Hartnell and Amies brought back to society, as led by the royal ladies.

The film *The King's Speech* ended with George VI's flawless broadcast to the nation in 1939 when war was declared. His life ended in 1952 while Princess Elizabeth and her consort, the Duke of Edinburgh, were on a tour of Kenya. The King died of cancer, largely caused by his lifelong addiction to cigarettes, which he was encouraged to smoke by his doctors to 'refresh the lungs'. His death devastated his Queen, who blamed the Duke and Duchess of Windsor for the rest of their lives for the premature passing of her husband.

The coronation of Queen Elizabeth II in 1953 ushered in a new Elizabethan Age and a radical shift in the fashion cycle. It also gave Royal Ascot a monarch who would elevate the social occasion to its greatest height since the reign of her grandfather, King

A view of the Royal Box on Gold Cup day with King George VI smoking a cigarette (far left) and Princess Elizabeth and Queen Elizabeth observing the trackside Royal Enclosure (1950). The Queen is swathed in arctic fox and both royal ladies wear crowd-pleasing hats designed to show their faces at every angle.

The royal family's private collection of pearls is one of the largest and finest in the world. The three-strand pearl necklace was the Queen Mother's signature and has subsequently become the Queen's. This 1950 photograph of Queen and Princess Elizabeth in the Royal Box at Ascot shows off a fine example; possibly the pearls with ruby clasp presented to Queen Victoria by the Maharaja Ranjit Singh in 1851.

Edward VII. It is appropriate, however, to bring Queen Elizabeth The Queen Mother's story to its conclusion in the chapter dedicated to her husband, King George VI.

The Queen Mother had first attended Royal Ascot in 1919, the year the Royal Meeting was reinstated on the social calendar after the First World War. Racing was her favourite sport, but passion for the turf only came to dominate her life in the early 1950s, after the death of her beloved Bertie. As her official biographer William Shawcross writes in *Queen Elizabeth the Queen Mother* (2009), the Dowager Queen was most amused by steeplechase equestrian sport, whereas the new Queen Elizabeth II chose to concentrate on the Royal Stud and flat racing. They owned a successful steeplechaser called Monaveen together but, as the Princess Margaret commented, 'She wouldn't share with anybody now.' In the many letters between the two Queens, the Queen Mother would invariably write of a new acquisition: 'He has something special, hasn't he darling.'

Shawcross writes that 'over the next five decades [after 1952], mother and daughter derived enormous pleasure from their shared passion for racing ... wherever they were, they exchanged the news and the gossip of the Turf. Reading *Sporting Life* every day of her life, [the Queen Mother] installed a loudspeaker system in Clarence House not dissimilar to a betting shop.' The Queen Mother never missed a Royal Ascot week. She would install herself and her house party at Royal Lodge, Windsor, and continued to host her daughter's dinners at Windsor Castle.

As Hugo Vickers writes in his biography *Elizabeth, The Queen Mother* (2005), 'In later life, the Queen did not disguise her dislike of certain nationalities, notably the Germans. When Crown Prince Naruhito of Japan, son of Emperor Akihito, was staying at Windsor Castle for Ascot Week, she insisted that the Japanese sword of surrender be put on display in the Royal Library for his "special interest". When the royal party processed in to dinner, the Queen said (in a stage whisper) "Come on everybody. Nip on! Nip on!"'

Until the end of her life in 2002, the Queen Mother was a much-loved presence at Royal Ascot in June and at the King George and Queen Elizabeth Stakes in July. She invariably rode in the carriage procession with the late Diana, Princess of Wales, in the years after the Princess married Prince Charles. The Queen Mother was the first Queen to have a winner at Royal Ascot since Queen Anne, and is still much missed as one of Royal Ascot's most popular leading ladies.

OPPOSITE
The Queen Mother, as she was remembered later in her long life, photographed with her racehorse Sunny Boy at Ascot in 1976.

The Queen Mother and Diana, Princess of Wales, were regular companions in the Royal Procession at Ascot, as pictured here in 1986. Diana, Princess of Wales, was loaned relatively little of the royal jewels, and chose instead to make a signature of the multiple-strand pearl choker, of which she owned several with opal, turquoise and diamond snaps.

THOROUGHBREDS: FABULOUS FILLIES AND GORGEOUS STUDS AT ROYAL ASCOT

'Royal Ascot is the best race meeting in the world – it has style, it has panache and it has class, all of which are reflected in the way people dress to impress. Royal Ascot brings out the best sport and the best in British fashion.'

CLARE BALDING, BBC RACING CORRESPONDENT (2011)

OPPOSITE AND OVERLEAF
The racing may be fun and games for racegoers, but for jockeys Royal Ascot is deadly serious. As veteran jockey Harry Carr wrote in his 1966 autobiography, 'At no meeting in the season is the betting more fast and furious than Ascot.'

Royal Ascot has had many champion jockeys in its three hundred years, but none as successful as the greatest English flat-racing jockey of all time, Lester Piggott, with his world record 3,500 career wins, 11 British Champion Jockey titles, 30 British Classic races and 11 wins at the Ascot Gold Cup. Piggott's father won the Grand National three times, but the twelve-year-old apprentice chose instead to race on the flat, winning his first title in 1948. Piggott was a star and, arguably, the first jockey to have achieved national and international recognition as much for his sardonic humour as his style in the saddle. He was known to growl, 'Move over, Granddad,' to his elder competing jockeys when he was all out to win at Ascot. Piggott's racing career ostensibly ended in 1985 and in 1987 he was jailed for tax evasion and stripped of his OBE. However, a true champion, he won the Breeder's Cup Mile within ten days of his return to the saddle in 1990, and rode his last winner in 1994, before retiring for good a year later.

William 'Willie' Carson is the fourth most successful jockey in Great British racing history to date, but is the most successful and popular of his peers at Royal Ascot, having combined a champion racing career with a second act as the BBC's racing correspondent alongside co-presenter Clare Balding. Carson was awarded the MBE in 1983 for services to horse racing; 1990 was his best season, when he rode 187 winners, including six winners on one card – a feat only achieved by four jockeys in the twentieth century.

In 1996, the *Times* leader read: 'To win seven races in an afternoon turns men into gods'. It referred to the Ascot Festival of British Racing, when Lanfranco 'Frankie' Dettori scored the Magnificent Seven: winning all seven races on the card. In 1990, Dettori became the first teenager since Lester Piggott to ride 100 winners in one season. Like Piggott, Dettori is a star in the media as well as at Ascot. In 2000 he was awarded the MBE, and a year later a David Roper-Curzon bronze of Dettori executing his famous 'flying dismount' was unveiled at Ascot. Dettori has three Championship Jockey titles, four Ascot Gold Cup winners and 39 winners at Ascot. He shows no sign of going quietly.

MARVELLOUS MILLINERY II:
THE GLORIOUS HATTERS
WHO CROWN ROYAL ASCOT

OPPOSITE AND OVERLEAF
The definition of a successful Ascot hat is that it be witty, pretty and not frighten the horses. Visibility is also a point of etiquette because a lady is never popular when her chapeau obscures the finishing post. The vogue at recent Royal Ascots has been for asymmetric brims and bravura vertical rather than horizontal displays. A notable exception to the rule is the divine Grace Jones (opposite, centre left), who attended the Royal Meeting in 2010 wearing a humbug-stripe broad-brimmed Philip Treacy hat accessorized by the milliner himself. Overleaf is a masterclass in marvellous millinery by Philip Treacy, Stephen Jones, James Lock & Co. and Ilda DiVico. See page 219 for a list of milliners whose work is shown.

'Hats are the important accessory. In fact, when worn with verve, they are often the raison d'être of many an outfit. But when magazines write articles on accessories, often they myopically feature only bags and shoes. Now I have nothing against Miuccia or Manolo, Louis or Lulu, but without the gloves, scarves, jewels – and hats? Why are they remaindered to the Timbuktu of fashion when they are in fact its Shangri-La?'

STEPHEN JONES IN *HATS: AN ANTHOLOGY* (2009)

Two milliners – Stephen Jones and Philip Treacy – share the honours as the Royal Enclosure's fashion leaders over the past two decades.

Treacy is a sculptor – the Naum Gabo of millinery – whose great respect for minimal shapes and balanced trim deployed to maximum impact creates Neoclassical shapes that respect the craft of couture millinery while giving us a contemporary redefinition of elegance. In 2000, he was the first milliner to be invited to show a hat collection at the haute couture shows in Paris.

Jones brings an irreverent punk and New Romantic sensibility, which he shares with long-time collaborator Vivienne Westwood, and combines it with a fascination for the history of hat making to push millinery to new heights of glamour, audacity and irresistible amusement. Stephen Jones's muse, *Vogue Italia* editor-at-large Anna

Piaggi, says that 'he is the maker of the most beautiful hats in the world', while US *Vogue* European editor Hamish Bowles observes that 'his genius is to enhance the mystery, allure and wit of the wearer'.

Both Jones's and Treacy's work has been honoured with world-touring exhibitions: 'Jones's Hats: An Anthology' for the Victoria & Albert museum and London's Design Museum-commissioned retrospective of Treacy's work with muse Isabella Blow, entitled 'When Philip Met Isabella'. Treacy is the favourite at Royal Ascot because it is his firm belief that 'hats are for everyone. We all have a head so we have the possibility to wear a hat. You feel better for wearing them.' Like Jones, he has collaborated with Royal Ascot since 2007, and whether worn ready-to-wear in the Silver Ring or couture in the Royal Enclosure, his work is unmistakable.

CHAPTER 5

QUEEN ELIZABETH II
The Golden Age of Ascot
1952 — PRESENT

'Once again a Queen ruled over Britain. The smiling
young girl who seemed to possess the hidden secret
of true happiness within her spirit had been summoned
to take upon her slight shoulders the burden which
two Kings had found almost beyond bearing and which
one had refused…'

COPE'S ROYAL CAVALCADE OF THE TURF, EDITED BY ALFRED COPE (1953)

? Ascot 1954

THE YEAR 1952 SAW THE FIRST ROYAL ASCOT OF THE NEW ELIZABETHAN AGE, AND EXPECTATIONS WERE HIGH. As Prime Minister Winston Churchill said in a radio broadcast, 'Famous have been the reigns of our Queens. Some of the greatest periods in our history have unfolded under their sceptre...'

There was already a marked change in the monarch's demeanour around the Royal racecourse, according to *Cope's Royal Cavalcade of the Turf*: 'Until the time of Queen Elizabeth II there had been a certain studied formality about the movements of the Royal family at the Royal meeting, but on this occasion race goers were astonished to see an absorbed young woman leaning casually on the paddock rails while watching the saddling of the horses ... so strange it was to see her mingling freely with her people that as she left the rails and walked back to the Royal Enclosure she was unrecognized by many.'

PRECEDING PAGES, LEFT
Queen Elizabeth II, not yet crowned, attends the Windsor Horse Show in 1952. Her Majesty's affinity with horses has proved to be a lifelong passion.

Light-weight wool dress with flared fullness at hem and silk bindings at neck and on the sleeves.

HARDY AMIES

HARDY AMIES

HARDY AMIES

OPPOSITE AND ABOVE
The British couture house of Hardy Amies has dressed the Queen for almost sixty years and was awarded the Royal Warrant in 1955. The archive, held at No. 14 Savile Row, contains hundreds of designs for Her Majesty with fabric swatches attached. One of the earliest (opposite, left) is a 1954 New Look model for Royal Ascot.

In keeping with this more relaxed royal aura at Ascot, a mere three years had elapsed since clothing rationing had been lifted and so the 1952 Ascot did not quite reach the dizzying heights of pre-war glamour. But the Royal Procession was reinstated for the first time since 1939, and the new Queen shone in Norman Hartnell couture with the dashing Prince Philip, whom she had married in 1947, at her side. This was in marked contrast to the Queen's first Royal Ascot in 1945, at which she wore the uniform of the ATS (Auxiliary Territorial Service) for which she was a Junior Commander.

The Queen's importance as a fashion leader in the early years of her reign is not to be underestimated, even though biographer Sarah Bradford writes in *Elizabeth: A Biography of Her Majesty the Queen* (2002): 'To her, clothes are props, part of her job, which is why she likes clear colours that stand out like cantaloupe and turquoise.' That the Queen is a pragmatist is not in dispute, but her first appearances as monarch at

Royal Ascot were not dissimilar to those of her daughter-in-law Diana, Princess of Wales, thirty years later.

Until her death in 1993, the Queen's formidable nanny, dresser and confidante Margaret 'Bobo' MacDonald ruled the royal wardrobe with an iron fist sans velvet glove. She was the only person outside the royal family allowed to address the Queen by her childhood nickname, Lilibet. 'Miss MacDonald to a great degree was the Queen's eyes and ears at the Palace and it didn't do you any good to fall foul of her,' writes Bradford. 'One of Bobo's particular spheres of interest was dealing with the Queen's dressmakers. She would attend the sessions with Norman Hartnell and Hardy Amies, and later Ian Thomas and a tailor, John Anderson. Mr Rayne, who went to the Palace in a morning suit, designed her shoes; and in those days, her milliners were Aage Thaarup, who was responsible for her much-criticized hats, and Simone Mirman.'

The sometimes caustic couturier Hardy Amies fell foul of Miss MacDonald when one of his unguarded remarks about his most famous client reached her ears. Amies was awarded the Royal Warrant in 1955 and he, or his lieutenants Ken Fleetwood and Jon Moore, dressed Her Majesty until well into the twenty-first century. But he remained on Miss MacDonald's blacklist, and she would routinely 'advise' the Queen to favour Hartnell. Bradford's suggestion that some Amies dresses were relegated to the back of

ABOVE LEFT
The British shoemaking dynasty of H. & R. Rayne of Bond Street held the Royal Warrants for Queen Mary, the Queen Mother and our present Queen until 1994. In 1958, the house collaborated with Wedgwood to produce these shoes with Jasperware heels decorated with Wedgwood cameos. The design was reissued in 1977.

ABOVE
Italian aristocratic couturier Elsa Schiaparelli's white organza and shocking pink slubbed silk gown for spring/summer 1953 echoes the pre-war, pre-austerity era of delicate 1930s fashion.

OPPOSITE
Vogue model Fiona Campbell-Walter (titled the Baroness Thyssen when she married in 1956) arrives at Royal Ascot 1953 in a neat, curvaceous, white corded skirt suit accessorized with a fur stole, black straw saucer hat and pearls.

the royal wardrobe until Miss MacDonald had retired seems rather unlikely, however. The house of Hardy Amies displays the Queen's mannequin in the archive room at No. 14 Savile Row; it is noticeable that over those years the mannequin has been padded with silk-covered wadding as the Queen's figure matured. The Amies archive also contains hundreds of sketches for the Queen, with embroidered fabric swatches still pinned to the paper, from the 1950s to the 2000s.

The eyes of the world were on Westminster Abbey in 1953 when Queen Elizabeth II was crowned in what was arguably the most lavish coronation since King George IV's in 1821. It had been sixteen years since her father's coronation, and fashion – not to mention that the new monarch was a Queen – necessitated more than simply dusting off ancient robes and refreshing ermine trim. It was the first coronation to be filmed in glorious Technicolor and televised for the nation, establishing the royal wardrobe as the most famous in the world, excepting perhaps that of a certain Miss Marilyn Monroe, who was starring in *Gentlemen Prefer Blondes*. Her Majesty wore Hartnell.

The first decade of the Queen's reign coincided with a golden age for Paris couture that was dominated by Christian Dior until his death in 1957. Spanish genius Cristóbal Balenciaga was sculpting arguably the most sublime silhouettes of the period, prompting *Harper's Bazaar* editor Diana Vreeland to declare, 'When a woman wearing Balenciaga entered a room, no other woman existed.' A seventy-one-year-old Coco Chanel made her comeback in 1954 and introduced the knitted skirt suit of the No. 5 collection, edged with distinctive multi-hued fringe; it remains the definitive Royal Ascot uniform for the ladies in the Enclosure, as worn with Chanel's 'gilt and quilt' handbags and two-tone flat leather pumps.

The rules of engagement in the Royal Enclosure did not relax under Queen Elizabeth II. Divorcees were still not welcome in either the Royal Household Stand or the extended Queen's Lawn (this rule being repealed only in the 1960s). Bare legs were anathema to the stewards who guarded the gates to the Enclosure. The 1950s and early 1960s were the era when fashion demanded that ladies be refined, ultra-feminine and immaculately turned out, like show ponies on the arm of a dashing chap. The full skirts currently enjoying another fashion moment thanks to US television series *Mad Men* were balanced by wasp waists and bosoms encased in the cantilever bra invented by billionaire aviator and film producer Howard Hughes for Jane Russell in his 1943 film *The Outlaw*.

For her formal day dress, such as Royal Ascot attire, the Queen was already developing a rigidity and uniformity that would increasingly distance her from fashion

LEFT
Audrey Tatou portrays Coco Chanel in *Coco Before Chanel* (2009); here she is poised on the mirrored staircase of her Rue Cambon flagship in Paris to watch reactions to her fashion show unobserved.

ABOVE
Chanel couture cream tweed suit and raspberry tweed suit (both early 1960s). Chanel's tweed skirt suits have been unimpeachably elegant propositions for Royal Ascot since the 1950s.

as the decade died. Sarah Bradford reported her telling one of her couturiers: 'That's too chic for me.' Princess Margaret, however, appeared to model herself on the late movie queen Elizabeth Taylor with her craving for the glamorous life that the racing, cabaret and cocktail crowd naturally obliged her with. Bon viveur Princess Margaret danced nightly at the Savoy with a group christened the 'Margaret set'. 'The Princess at this time seemed an almost impossibly glamorous figure,' writes Tim Heald in *Princess Margaret: A Life Unravelled* (2007). 'Hats, bouquets, handbags are all apparently permanent fixtures, as is a wide seductive smile.'

In 1953, Princess Margaret inadvertently found herself at the centre of the most profound constitutional crisis since King Edward VIII's abdication. At the Queen's coronation, the press noted a moment of intimacy when Margaret brushed an imaginary tuft of fluff (possibly errant ermine?) from the uniform of Group Captain Peter Townsend. Captain Townsend was controller of Queen Elizabeth The Queen Mother's household at Clarence House, where Princess Margaret also resided after the death of her father. He was divorced. After Prince Charles and Princess Anne, Princess Margaret was the third in line to the throne and thus the marriage was untenable. Nowhere would this have been more marked than at Royal Ascot, where in principle a divorcee husband of a Royal Princess would not have been admitted to the Royal Enclosure.

'The Queen was naturally sympathetic to her younger sister and she liked Townsend,' writes Heald, 'but she was still a crucial part of the exercise. Townsend felt bounced, particularly with regard to timing. He claimed that he was promised an opportunity to say a proper farewell to Margaret but that this was denied. He was, unexpectedly, ordered to leave [the country] before Margaret and her mother returned from an official visit to Rhodesia.'

Until her death in 2002, Princess Margaret's star gradually declined. Her marriage to society photographer Lord Snowdon mirrored that of Elizabeth Taylor and Richard Burton, who attended Royal Ascot in the 1960s with Noël Coward. Later, her escape to the island of Mustique unfairly distanced her from the affection of the public. However, Princess Margaret retained her poise until increasing ill health confined her to a wheelchair and, more importantly, she retained her love for Royal Ascot and loyalty to the Queen.

The 1960s saw a profound shift in attitudes towards the establishment, and towards fashion at Ascot – but not before royal photographer and celebrated costume

designer Cecil Beaton gave one last hurrah for the age of empire, with his now-legendary Ascot scene in the 1964 film *My Fair Lady* (see page 76). 'He had been drawing Ascot fashions since he was a child,' writes Hugo Vickers in *Cecil Beaton: The Authorised Biography* (1985). 'He had even published sketches in an article called "Ascots of the Past" in *Vogue* on 28 May 1930.'

Beaton had sketched out the costumes for the Ascot scene of the stage musical version of *My Fair Lady* starring Julie Andrews. 'His black and white scene – the motionless frieze of ladies like magpies against a white drop – upon which the curtain rises towards the end of the first act brought a gasp of astonished wonder night after night, combining all Cecil hoped for – elegance, beauty, surprise and wit,' writes Vickers.

But Beaton was to surpass himself with the assistance of the formidable costume department at Warner Brothers in Hollywood for the Audrey Hepburn film. As Hepburn writes in *Cecil Beaton's Fair Lady* (1964), 'I'll never forget the sight of the

ABOVE AND OPPOSITE
In 1992, Jasper Conran was invited to design the costumes for Simon Callow's theatrical revival of *My Fair Lady*. To follow in the footsteps of Cecil Beaton, who designed the original stage and screen productions of *My Fair Lady* to great acclaim and Oscar-winning success, was daunting, but Conran rose to the challenge. The sketches above are for Conran's interpretation of the Ascot scene, drawn by Julie Verhoeven; and Stephen Jones crafted the overblown flower-head hats for Conran's Ascot scene, dramatically photographed in the image opposite by Tessa Traeger.

enormous laboratory with hundreds of women sewing and doing and the beauty of the costumes which were on stands, of embroidery being done, of masses of beautiful aigrettes and feathers and velvets and ribbons, and violets which had been made I don't know where.' One of the costumers turned to Beaton as he worked on designs inspired by his childhood heroines, musical actresses Lily Elsie and Gaby Deslys, and said, 'What does it feel like, Mr Beaton, always to be right?'

Beaton's costumes were informed by the Black Ascot of 1910, but he leavened the palette with accents of white (royal mourning) and purple, which were appropriate after the initial period that demanded an all-black wardrobe. With the exception of Rex Harrison's Professor Higgins, who would not have been admitted into the Royal Enclosure wearing brown tweed, Savile Row firm Sullivan, Woolley & Co. tailored all the chaps' costumes in the scene. As visitor to the set Eddie Goetz reported to Beaton, 'I have just returned from the Ascot scene at Warner's and I am literally in a daze. These costumes are without doubt the most breathtakingly beautiful, exquisite creations ever wrought by man. And as you are the man, I bow low in your direction.' Cecil Beaton won both the Best Costume and Best Colour Art Direction Oscars for the film.

The decline of the nostalgic Hollywood musical, the decline of Parisian haute couture and the decline in dress at Royal Ascot occurred in tandem as the 1960s

Social mobility en route to Royal
Ascot: a dapper chap rides pillion
in full morning dress on his date's
scooter.

gathered pace. In 1961, the old Grandstand was razed to the ground to make way for
the Queen Elizabeth II Stand. In 1964, the Royal Enclosure doubled in size to a capacity
of 7,500 people, opening the floodgates to the new Swinging Sixties rock, fashion and
photography aristocracy, and also widening the margin for error in dress. Social
mobility was at its most aggressive in this era, with working-class boys and girls such
as photographer David Bailey, model Jean Shrimpton, and Justin de Villeneuve with his
protégée model Twiggy leading the 'Youthquake'.

The Queen continued to appear at Royal Ascot throughout the decade in elegant,
simple silk and wool day dresses in the style of former US First Lady Jacqueline
Kennedy – invariably accessorized with matching hats, gloves and handbags, not to
mention magnificent diamond brooches and pearls from the Windsors' private jewel
collection – but her subjects were sorely trying the patience of Her Majesty's
Representative, the Duke of Norfolk. As Sean Magee writes in *Ascot: The History*
(2002), 'Female fashion presented far more tricky problems and in 1967 the Duke
of Norfolk imposed a formal ban on trouser suits in the Royal Enclosure. In 1968 a
nineteen-year-old heiress named Jayne Harries, and a year later Maria Subiza, wife
of an Argentinean diplomat, both wrote footnotes in Ascot history by being turned
away from the Royal Enclosure for wearing such outrageous garb.'

A rare Paco Rabanne chain-linked armour-plated mini dress (1967). It was not only skirt length, trouser suits and hot pants that challenged the Duke of Norfolk, Her Majesty's Representative at Royal Ascot, in the 1960s. Fashion quite literally appeared to be from another planet, with couturiers such as Paco Rabanne creating space race-inspired collections using metal sheeting, moulded plastic and patent fetish rubber, as epitomized by Jane Fonda in the 1968 film *Barbarella*.

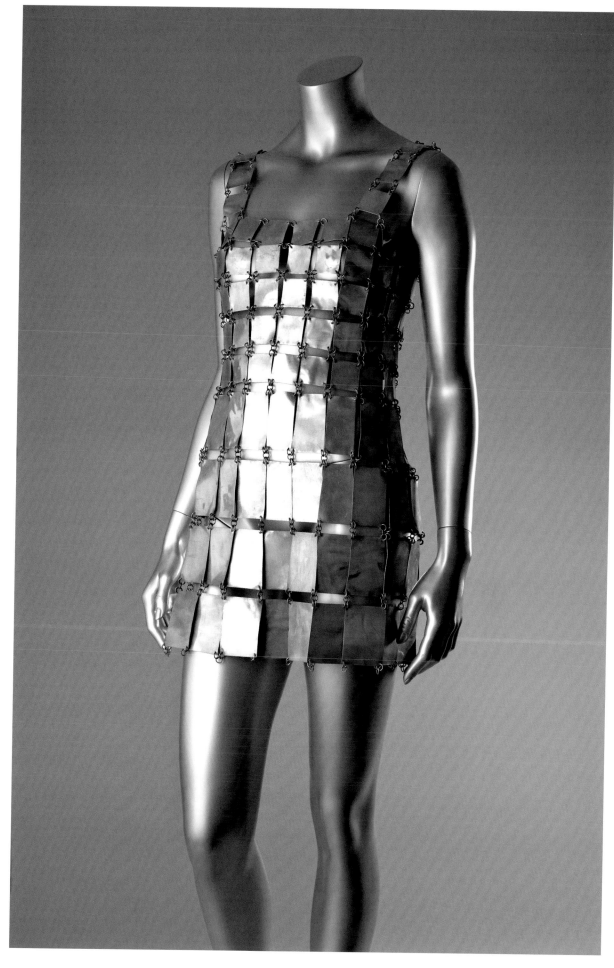

'In the Sixties, fashion began to focus upon teenagers', writes James Laver in *Costume & Fashion*. Compared with the calmer 1970s, the 1960s seemed to be one frenetic dash by girls to buy the latest look and by designers to produce the next one. Fashion effectively crossed the floor from elegant attire to fantasy fancy-dress costume, with Parisian couturiers such as Paco Rabanne, Pierre Cardin and André Courrèges being inspired by the space race to design minidresses fashioned with chain mail, plastic discs and white plastic; all worn with kinky knee-high boots.

If Paris couture still nominally led fashion within the Royal Enclosure, Swinging London led the charge outside it, with the new Carnaby Street and King's Road boutique culture selling faux-naive and ever-so-jejune ready-to-wear. The darling of them all was Mary Quant, the woman fashion history has credited with the rise of the miniskirt. As racing commentator Peter O'Sullevan observed in 1967, 'The miniskirt fashion seems to be exploited by those least suited to exposure.' Observers of the Royal Enclosure today may be tempted to whisper 'plus ça change'.

The miniskirt, worn bare-legged or with luridly coloured tights and Mary-Jane shoes or boots, was everything that the Royal Enclosure stewards despised. London was also leading the way in a hairdressing revolution, with Vidal Sassoon's asymmetric bob perfected on Mary Quant and Twiggy's urchin crop necessitating a decline in the wearing of hats. The 'dolly bird' look of late-1960s make-up – false eyelashes like a burlesque dancer's fan, pearly pink lipstick and white foundation

— was equally confrontational when placed in the context of formal day dress at Royal Ascot.

One would imagine the Royal Household was starting to hear the creak of tumbrel wheels when confronted with the hippy culture of the last years of the 1960s, when even swinging aristocrats followed The Beatles in their experiments with Maharishis, hallucinogenic drugs, floral smocks and love beads. Equally unacceptable to the old establishment was the brief flowering of the peacock male in London's Savile Row, when bespoke wild child Tommy Nutter and his cutter Edward Sexton dressed society rebels such as Mick Jagger, Lord Montagu of Beaulieu, Elton John, John Lennon and Lord Snowdon in wildly patterned and coloured bespoke suits with characteristic roped shoulders, madly splayed lapels and crotch-hugging flared trousers.

Savile Row tailor Bobby Valentine cut a morning coat in bubblegum-pink for society hairdresser Raymond 'Mr Teasy-Weasy' Bessone, the Nicky Clark of his day. East End tailor Timothy Everest, who worked for Nutter in the autumn of his life, owns a dogtooth morning coat, waistcoat, trousers and matching top hat that Nutter crafted for one of his peacocks to display at Royal Ascot. What's more, fashions in male hair between 1968 and 1976 favoured long locks and sideburns that somehow seemed totally disrespectful when worn under a black silk top hat.

Not that the Royal Enclosure was quite comparable in its free-love Age of Aquarius fashions to the Woodstock music festival held in San Francisco in 1969. Standards were

The minidress looking surprisingly frumpy at Royal Ascot in 1966: less Carnaby Street than Lucie Clayton.

ABOVE LEFT
An Ossie Clark/Celia Birtwell tulip print chiffon tunic, and an Ossie Clark/Celia Birtwell for Radley printed rayon maxi dress, both early 1970s. This period saw a revival of interest in retro fashion movements such as the Ballets Russes and Art Nouveau, and 1920s style.

ABOVE RIGHT
In 1971 these three ladies attended Royal Ascot wearing flares, miniskirt and maxi dress trimmed with multicoloured plastic computer keyboard keys. It is the tradition for certain ladies to make their own outfits at the Royal. Suffice to say, you won't see them in the Enclosures.

still upheld; almost as though the Royal Meeting were a last bastion of civilization, holding back the floodgates of a more ugly, aggressive world outside. Still, by 1967 it was already too much for Cecil Beaton, whose disdain for the event may, admittedly, be coloured by a snub long since passed. As he writes in his *Self-Portrait with Friends*, edited by Richard Buckle (1979), 'As a snobbish boy I was always disappointed when my mother's request for tickets to the Royal Enclosure at Ascot were turned down. But the slap in the face came again and again from Lord Churchill on behalf of the King. … However, nowadays anyone who can pay [the] few guineas necessary is welcomed, and with the opening of the floodgates that allowed in [band leader] Jack Hylton, [theatrical impresario] Binkie Beaumont and any little starlet, I was given the OK.' Despite declaring that the days of 'the grand ladies in their fantastic dresses and the exclusiveness had all gone', Beaton does concede: 'The colour of Royal Ascot has changed – Edwardian Ascot must have been entirely pastel-coloured. But this was a

The major 1920s revival in early 1970s fashion is reflected by creative director Marc Bohan in this Christian Dior rose weave coat trimmed with purple fox fur on the collar, cuffs and hem, *c.* 1975. Both the pattern and the extravagant fur trim are reminiscent of Paul Poiret's work in the first decades of the twentieth century.

The 'Ascot Mascot', Mrs Gertrude Shilling, sallies forth in 1969 wearing an apricot feathered get-up, with a supersized cartwheel picture hat also trimmed with apricot feather fringe, as designed by her son, milliner David Shilling. Mrs Shilling delighted and shocked the Royal Enclosure in equal measure. Pity the poor racegoer who happened to be behind her on the trackside lawn when the Royal Procession came by.

transformation that I enjoyed. Everywhere there were large touches of brilliant magenta, orange and viridian. The Maharaja of Jaipur in a marvellous turban of ochre and scarlet. Yet the retina-irritant mutation of the plastic and the nylon looked crummy in the outdoors; the crocheted shift, the mini skirts and little-girl fashions were hardly right.'

Thus the battle lines between those who want to uphold the traditions of propriety and elegance at Ascot and those who come for a knees-up dressed inappropriately were drawn, and still exist to this day. The public mood was ugly when Beaton visited Ascot in 1967, with protestors holding up the Royal Procession while waving banners that read 'stop the murder in Vietnam'.

In 1969, the Queen allowed the BBC and ITV to collaborate on a documentary, *Royal Family*, depicting the Windsors' domestic life. As broadcaster David Attenborough quite rightly said to producer–director Richard Cawston, 'You're killing the monarchy you know, with this film you're making. The whole institution depends on mystique and the tribal chief in his hut. If any member of the tribe ever sees inside the hut, the whole system of tribal chiefdom is damaged.'

The first five years of the 1970s saw the unfurling of peacock male tailoring, as led by Savile Row tailor Tommy Nutter and his cutter Edward Sexton. It was arguably the last era of the twentieth century in which men outshone their lady friends. This image shows Ken and Rose Calder at Waterloo station en route to Royal Ascot in 1970: he is sporting a white single-breasted suit with extravagant lapels and sharp shoulders, and she wears patchwork platform boots, an artisanal smock and a satin blouse with vast pussycat bow.

In 1970, Royal Ascot had to bow to fashion and feminism by allowing trouser suits of a matching fabric into the Royal Enclosure. 'By 1971 the Enclosure was under attack from an even more insidious fashion of the time – hot pants,' records *Royal Ascot: The History*. 'The *Daily Mail* reported, "There is now a hot-bed of confusion on whether women wearing hot pants will be allowed into the Royal Enclosure at Ascot races. On Monday an Ascot racecourse official ruled them OK. But yesterday the Duke of Norfolk issued a statement declaring shorts out." A lady named Denise Lee got round Norfolk's decree by wearing a cutaway skirt over clearly visible orange pants. But other excesses, such as the bare midriff, remained well beyond the pale.'

By 1971, the Queen was forty-five years old, her wardrobe was still directed by Miss MacDonald, now sixty-seven, and her favoured couturiers, shoemakers and hatters had remained unchanged. The Queen's hairstyle was largely as it had been on coronation day in 1953. However, the Queen Mother – invariably a vision in pastels, veils, feathers and furs – remained in the fashion limelight as the nation's sugar-coated grandmother.

After being the leading winner/owner in 1954, the Royal Stud was not enjoying much success at Royal Ascot or any other race meeting in the 1970s. However, the Queen always lit up when surrounded by her horse-racing and -breeding circle at Royal Ascot, such as racing manager Sir Peter Cazalet, the Aga Khan (whose father had given the Princess a filly foal she christened Astrakhan in 1947) and Lord 'Porchy' Porchester

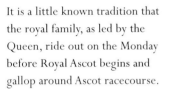

It is a little known tradition that the royal family, as led by the Queen, ride out on the Monday before Royal Ascot begins and gallop around Ascot racecourse.

(later the 7th Earl of Carnarvon), whom she had known since she was a girl. As Sarah Bradford writes, 'Breeding and training gun dogs and thoroughbreds are her two private interests, both of which she approaches with her usual professionalism. … Elizabeth is competitive. She looks for excellence and likes to win.'

The Queen's Silver Jubilee in 1977 coincided with what was perhaps one of the most shocking, aggressive anti-establishment fashion moments to emanate from London's streets: punk. While the nation planned bunting-strewn street parties and the Queen made her annual appearance at Royal Ascot in the carriage procession, Derek Jarman released his irreverent, anarchic celluloid tribute to punk, *Jubilee*, impresario Malcolm McLaren unleashed the Sex Pistols' *God Save the Queen (the Fascist Regime)* and punk fashion's high priestess Vivienne Westwood sold T-shirts of the Queen with a safety pin through her nose from her King's Road boutique, Sex.

Punk did not permeate the Royal Enclosure except in the painted-chiffon torn, slashed and knotted dresses crafted by Zandra Rhodes. Much more appropriate were the nostalgic 1920s- and 1930s-inspired dresses sold by High Street Kensington super-boutique Biba; the neat navy jersey dresses designed by Jean Muir; and the chiffon and silk velvet tea dresses cut by Ossie Clark from wife Celia Birtwell's whimsical prints, worn with tiny lacy, netted 1940s retro 'Hollywood hats'. The vogue for platform shoes and boots did walk all over the lawns of the Royal Enclosure, as did the 'sport couture' aesthetic of easy silhouettes in luxe fabrics, as perfected by the Studio 54 generation of Halston, Gucci and Fiorucci.

The couturier who dominated 1970s Royal Ascot was Yves Saint Laurent, who released a string of fashion pearls such as the Safari collection, Le Smoking collection and a revival of the Ballets Russes' early twentieth-century oriental exoticism. The sight of Saint Laurent storm troopers Jacqueline Kennedy Onassis, model Iman and actress Catherine Deneuve in tuxedo jackets, slim cigarette pants and killer heels couldn't have been in more marked contrast to the royal ladies at Ascot in their sensible knee-length tweed coat dresses with increasingly anachronistic hats. Bohemian-chic Diane Keaton in her mannish Ralph Lauren slouch pants was where high fashion resided, not at the Royal Meeting.

With timing that would put Cinderella to shame, a nineteen-year-old Lady Diana Spencer announced her engagement to Prince Charles (wearing the same sapphire ring her son Prince William gave to Miss Catherine Middleton almost thirty years later) and placed the fashion spotlight firmly back on the royal family and the Royal Meeting.

ABOVE
A Vivienne Westwood/Malcolm McLaren 'God Save the Queen' pink cheesecloth bondage shirt from 1977. While the nation celebrated the Queen's Silver Jubilee with street parties, bunting and flag-waving reminiscent of VE Day, the subversive king and queen of London's punk scene were printing T-shirts bearing jubilee portraits of Her Majesty with a safety pin through her nose.

OPPOSITE
Milliner Stephen Jones revisits his punk and New Romantic past with a tiny Union Jack top hat, modelled at Royal Ascot in 2008 by Olivia Inge and photographed for a fashion advertising campaign for the Royal Meeting in the same year.

'Shy Di', a stereotypical 'Sloane ranger', as posh Chelsea girls in pearls were christened, made her first appearance in the Royal Procession at Ascot in June 1981. As *Royal Ascot: The History* relates, 'Shrugging off a potentially treasonable incident when a gateman tried to stop her entering the Royal Enclosure as she was not displaying her badge – she just looked startled, then somebody said it was Lady Diana, and she gave a wonderful smile and walked on.'

In her early Ascot years, the Princess of Wales, as she was styled, did not exactly set the fashion world on fire. Her overblown ivory silk wedding dress with its train the length of St Paul's Cathedral, designed by David and Elizabeth Emanuel, established her as a fairytale princess. But in the formal day dress of a working royal, she appeared to be dressing twenty years too old for her age, and the fussy pussycat-bow blouses and stiff skirt suits in the sugary New Romantic pastel palette of the early 1980s did not become a young, modern princess; Prime Minister Margaret Thatcher, perhaps, but not a princess.

The Princess of Wales wisely decided to consult the then editor of *Vogue*, the late Elizabeth Tilberis, who introduced her to a new generation of great British fashion designers such as Amanda Wakeley, Bruce Oldfield, Arabella Pollen, Catherine Walker, Jasper Conran and Tomasz Starzewski. Taking her cue from Nolan Miller, who designed Joan Collins's costumes for the US soap *Dynasty*, Princess Diana developed the 'Dynasty Di' wardrobe of bold, angular, primary-coloured dresses with shoulder pads like a rugby fullback, worn with hats that were crafted to frame her face and add drama and height to her model figure, and which, incidentally, dwarfed her husband, the Prince of Wales, physically and metaphorically.

The *Telegraph*'s garrulous fashion editor Hilary Alexander (a Royal Ascot veteran) wrote in 1988: 'Spurred on by the Princess of Wales's recent appearances, clad head to toe in polka dots, everyone predicted a spotty Royal Ascot opening day. They weren't wrong … but predictably, after such a rush of spotty outfits, the Princess of Wales eschewed spots altogether. She picked instead the coolest of cream silks for a suit and perfectly toning Spanish hat.'

The Princess of Wales continued to lead fashion at Royal Ascot for the rest of the decade, though her elegance reached its apogee in 1988, when she wore a cool, understated dove-grey coat, echoing male morning tails, over a white Catherine Walker dress, accessorized with a white Philip Somerville picture hat and pearls. She wowed the crowd for a second time with a black-and-white polka-dot dress designed by

TOP
An early 1980s Hardy Amies Couture royal blue skirt suit made for the late Diana, Princess of Wales. The suit is not dissimilar to the model then Lady Diana Spencer wore in the gardens of Buckingham Palace when her engagement to Prince Charles was announced. However, the pronounced shoulders suggest this piece was made later in the decade.

ABOVE
Early supermodel girls in pearls Jerry Hall and Marie Helvin arrive in the Royal Enclosure at Ascot in 1982. The wives of Rolling Stones rock god Mick Jagger and fashion photographer David Bailey respectively, Hall and Helvin are two of British fashion's most enduring muses and models.

A memorable 1988 appearance at Royal Ascot by Diana, Princess of Wales, who was the undisputed queen of Ascot fashion in the 1980s. Here she models arguably her most elegant Ascot attire: a dove-grey 'morning tails' linen coat with exaggerated mother-of-pearl buttons and a white linen shift dress tailored by one of her favourite British fashion designers, Catherine Walker, who died in 2010. The Princess's picture hat is designed by Philip Somerville.

Victor Edelstein and a matching hat trimmed with polka-dot cloth, again made by Somerville. The 'Diana effect' on fashion and on Royal Ascot encouraged high-profile fashion icons, such as Joan Collins (a great Ascot favourite), Ivana Trump, Jerry Hall and Marie Helvin, as well as designer Valentino and supermodel Elle Macpherson, to attend the Royal Meeting and inject some much-needed va-va-voom.

While the Princess of Wales was growing into her role as international ambassador for British fashion, the industry's focus had fixed firmly on the high-octane glamour of Italian stallion Gianni Versace's baroque Medusa-printed, beaded cocktail dresses; Franco Moschino's 'greed is good' surreal suits inspired by Elsa Schiaparelli – one scarlet skirt suit was trimmed with gold knives and forks in place of buttons; 'King of Cling' Azzedine Alaïa's thigh-skimming little black dresses; and Hervé Léger's body-conscious, multicoloured ribbon dresses sculpted skin-tight. Backed by LVMH, the mighty French luxury goods group, Christian Lacroix opened the first new haute couture house in Paris in 1987 and was an instant hit with the ladies of the Royal Enclosure. The statement accessories to display in the Enclosure were a pair of Chanel sunglasses designed by creative director Karl Lagerfeld, and a designer-logo handbag such as the Hermès Kelly or Chanel's 'gilt and quilt'.

Needless to say, Royal Ascot had little time for the dark, inscrutable aesthetic of the Japanese school of Comme des Garçons, Issey Miyake and Yohji Yamamoto, and neither were British fashion heroes Vivienne Westwood, Rifat Ozbek, Bodymap and Katharine Hamnett overly conspicuous in the Royal Enclosure; however, Lady McAlpine was an early adopter of Westwood, and would receive compliments from Margaret Thatcher whenever she wore her Westwood Boucher print corset dresses with exaggerated bustles and teetering platform hobble heels.

The years of ostentation and excess teetered on into the 1990s, but the line was drawn in 1992. In a speech to the Guildhall, the Queen said, with bittersweet humour, 'Nineteen ninety-two is not a year on which I shall look back with undiluted pleasure. In the words of one of my more sympathetic correspondents, it has turned out to be an *annus horribilis*.' Prince Andrew and the Duchess of York separated 'after the Duchess had been guilty of some spectacularly vulgar and well-publicized indiscretions with a rich American playboy,' as Philip Ziegler writes in *Queen Elizabeth II: A Photographic Portrait* (2010). Princess Anne's marriage to Captain Mark Phillips ended, a fire destroyed large parts of Windsor Castle and the troubles between the Prince and Princess of Wales had become increasingly acrimonious and public.

OPPOSITE
Naomi Campbell, photographed by Kevin Davies, getting ready for a 2002 appearance at Royal Ascot wearing a sublime Philip Treacy flying saucer hat trimmed with corkscrew-curled matching feathers.

Fashion, too, had once again turned on Royal Ascot, with a new mood of minimalism, if not quite austerity, and a new crop of edgy, young designers rejecting the slick polish of 1980s fashion gods such as Jil Sander, Helmut Lang, Ann Demeulemeester, Raf Simons and Martin Margiela. Things took a turn for the worse in 1994, when Marc Jacobs sent his now-infamous Grunge collection, inspired by downtown New York vagrant chic, down the runway at Perry Ellis and designed his way out of a job. In place of the glossy trinity of supermodels Naomi Campbell, Linda Evangelista and Christy Turlington, a skinny little fourteen-year-old called Kate Moss was introducing waiflike vulnerability not seen since Twiggy and a look that was to be christened 'heroin chic' because the girls looked so washed-out and wasted.

In 1995, *The Times* correspondent Richard Evans wrote: 'For all its success, Royal Ascot has been in danger in recent times of losing its charm because of fussy formality and unnecessary intransigence. In the 1990s, people do not take kindly to having their belongings searched after paying good money to attend a sports event; they do not expect to be subjected to endless notices telling them "By Order" what they must not do. Above all, they expect to enjoy themselves.' Faltering crowd figures at Ascot told their own story.

To add insult to injury, two actors dressed up as game-show characters Mr and Mrs Blobby were photographed being turned away from the Royal Enclosure. Dignity was restored when rising star jockey Lanfranco 'Frankie' Dettori rode the Queen's filly Phantom Gold to victory in the Ribblesdale Stakes in 1995. When he asked the Queen's permission to plant a kiss on the horse's muzzle in the paddock, Phantom Gold's trainer Lord Huntingdon overheard Princess Anne quip, 'I hope the kissing will stop at the horse.' The ever-dapper Mr Dettori is one of the true dandies of the Royal Meeting and was confirmed as an Ascot legend in 1996, when he scored 'the Magnificent Seven' – winning every event on a seven-race card. David Roper-Curzon's bronze of Dettori making his victorious signature 'flying dismount' was unveiled at Ascot in 2001.

By the time she divorced in 1995, surrendering her position in the royal family, the Princess of Wales had expanded her fashion horizons and was seen modelling increasingly fashion-forward dresses designed by Versace, Christian Lacroix, Valentino and Chanel. But her presence was no longer felt at Royal Ascot. In August 1997, Diana, Princess of Wales, was killed in a car crash in Paris. The somewhat disproportionate outpouring of public grief – more appropriate to the Oprah Winfrey sofa than a semi-state royal occasion in London – caused thunder to roll around the throne once more.

The Queen's popularity reached its nadir in that year, although the 2006 film *The Queen* starring Helen Mirren may have overestimated the role of then Labour Prime Minister Tony Blair in reversing public opinion.

Suffice to say, in 2002 the largely republican New Labour government was caught firmly on the back foot by the British public's response to the death of the Queen Mother, when tens of thousands of people queued to file past the coffin lying in state in the Palace of Westminster. As Her Majesty's Representative, the Marquis of Hartington (now Duke of Devonshire) ordered a minute's silence for the Queen Mother at Ascot, just as he had led three cheers and a rendition of 'Happy Birthday' for the Queen Mother's 100th birthday in 2000. Similarly, both the BBC and Mr Blair were surprised by the enthusiasm with which Britain marked the Queen's Golden Jubilee in 2002. To celebrate the Jubilee, the Queen commanded that the Royal Procession ride out on the Saturday of Royal Ascot, as it does to this day.

With the passing of Diana, Princess of Wales, Princess Margaret and the Queen Mother, Royal Ascot was introduced to a new generation of fashionable young Windsor girls in the new millennium, including Lady Helen Taylor, an ambassador for Giorgio Armani; Sophie, Countess of Wessex, who married Prince Edward in 1999; Ella Windsor, the statuesque daughter of Prince and Princess Michael of Kent; Princess Anne's gung-ho, sportswoman daughter, Zara Phillips; and the Duchess of York's daughters, the Princesses Beatrice and Eugenie – not to mention the new crop of handsome royal males.

Much has been made of the Queen's 'new flair for elegance' in the twenty-first century. The secret weapon in Her Majesty's sartorial artillery is her personal assistant and curator of dress and jewelry, Angela Kelly, who first joined the royal household in 1993 as one of the Queen's dressers, and has risen through the ranks to be the Queen's first personal assistant and a member of the Victoria Order: an honour in the monarch's personal gift. The *Daily Mail* rather uncharitably called Mrs Kelly 'a crane driver's daughter with a broad Scouse accent' in 2006 and noted a growing closeness with the Queen since her mother and sister died in 2002.

Acknowledged in palace circles as the 'gatekeeper' to the Queen – a cliché since Margaret 'Bobo' MacDonald's era – it appears that Mrs Kelly and the Queen share a sense of humour and a bond of trust that moved the Queen to comment: 'You and I do work well together. I think we are a good team.' The Queen even allowed Mrs Kelly to comment on their working relationship to the *Daily Telegraph* in a 2007 feature by

The Queen enters the Royal Box in 2009. After Royal Ascot returned from its 2005 posting to York while the new Grandstand was being built, the views from the trackside Royal Enclosure lawn, which had not been raked (angled), were not satisfactory; the ladies and gentlemen in the Enclosure could not see above the top hats in front of them. Structural amendments were swiftly made in time for 2007.

Andrew Alderson, 'The Queen and I'. Mrs Kelly is quoted as saying, 'My job is to ensure that when the Queen meets people she looks right. I would never overstep the mark and I remain in awe of the Queen … she is the one in control. She always makes the final decision [but] we are two typical women. We discuss clothes, make-up, jewellery.' However, she concludes: 'I am not there to replace her mother or sister. I know my place. I come from a humble background and I like to think that I have stayed humble.'

In 2004, the last Royal Ascot was held before the old Grandstand was again demolished and the entire racecourse – including two-thirds of the turf – was realigned to reflect Ascot's ambition to remain at the apex of the international racing calendar. This was also the first year that the author was invited to commentate on Royal Ascot fashion for the BBC with Suzi Perry. Owing to the gargantuan building programme in Berkshire, Royal Ascot 2005 was relocated to York.

For commentary on the Royal Procession at Ascot, it is the form for the Palace to relay by telephone the details of the Queen's attire; this is then handed into the commentary box by a runner, timed precisely to coincide with the carriage's first appearance at the Golden Gates. This cloak-and-dagger ritual is doubly important on Ladies' Day, when punters traditionally place bets on the colour of the Queen's hat. Security was even tighter in York when it was noted that bets were placed in Windsor on the Queen's hat being brown. The York Royal Ascot was the first occasion when the instructions from the palace read: 'in-house design by Alison Pordum and Angela Kelly'.

As BBC anchorwoman Clare Balding has pointed out many times since, the Queen has had more prime ministers than she has dressmakers, so it would stand to reason that she knows better than they do how to dress appropriately for Royal Ascot. Formal day dress is her working wardrobe. The flair for elegance detected in recent

PRECEDING PAGES, LEFT
Despite a faux pas in 2003, when she appeared in a one-shoulder tropical-print dress split to the thigh, Zara Phillips is an elegant presence at Royal Ascot, rather in the spirit of her mother, Princess Anne, who always cuts a dash for the Royal Meeting. Here Miss Phillips wears a delightful Philip Treacy flower-trimmed flying saucer hat at Royal Ascot in 2008.

PRECEDING PAGES, RIGHT
The Duchess of Cornwall, looking increasingly like a Queen Consort, photographed in the Parade Ring with the Prince of Wales at Royal Ascot in 2009. The Duchess, like the Princesses Beatrice and Eugenie, orders her hats from Philip Treacy. The Prince wears a grey three-piece morning dress cut by Savile Row tailors Anderson & Sheppard.

LEFT
Left to right: Princess Beatrice, Princess Eugenie and Mrs Peter Phillips (daughter-in-law of Princess Anne) share a joke in the Parade Ring at Royal Ascot in 2008. The princesses both wear hats by Philip Treacy.

OPPOSITE
Sophie, Countess of Wessex, wife of the Queen's youngest son, Prince Edward, attends Royal Ascot in 2006. The Countess is arguably the most consistently elegant, understated member of the royal party, and excels at formal day dress in the spirit of Hubert de Givenchy's designs for Audrey Hepburn. Here the Countess wears a Philip Treacy flying saucer hat trimmed with black feathers. She is also a great fan of Stephen Jones's millinery. Many of her day dresses are designed by Pimlico couturier Ulrich Engler.

years is doubtless due to Mrs Kelly's relationship with the Queen, and also due to her patronizing younger British couturiers such as Karl Ludwig, who has held the Royal Warrant since 1997, and Stuart Parvin, who was awarded the royal crest in 2007.

The Queen's hats – many in the style of the asymmetric 'tipsy-top hat' that shows off her face – have also been injected with a little more wit and flair by milliner Rachel Trevor-Morgan, who scored the golden grand slam in 2009 and made all five of the Queen's Royal Ascot hats. With her hair a forgiving soft silver that confirms her status as the nation's grandmother, the Queen now occupies a position above fashion that is entirely her own – though not dissimilar to that of her late mother – and remains consistently elegant at the Royal Meeting.

The supporting cast that surrounds the Queen in the Royal Processions of late has done much to strengthen the bonds between the Windsors and great British fashion. Prince and Princess Michael of Kent, a perennially glamorous royal couple, always strike a pose in Savile Row bespoke morning coat and haute couture respectively. In 2009, the Duchess of Cornwall wore Vivienne Westwood on the Ascot opening day with an audacious Philip Treacy hat. Treacy also scores as the milliner of choice for the Countess of Wessex and the Princesses Beatrice and Eugenie, who have been known to wear anything from Prada diffusion line Miu Miu to natty little high-street frocks and L. K. Bennett kitten heels at Ascot. The Countess of Wessex is perhaps the most consistently chic and demure fashion figure at Royal Ascot with her wardrobe of 1950s-inspired formal day dress cut by London couturier Ulrich Engler, who also dresses the glamorous Countess of Derby.

Arguably the strongest sartorial message to come from Royal Ascot in recent years was the 2010 advertising campaign photograph shot at Cliveden House, which featured an opulent guest list reminiscent of the parties led by that social cocktail-shaker, King Edward VII. The Duke of Devonshire is posed on a gilded chair surrounded by young aristocrats, socialites, celebrities and racing legends such as milliner Stephen Jones, Cilla Black, Nigel Havers, Frankie Dettori, fellow jockey Hayley Turner, Lorraine Chase, Ronnie Corbett and BBC presenters Clare Balding and Rishi Persad. The ladies are dressed in Westwood and the chaps in Gieves & Hawkes, both of whom presented fashion shows in the Bessborough Suite at Royal Ascot that year along with Amanda Wakeley and Matthew Williamson.

The message was clear: Royal Ascot is an inclusive occasion where everyone is welcome to dress in their best as guests of Her Majesty The Queen. In 2011,

Royal Ascot celebrates its tercentenary and continues on into another century in fine fettle.

The *Racing Post* really said it all in a 2001 editorial penned by Laura Thompson: 'For most people, the meeting is a delight, a place that they yearn to inhabit, a golden time suspended from real life for which they plan (dress/hat/shoes/matching bag/hire car/six for the price of five vintage champagne/organic guacamole/awning) with the attention to detail given by Napoleon to the Battle of Austerlitz. One dresses up, one swans around all day amongst top hats and bright colours, one has picnics, one cheers when Frankie Dettori does his wretched leap, one reverts cosily to the class system of a century ago. These are all things that, given half a chance, the British love to do, and that racing – being a world unto itself – allows.'

CATWALKING:
FASHION AT ROYAL ASCOT

'Everywhere are to be seen signs of a desire to move with the times, and to make Ascot as attractive socially as it is interesting from the racing point of view.'

THE *TIMES*, 1903

OPPOSITE AND OVERLEAF
Highly successful catwalk shows staged annually since 2007 have cemented the close relationship between British fashion and Royal Ascot. See page 219 for a list of designers and milliners whose work is shown.

In 2010, champion jockey and BBC commentator Willie Carson told the author that fashion at Royal Ascot was a divisive subject amongst the racing fraternity. It has ever been thus, with 50 per cent of viewers who watch the BBC coverage wishing to see more frocks parading and 50 per cent wishing to see more thoroughbreds racing. Suffice to say, Royal Ascot is a unique date on the international racing calendar on which horses and haute couture take equal precedence. One without the other would diminish, not enhance, the race meeting's global appeal.

Since 2007, Royal Ascot has hosted fashion shows in the custom-built Bessborough Suite and has attracted stellar names such as Vivienne Westwood, Amanda Wakeley, Stephen Jones, Philip Treacy, Luella, Matthew Williamson, Gieves & Hawkes and Hardy Amies to present catwalk-show lunches before the racing begins. The mastermind behind this injection of glamour is Ascot Hospitality's Gary England.

The BBC fashion team showcases each of the designer collections on an al fresco catwalk twice daily at Royal Ascot, and these glimpses into the world outside formal day dress and morning coats has proved one of the most popular additions to the day's television coverage. Having co-hosted all of these shows for the BBC with Suzi Perry, the author has license to share some of Royal Ascot's most magical fashion moments.

More than one dowager choked into her gin and tonic when Luella presented a collection inspired by 'Princess Anne on Acid'; not a few eyebrows were raised when Vivienne Westwood's special envoy to Ascot appeared on television sporting a Stetson and cowboy boots worn with one of Dame Vivienne's Propaganda print dresses; memories of Alfred Hitchcock's *The Birds* were evoked by Stephen Jones's black feathered headdress worn by Jasmine Guinness that was reported to have been inspired by Minnie Mouse's ears (see page 46); and few who witnessed it will forget Grace Jones sporting a vast black-and-white Philip Treacy picture hat and answering the question, 'Is this your first Royal Ascot?' with, 'No, darling, I first attended Ascot when I was shooting the Bond movie [*A View to a Kill*] with Christopher Walken and Roger Moore' (see page 143).

LONGINES CHAMBORD

proudly present

ROYAL ASCOT
FASHION
SHOW
2009

ROYAL ASCOT

Luella.

MRS SHILLING: A MEMOIR

BY DAVID SHILLING

For as long as I remember, my mother, Gertrude Shilling, had always asked me to help with her fashion choices and I loved to do so. Even if the designs were more and more mine, she always added that special magic. I was at school that first Tuesday of Royal Ascot in 1965 when my mother made her debut and changed the Royal Meeting forever, adding a splash of fizz to an already heady event. No one could have predicted that this mutual fascination between the media and my mother would last over three decades.

If you want to know what Mrs Shilling loved about Ascot, I can tell you. She loved 'everything!' My mother's annual appearances coincided with vintage years at Royal Ascot. Would she have loved the new Grandstand that she never lived to see? Yes, especially if I designed a hat for her tall enough to really take advantage of the new atrium. It seemed my mother loved every day she went to Ascot. Of course, it meant being with my father, whom she adored. He was equally devoted to her happiness and made sure he had long-wheelbase Rolls-Royces to best accommodate her hats.

The year that my father Ronald died, 1988, was the first year my mother missed going to Ascot with him since 1965. She was back the next year and every year until she died in 1999. There could be so many reasons why people around the world loved seeing my mother appear at Ascot; maybe one important one was that it was always a joy for us and she was able to share and transmit that joy.

TOP
A studio portrait of Mrs Shilling wearing a 1970s trapeze-line floral dress and gargantuan cartwheel hat designed by David Shilling.

ABOVE
Mrs Claridge, who has picked up the mad-hatter baton of Mrs Shilling, attends Royal Ascot in 2010 wearing a hat designed by David Shilling.

OPPOSITE
In the spirit of Cruella de Vil, Mrs Shilling attends Royal Ascot in 1990 wearing one of her signature costumes, comprising a black-and-white marabout feathered floor-length dress and pointed feather-trim coolie hat.

RULE BRITANNIA: PATRIOTISM AND PRIDE AT ROYAL ASCOT

'Royal Ascot racegoers might not always quite know what to do with themselves when they actually get on the course. But, boy, do they want to be there. For Ascot has learnt how to perform an immaculate two-step: it has moved into the present while never, for a moment, forgetting that what it offers is an image of the past.'

LAURA THOMPSON IN THE *RACING POST* (2001)

OPPOSITE AND OVERLEAF
The Band of the Irish Guards entertains the crowds in the Parade Ring in anticipation of the arrival of the Royal Procession at 2 p.m. After the last race, the band returns to the bandstand and leads the Union Flag-waving crowds with a selection of patriotic and popular songs. In 2009, the Band of the Irish Guards was joined by opera singer Katherine Jenkins, who performed an impromptu rendition of 'We'll Meet Again'.

It is one of Royal Ascot's great traditions to end the day's racing with a singalong around the bandstand, with Union flag-waving as robust and enthusiastic as at the Last Night of the Proms at the Royal Albert Hall. No doubt aided a little by that last bottle of champers, the assembled throng join as one to sing 'Rule Britannia' with as much gusto as when they serenaded the late Queen Mother with 'Happy Birthday', led by the Duke of Devonshire, in the year 2000. But many vocal chords are held in reserve for the anthem that is the most appropriate conclusion to another marvellous Royal Meeting:

God save our gracious Queen,
Long live our noble Queen,
God save the Queen!
Send her victorious,
Happy and glorious,
Long to reign over us,
God Save the Queen!

Rule Britannia

When Britain first at heaven's command,
Aro-o-o-ose from out the azure main.
Arose, arose, aro-o-o-ose from out the azure main.
This was the charter, the charter of the land,
And Guardian Angels sang this strain:

~~e~~ Britannia, Britannia rule the waves,
~~ns~~ never never shall be slaves.
~~ritannia,~~ Britannia rule the waves,
~~ever~~ never never shall be slaves!

Jerusalem

And did those feet in ancient time
Walk upon England's mountains green?
And was the holy Lamb of God
On England's pleasant pastures seen?

And did the Countenance Divine
Shine forth upon our clouded hills?
And was Jerusalem builded here
Among these dark Satanic Mills?

Bring me my bow of burning gold!
Bring me my arrows of desire!
Bring me my spear
Bring me my char

I will

RACING'S FASHION CALENDAR

Dubai World Cup — MARCH

Despite being one of the youngest world-class international race meetings at only fifteen years old, the Dubai World Cup is now big business, with a purse standing at $10 million. It was created by HH Sheikh Mohammed bin Rashid Al Maktoum after he had established the world-famous thoroughbred racing stable Godolphin in Newmarket in 1992. Before the free movement of horses in and out of the United Arab Emirates was permitted, the race meeting gained the world's attention by inviting famous and successful jockeys to ride in the Dubai International Jockeys' Challenge.

The DIJC developed into the Dubai World Cup, and today champion horses are exclusively invited to race by Sheikh Mohammed and flown in, all expenses paid, from all corners of the world to race on this former camel-racing course, which has recently been upgraded to a state-of-the-art Tapeta all-weather track.

Each year the sponsor holds a Style Stakes competition for the best-dressed racegoer and the prizes are suitably mink-lined, gold-plated and ocean-going, as is the style of high-rolling Dubai itself. This being an Arab state, rules of dress for ladies are inevitably stricter than in the Western world on religious grounds. It is terrific fun to see how ingenious the Arab ladies can be, matching their jewel-coloured headscarves with Philip Treacy butterfly-trimmed saucer hats.

However, the Dubai World Cup has its own royal lady to lead fashion at the meeting, Sheikh Mohammed's Western-dressed wife, Princess Haya, and she is arguably one of the best-dressed women in the world. This does not prevent some of the expat community making an awful show of themselves in monsters of frock more reminiscent of Ascot's Silver Ring than the Royal Enclosure. Nevertheless, it is lovely to see the nation's princesses dressed in the finest Parisian haute couture, dripping with a king's ransom of finest coloured diamonds.

MEYDAN RACECOURSE, NAD-AL-SHEBA, DUBAI, UAE
WWW.DUBAIWORLDCUP.COM

The Kentucky Derby — MAY

The Kentucky Derby is a direct descendant of the British Epsom Derby and has been in existence since 1875. It is America's second oldest thoroughbred race. A number of traditions have developed over the years, including the draping of the race winner in a giant garland sewn with over 400 fresh roses, said to have been inspired by the presentation of roses to visiting southern belle socialites in the 1880s. Consequently, the race is known as the 'Run for the Roses'.

It is the tradition at the Kentucky Derby to imbibe whiskey, mint and sugar syrup served in an iced silver julep cup or a frosted glass printed with the names of previous Derby winners. When the Earl of Derby attended the Kentucky race meeting in 1930 during Prohibition, he expressed his disappointment at not being able to taste a julep by saying: 'You have a great many advantages I should like to copy for England but Prohibition is not one of them.'

This being the deep south, impeccable manners are expected in the enclosures at the Kentucky Derby and the social snakes-and-ladders board is as perilous if not even more strict than at Royal Ascot. There are no official dress codes for the Kentucky Derby, but the unwritten rule is that ladies who have reserved seats in the Grandstand and Clubhouse wear delicate, pastel skirt suits in the spirit of late First Lady Jacqueline Kennedy, or floral chiffon dresses with immaculately matched cartwheel picture hats. Gentlemen favour old colonial pale linen suits worn with formal shirts and impeccably knotted ties or silk cravats and Panama hats. In the Infield, however, which is the central part of the track, there is a party atmosphere of general abandon and fashion submits to fancy dress.

CHURCHILL DOWNS, LOUISVILLE, KENTUCKY, USA
WWW.KENTUCKYDERBY.COM

The Derby — JUNE

The town of Epsom was founded in 1618, when the health-giving properties of the natural spring on the Downs brought the fashionable courtiers of King James I's court from the capital to recover from the debauches of London town life. Over 160 years later, the first official thoroughbred horse race was recorded, and the two friends who organized it, the 12th Earl of Derby and Sir Charles Bunbury, flipped a coin to name their new race. Lord Derby won the toss.

This friendly race over the Surrey Downs has become one of the most keenly fought contests in the world, and has inspired similarly named international races such as the Kentucky Derby in the USA. In 1913, the suffragette Emily Davison gave up her life at the Derby when she walked in front of King George V's horse in clear view of the King and Queen Mary to plead the cause for votes for women.

It is said that the name of the Derby winner will mysteriously appear in chalk on the Sunday before the race on a 'magic well' in front of local pub The Amato (named for a previous Derby winner). The Derby Festival is the official title for the English Classic races, comprising the Oaks, the One Thousand Guineas and the Two Thousand Guineas at Newmarket's Rowley Mile and the St Leger at Doncaster.

Because the Queen traditionally attends Derby Day, dress in the Queen's Stand is strictly morning coats and top hats. As with Royal Ascot, service dress and full national costume are also appropriate. Ladies are asked to wear formal day dress, including hats or substantial fascinators. Fancy dress does abound outside the Enclosures, with the usual suspects wearing Las Vegas showgirl plumes, skimpy dresses more suited to a beach on Ibiza and enough fake tan to rub down a thoroughbred.

EPSOM DOWNS, SURREY, UK
WWW.EPSOMDERBY.CO.UK

The July Cup – JULY

The medieval market town of Newmarket stands just off England's oldest road, the Icknield Way Path. In the early seventeenth century, King James I used this road to travel to the north, and Newmarket became a natural stopping point to rest the horses and hold court. To alleviate boredom the king hunted, hawked and raced horses on the expansive heath, eventually building a palace there, parts of which are still in existence today. James I's grandson, King Charles II, famously built a passageway from the palace to the Newmarket home of his favourite mistress, Nell Gwynn.

Newmarket is known as the International Headquarters of Horseracing, and is unique in that there are two courses, the Rowley Mile and the July Course, both of exceptional international race quality. It is also home to over 2,500 horses in training, 65 racing stables, a jockey training school, world-class equine and animal health trust facilities, the Jockey Club, the National Horseracing Museum, Tattersalls (the largest bloodstock sales in Europe) and the largest expanse of cultivated heathland in the world.

Sheikh Mohammed is the world's leading thoroughbred owner and breeder, and his racing headquarters (the Darley Stud and Godolphin Racing Stables) are also based in Newmarket. The July Course prides itself on being a very pretty, intimate course with manicured gardens, lawns and flowerbeds, forming a perfect mise-en-scène for showing off new-season fashion.

Newmarket's July Course consequently attracts an extremely good-looking, not to mention well-dressed, group who are as passionate about correct attire as they are about the racing. Gentlemen wear either lounge suits or country separates, such as a check tweed coat and complementary corduroy trousers, with neat brown felt fedoras the form for headwear. Ladies are encouraged to wear hats or substantial fascinators and, as at the Melbourne Cup, there is a fashion parade and competition on Ladies' Day that attracts the best and the worst in show.

JULY COURSE, NEWMARKET, SUFFOLK, UK
WWW.NEWMARKETRACECOURSES.CO.UK

The Sussex Stakes – JULY

In 1801, the 3rd Duke of Richmond, whose family seat, Goodwood House, was a favourite of the Prince of Wales, resolved to add a racecourse to the grounds of his magnificent Jacobean house to benefit his royal friend and the officers of the Sussex Militia, of which he was Colonel. With royal patronage, Goodwood instantly won a place on the social race card, and the following year, Goodwood hosted three days of racing run under Jockey Club rules; somewhat unsurprisingly, both the Duke and the future King George IV's horses romped home.

Informally known as one of the greatest garden parties in the English social season, Glorious Goodwood is famed for serving Pimm's on the present Earl of March's lawns and in the Richmond Enclosure. Since the 1930s, a distinct dress code has emerged for Glorious Goodwood: light linen suits not dissimilar to those worn at the Kentucky Derby for chaps, teamed with Tattersall check shirts and claret spotty ties, brown suede brogues, and topped off with a classic Panama hat as popularized by King Edward VII in 1906.

For the ladies, Goodwood encourages formal day dress, but with more of a tweedy, country mood, as in classic 1930s Mitford-sister skirt suits, pearls, low-heeled brogues or boots, and a more robust country hat trimmed with pheasant feathers or suchlike. Of course, such is the popularity of race meetings with fashionable ladies that you will see flocks of chiffon-clad lovelies in towering hats trimmed with feathers, bows, flowers and furbelows more suitable to a carnival float than the West Sussex Downs.

GOODWOOD, CHICHESTER, WEST SUSSEX, UK
WWW.GOODWOOD.CO.UK/HORSE-RACING

Prix de l'Arc de Triomphe - OCTOBER

The Prix de l'Arc de Triomphe was inaugurated in 1920 to showcase the quality of breeding in French thoroughbred racehorses, and winners of the race today have become extremely sought after at stud. Before the Arc, the governing body of French racing had only allowed horses bred nationally to race in France; the Arc opened the field to international thoroughbreds, thus making it the star race on the French national calendar, and today it has the richest purse in Europe. It was named the Arc de Triomphe because the First World War was still in recent memory and race organizers felt the name was a fitting tribute to the French resistance soldiers who had served their country and fought shoulder to shoulder with the British.

As befitting a race meeting of such calibre, the appropriate dress for ladies is easily as extravagant as in Ascot's Royal Enclosure. This being in the environs of Paris, one inevitably sees more haute couture per head than Ascot could possibly match. The Arc attracts both the fabulous international new money and the old 6th arrondissement French aristocracy; 1950s Balenciaga rubs shoulders with the new-season collection designed for the house by present creative director Nicolas Ghesquière.

Ladies at the Arc tend to dress more extravagantly and inappropriately for the races than at Royal Ascot, and it has to be said that the Parade Ring and Enclosures look all the prettier for it. Sadly, gentlemen are not required to wear morning dress, and their suits, shirts and ties are more reminiscent of modest sparrows than the peacock gentlemen at the Royal Meeting.

LONGCHAMP, FRANCE
WWW.PRIXARCDETRIOMPHE.COM

The Melbourne Cup – NOVEMBER

This 150-year-old race is so popular nationally and internationally that it is a public holiday for all citizens of Victoria, although, unofficially, it actually causes the whole of Australia to shut down, hence its nickname, the 'Race that Stops a Nation'. The Melbourne Cup also attracts monarchists keen to celebrate a little of the grandeur and pomp of Royal Ascot.

The city of Melbourne was founded a mere thirty years prior to the Melbourne Cup, and was at the time in the grip of the Gold Rush. Consequently, the original trophy for the race was a gold watch. This has evolved over the years to become the hand-beaten, three-handled loving cup presented today. This eighteen-carat gold cup has become an iconic part of Australia's cultural fabric and is one of the most identifiable sporting trophies in the world.

During the 1960s the race organizers created 'Fashions on the Field' to encourage more ladies to visit the race, rightly believing that when ladies were present, gentlemen (ergo money) would flock to the races, even if they were not gentlemen of the turf. Fashion on the Field quickly became a national spectator sport, with prizes given to outfits costing less than £30 and those less than £50. The criteria stipulate that the outfit should be stylish, original and appropriate for the race meeting and climate, with hats mandatory. This being Australia, every Royal Enclosure rule is broken, so expect to see hot pants, off-the-shoulder dresses, micro miniskirts and all manner of mad millinery that even Mrs Shilling would have thought twice about sporting at a race meeting.

FLEMINGTON RACECOURSE, MELBOURNE, AUSTRALIA
WWW.MELBOURNECUP.COM

RACING COLOURS:
THE HISTORY OF JOCKEY SILKS

'Reading a race is a telling phrase and a difficult art,' writes Dorothy Laird in *The Benson & Hedges Book of Racing Colours* (1973). 'It requires a good knowledge of colours, which adds immeasurably to the interest of each and every race.' Before the advent of the BBC at Royal Ascot in 1953, judges, stewards and commentators would have to read the race with nothing more sophisticated than a pair of binoculars. Easily identifiable racing colours in the original eighteen basic colours devoid of the insignia and monograms popular on the continent simply made it easier to identify jockey and horse.

Racing colours were first used in the mid-eighteenth century but, in 1762, the Jockey Club ordered that 'for the greater conveniency of distinguishing the horses in running, as also for the prevention of disputes arising from not knowing the colours worn by each rider, the underwritten gentlemen have come to the resolution and agreement of having the colours annexed to the following names.' Of the original eighteen names, only the Duke of Devonshire's straw colours and Lord Grosvenor's orange silks are still in the same ownership today.

In the early history of racing silks, owners were largely aristocratic and chose their colours according to the livery of their coachmen and postillions. They were registered, and still are, at Weatherbys in Newmarket, whose earliest book in the archive dates back to 1780. One of the most identifiable historic silks is the rose-and-primrose stripe of Lord Rosebery (whose family name is Primrose). A bolt of Lord Rosebery's silk as vivid as the day it was woven was recently discovered in the Henry Poole & Co. archive on Savile Row, in a bound leather book embossed with the title 'Jockey Silks'.

Superstition is rife on the turf, and silks fall at the mercy of lady luck: Lord Derby retained a white button on his black colours because a winning jockey had dressed in a hurry and buttoned his white stock (neckerchief) over one black button; Anne, Duchess of Westminster, did not like her winning horse Arkle's colours to be washed too frequently for fear that 'it washed the luck away'.

Today, there are approximately 10,000 racing colours registered at Weatherbys, with 'cherished colours' changing hands for as much as £10,000. One does not need to own a horse to register. The intent of owning in the future or a family history of owning colours are sufficient reasons to acquire your family silks.

OPPOSITE
A bolt of Lord Rosebery's rose-and-primrose stripe racing colours preserved in the Henry Poole & Co. archive at No. 15 Savile Row, dated c. 1930.

BELOW
A collection of vintage cigarette cards depicting famous jockeys. On the far left, Childs is wearing the royal racing colours.

J. CHILDS   C. SMIRKE   B. CARSLAKE   G. RICHARDS

Earl of Rosebery

rose stripe satin.

#734 yds.
made i
L

ROYAL LIVERIES

'Trotting down the narrow lanes to reach the racecourse, our route was lined with onlookers who, I imagine, had no idea that whatever they said could be heard by the occupants of the carriages: "Doesn't she look awful in that hat?" "Who's he?" as well as admiring words for the Queen. When it was our turn to drive between the lines of critics there was an audible "Ohhh", a groan of disappointment when they realized that all the royals had passed and they were left with a few unknowns, not even a movie star.'

DEBORAH, DOWAGER DUCHESS OF DEVONSHIRE,
WAIT FOR ME! MEMOIRS OF THE YOUNGEST MITFORD SISTER (2010)

The Royal Procession at Ascot that rides out from the Golden Gates at precisely 2 p.m. is one of the great moments in the royal calendar. The Queen's carriage leads three further landaus pulled by Windsor Greys, with two postillions riding each team of horses. The state liveries that these postillions wear are reserved only for the Royal Meeting and are still tailored on Savile Row by august houses such as Dege & Skinner and Gieves & Hawkes, although Henry Poole & Co. now makes the lion's share, including two new tunics for the 2011 Royal Meeting.

'Each Ascot livery takes an average of 120 hours to complete,' says Keith Levett, head of ceremonial tailoring for Poole's. 'The Ascots are embellished with between 30 and 36 yards of pure gold lace (containing 2½ per cent gold) and the lace is sewn down with between 10 and 14 hand stitches per inch.' The investment of time and money in liveries for the Royal Mews is sound. The Mews stores Poole's walking groomsman state liveries dating from 1875, which are still perfectly serviceable and in commission. The oldest Ascot livery on parade is late

twentieth-century purely because, as Levett observes, body shapes have changed radically and today's postillions are much larger in frame than their forebears. Also, for 2011, the Mews has appointed a female postillion.

Those who remark upon the cost in public taxes for all the pomp and circumstance surrounding the British royal family should not only consider whether any of their clothes date from 1870, but also whether any of the buttons on their best bib and tucker date back to King William IV (1830–37) as do some of those adorning the Royal Ascot liveries.

DRESS ETIQUETTE

Royal Enclosure Form for Gentlemen

TOP HAT: Black silk plush, the traditional material from which top hats are fashioned, is no longer manufactured. So the smartest toppers are now family heirlooms, or reconditioned antique black silk top hats produced by James Lock & Co. on St James's Street (the oldest hatter in the world). Top hats made today are crafted from polished fur felt but they don't have the vinyl sheen of the real deal.

COLLARS/SHIRTS: Traditionally, Ascot shirts are cut with detachable stiff stud collars that are now manufactured only by Ede & Ravenscroft, but for off-the-peg shirts, palest base colours, or stripes with a white collar and cuffs, are preferable. Button-down collars are to be discouraged, as are oikish patch pockets.

TIES: The Royal Enclosure code does allow chaps to wear cravats, but they tend to look too flouncy for the Enclosure. A definitive Ascot tie is made in woven silk, and will mismatch but complement the colour of the shirt, waistcoat and handkerchief. A simple four-in-hand with neat dimple beneath the knot is correct, as is a tight knot with a tie stud or pin to hold the tie in a slight billow.

MORNING COATS: A black bespoke morning coat is the fashion in the Royal Enclosure, though grey three-piece morning dress is enjoying a revival thanks to the patronage of the Prince of Wales. The key points are the neat shoulder, the sleeve that finishes 1 ½ inches above the shirt cuff, working cuff buttons, and tails that finish just below the knee. It is understood that the Queen likes to see chaps with their one-button morning coats fastened rather than flying free.

POCKET HANDKERCHIEFS AND BOUTONNIÈRES: A silk, linen or cotton pocket square that mismatches the rest of the ensemble is a nostalgic touch. The rule for handkerchiefs is 'one for showing and one for blowing'. How you display your pocket handkerchief is open to artistic interpretation. Boutonnières are quintessential Royal Ascot, but do keep them neat and discreet. The most popular are the royal favourites: the red carnation, yellow rose or cornflower.

WAISTCOATS: Single or double-breasted is appropriate in the Enclosure, with a bias towards traditional buff or grey wool. However, the Edwardian fashion for ivory linen waistcoats is gaining ground, as is the time-honoured courtesy of a chap wearing a sober waistcoat on Ladies' Day to allow the ladies to shine. Fancy waistcoats are too reminiscent of weddings for Royal Ascot. A nice touch is to ask your tailor to include a fob watch tab and pockets from which to display your grandfather's watch and chain. Should you wear single-breasted, the lowest button is left undone in homage to Edward VII, who set the fashion when Prince of Wales.

TROUSERS: Bespoke trousers are cut high on the waist and worn with braces so that a gentleman will never commit the cardinal sin of 'showing shirt' between waistcoat and trouser tops. The cloth for a Royal Ascot trouser is pinstripe or puppy-tooth, though herringbone made a surprising comeback in 2010. Turn-ups and pleats are a matter for a chap and his tailor, not the dress code at Royal Ascot, to dictate.

SOCKS: The long sock prevents any display of unsightly ankle flesh when a chap takes his seat at lunch. Though few houses make them in anything other than black, navy and grey, Huntsman on Savile Row always has a collection of jolly pastels, such as the lemon-yellow socks favoured by the late Duke of Devonshire.

SHOES: It is acceptable to wear a black Chelsea boot because the morning tailcoat had its roots in equestrian tailoring, but the form is a black cap-toed Oxford.

ADORNMENT: A word on jewelry: apart from your fob watch, family ring, gem-set cufflinks and tie stud, any other embellishment is to be discouraged.

Right: Morning dress as tailored by Ede & Ravenscroft.

Royal Enclosure Form for Ladies

HATS: Of course, one will always see braver fashionable ladies, such as Knightsbridge couturier Isabell Kristensen, stalking the photographers' lawns at Royal Ascot wearing audacious hats that defy gravity and remind one of the excesses of Georgiana, Duchess of Devonshire, and to those, we say, 'Bravo!' But the Royal Enclosure ladies who attend for the fillies rather than the frocks understand that elegance and practicality must go hand-in-glove. As the late *Vogue* editor Diana Vreeland said, 'Elegance is refusal.' So the shapes we invariably see in the Enclosures are the tipsy-top hats favoured by the Queen that allow one to see a race, as well as the flying saucer and the tall feathered fountains popularized by Philip Treacy. Variations on the turban, the pillbox and the beret are always Ascot staples, as are asymmetric brims. The virtue of a picture hat is its function as well as form. It prevents random chaps attempting to kiss you.

ASCOT DRESSES: The rules are terribly simple for formal day dress. Shoulders should be covered and hems should touch the knee, but you are urged not to mistake day dress for cocktail dress: satins, paillettes and sequins are frowned upon in the Royal Enclosure. The coat dress is a popular choice – not least with the Queen – because it allows for the 'four seasons in five days' weather at Royal Ascot. A simple shift dress in the spirit of Hubert de Givenchy for Audrey Hepburn is indisputably elegant, as is the Chanel tweed skirt suit. Trouser suits are admissible, but only in matching colour and fabric. However, it does seem rather a pity for ladies to opt for the kind of outfit you'd see behind the teller's desk in a local bank when they have a rare opportunity to wear formal day dress.

ACCESSORIES: The handbag needs to allow for a race card, sunglasses and cigarettes (should you partake), and some of the more seasoned racegoers like to suspend their badges from the gilt chain of a Chanel or Hermès handbag. Anything too logo-a-go-go or large tends to look try-hard, as do vintage beaded evening bags. Gloves are a delightful addition and should, like cars, strictly be either black or white. However, such is the talent of London's glove-makers, such as Pickett in the Burlington Arcade, that one can have one's gloves dyed to match one's hat.

JEWELS: Ropes of family pearls with intricate jewelled clasps are always appropriate, though the late Diana, Princess of Wales, went some way towards reviving the Edwardian pearl choker with amethyst, sapphire or diamond clasp. Royal Ascot is one of the few occasions at which diamonds may be worn for daytime. The Queen leads the field with eye-popping diamond brooches from one of the largest collections of historic jewels in the world. Some racegoers, including Lady Derby and Princess Haya, favour 'lucky' jewels, such as diamond-set equestrian brooches. Earrings should never be too 'cocktail', dangling like the chandeliers in the Hall of Mirrors at Versailles. A simple pearl button is always a lovely sight and is perfectly displayed when hair is dressed up. As with tiaras, hats always look more soigné when worn with dressed hair.

SHOES: A low-heeled court is a popular choice in the Enclosure, considering that the ladies spend the lion's share of their day walking on turf. However, some of the flashier ladies in Grandstand boxes can feasibly be at Ascot for an entire day, and their Louboutin heels won't even touch a tuft of grass. Soaring heels may be the rage at the moment but they aren't terribly user-friendly at Ascot. And God forbid you join the ranks of the poor unfortunates who have to buy flip-flops at the end of the day because their Manolos have crucified their toes.

ALL-WEATHER ACCESSORIES: If a lady likes to fly close to limit of the Royal Enclosure Dress Code, she may wear a strappy dress but drape a silk cashmere pashmina over her shoulders and pass muster. A pashmina is as essential at Royal Ascot as a very tall escort to hold your umbrella when the heavens open.

Right: Suzi Perry attends Royal Ascot in 2009 wearing millinery by Philip Treacy and dress by Ralph Lauren.

NOT APPROPRIATE

A ARMS: An artfully draped pashmina covers a multitude of sins

B BRA STRAPS: Should never be seen at Royal Ascot

C COURT SHOES: Those with low heels are best on the turf

D DRESSES: Remember, this is a race meeting, not a cocktail party

E ELEGANCE: As Mrs Vreeland says, elegance is refusal

F FASCINATORS: A dodgy tuft of chicken feathers is hardly an object of fascination

G GLOVES: Kid to the wrist, not satin to the elbow

H HATS: Be bold, but don't panic your pets and small children

I IRONING: Do steam and press your morning coats, chaps

J JEWELRY: Diamonds for daytime are acceptable at Royal Ascot

K KNOTS: The definitive Ascot tie knot is a tight four-in-hand with a neat dimple

L LEGS: Hose are no longer compulsory in the Enclosure, but go easy on the Fake Bake, ladies

M MORNING DRESS: A black cutaway coat and puppy-tooth trouser is the fashion, but not the rule

N NAILS: Acrylics are common even if you are wearing Chanel Couture

O OSTENTATION: It is always advisable to remove one accessory or piece of jewelry before embarking for Royal Ascot. Tone it down.

P PANTIES: Yes, please, ladies, but not on show

Q THE QUEEN: Watch and learn

R RAINWEAR: Brollies are never folly at Ascot, and make rather smart walking sticks for our elders and betters

S SATIN: Never, ever at Ascot

T TIE STUDS: Gentlemen prefer studs at Ascot. Tie clips are for bankers

U UNACCEPTABLE: Tattoos, piercings, strapless, too short, too tight, too tarty

V VEST: The Savile Row term for waistcoats. Yes, please, but not shiny, embroidered or comedic

W WHITE SHIRTS: Not in the Royal Enclosure

X X-RATED: Do remember, this is the Royal Meeting, not *My Big Fat Gypsy Wedding*

Y YOBBISH BEHAVIOUR: Well dressed and well behaved go hand in hand at the races

Z ZIP FASTENERS: A marvellous invention, but an aberration if clearly visible

ROYAL ENCLOSURE DRESS CODE

Her Majesty's Representative wishes to point out that only formal day dress with a hat or substantial fascinator will be acceptable. Off the shoulder, halter neck, spaghetti straps and dresses with a strap of less than one inch and miniskirts are considered unsuitable. Midriffs must be covered and trouser suits must be full length and of matching material and colour.

Gentlemen are required to wear either black or grey morning dress, including a waistcoat, with a top hat. A gentleman may remove his top hat within a restaurant, a private box, a private club or that facility's terrace, balcony or garden. Hats may also be removed within any enclosed external seating area within the Royal Enclosure Garden.

THE LANGUAGE OF THE TURF

ABANDONED: A race meeting cancelled because a club did not receive sufficient nominations or because of inclement weather rendering the track unsafe.

ACCUMULATOR: A multiple bet, making simultaneous selections on two or more races with the intent of pressing the winnings of the first win on the following bet, and so forth. All bets must win to roll over or the accumulator is lost.

ACEY-DEUCY: Uneven stirrups popularized by jockey Eddie Arcaro, who rode with his left (inside) iron lower than his right to achieve better balance on turns.

ACROSS THE BOARD: A bet on a horse to win, place or show.

ACT IN THE DIP: To put on a spurt at the dip in the ground at Ascot (see Swinley Bottom), after which the track rises to the winning post.

ACT OF ENCLOSURE: The 1813 Parliamentary Act of Enclosure that ensured Ascot Heath, the property of the Crown Estate, would be kept and used as a racecourse for the public in the future.

ACTION: A horse's manner of moving.

ADDED PURSE: Purse money that was enhanced by payments made by owners and/or breeders.

ADDED WEIGHT: A horse carrying more weight than the conditions of the race require, usually because the jockey exceeds the stated limit.

AGE OF A HORSE: All thoroughbreds share the same official birthday, 1 January, making it easy to enforce the age restrictions that go with every race.

AGED: A horse of seven years or older.

AGENT: A person empowered to transact business of a stable owner or jockey.

AIDS: Signals used by a rider to pass instructions to his mount. Artificial aids include the whip and spurs. Natural aids include hands, legs, voice cuts and weight cues.

AIRING: Not running at best speed.

AJAX (OR BEESWAX): Slang for betting tax.

ALL CLEAR: Signified by a siren at the end of a race; means that the stewards deem the finishing order of horses correct so bets can be paid out. It also means no protest or objection has been made.

ALL OUT: A horse who is trying to the best of his ability.

ALL-THE-WAY WIN: To lead from start to finish in a race.

ALLOWANCE RACE: A race for which the racing secretary drafts certain conditions to determine weights to be carried based on the horse's age, sex and/or past performance.

ALSO RAN: Any selection of horses not finishing 1st, 2nd, 3rd or 4th.

ALTERED: A horse that has been gelded.

ANTE POST: Bests placed in advance predicting the outcome of a future race in return for the chance of better odds. Punters risk no return on stakes if their selection pulls out.

APPRENTICE: A rider who has not ridden a specified amount of winners within a specific time period. These riders get weight allowances on all their mounts based on the number of winners they have.

APPRENTICE RIDER (BUG RIDER): A student jockey.

APPROXIMATES: The approximate price a horse is quoted before a race begins.

ART: Artificial turf.

ARTIFICIAL BREEDING: Includes artificial insemination/embryo transplants not approved by the Jockey Club.

ASCOT AUTHORITY: Established in 1813 by an Act of Parliament, the Ascot Authority was led by His Majesty's Representative, who became Chairman of the Authority with the Clerk of the Course acting as Secretary.

ASSISTANT STARTER: The employee of a racetrack who, under direct supervision of the starter, helps to place the starting gate for a race, leads horses into the gate, helps jockeys and handles horses while in the gate until the start.

ASSISTANT TRAINER: In many cases one trainer may have many horses under his care and these are spread out at several racetracks on any given day. The assistant deputizes for the trainer.

AT THE POST: The time when the horses have arrived and are ready to be loaded into the starting gate.

ATTACK: To challenge the leading horse during a race in an attempt to take the lead. An attack can sap the horse's energy, as well as that of the leader, leaving both with little reserve for the finish.

AVERAGE EARNINGS INDEX: A breeding statistic that compares racing earnings of a stallion or mare's foals to those of all other foals racing at the time.

AWT: All weather track.

BABY RACE: A race for two-year-olds.

BACK: To bet or wager.

BACK END: The last few weeks of the flat racing season; sometimes offers late-maturing horses a chance to win a race.

BACK MARKER: The horse given the biggest handicap.

BACK STRAIGHT (BACKSTRETCH): The straight length of the track furthest away from spectators and the winning post.

BACK UP: The action of a horse slowing down noticeably.

BACKSIDE: The stable and training area of the racetrack.

BAD ACTOR: A fractious horse.

BAD DOER: A horse with a poor appetite, a condition that may be due to nervousness.

BALANCED BOOK: A legal on-course bookmaker who takes bets on horse racing aims to adjust the odds in his favour and guarantee profit by achieving a balanced book, regardless of the outcome of the race. This is also known as spread betting.

BANKER: Highly expected to win.

BAT: A jockey's whip.

BATTERY: Illegal electrical device used by a jockey to stimulate a horse during a race.

BAY: Colour of horse, from yellowish tan to brown, or dark, rich mahogany.

BEARD: A friend or acquaintance employed to place bets so the bookmaker will not know the identity of the bettor.

BELL: Rung in the home straight to warn jockeys they are about to commence the final lap of the race.

BETTING BOARD: A board used by bookmakers to display the odds of the horses engaged in the race.

BETTING RING: The allocated area at the paceway where bookmakers work.

BISMARCK: A favourite that the bookmakers do not expect to win.

BIT: Stainless steel, rubber or aluminium bar attached to the bridle that fits into the horse's mouth; one of the means by which a jockey exerts guidance or control.

BLANKET FINISH: When the horses all finish so close to the winning line you could put a single blanket across them.

BLAZE: A white mark covering much of the horse's face.

BLEEDER: A horse with a tendency to break blood vessels during a race.

BLIND BET: A bet made by a racetrack bookmaker on another horse to divert other bookmakers' attention from a sizeable bet on the main horse.

BLIND SWITCH: When a horse is pocketed behind other horses in a race and the jockey decides whether to hope for an opening or take back and go around.

BLINKERS: A cup-shaped device applied over the sides of the horse's head to limit vision and help prevent the horse swerving or being distracted.

BLOODSTOCK AGENT: A person who advises or represents a buyer or seller of thoroughbreds at a public auction or private sale.

BLOW OUT: A short exercise to limber a horse before a race.

BLOWING UP: A horse that has had a hard run and is not at peak fitness may be referred to as 'blowing up' after the run:

breathing vigorously and excessively.

BOBBLE: A bad step from the starting gate, usually caused by the track surface breaking away from under a horse's hooves.

BOLT: When a horse swerves sharply from its lane.

BOMB: A winning horse sent off at very high odds.

BOOK: The group of mares being bred to a stallion in a given year.

BOTTLE: Odds of 2 to 1.

BOTTOM: Stamina in a horse.

BOUNCE: A poor race run directly following a career best.

BOXED IN: To be trapped between, behind or inside other horses.

BREAK A HORSE: To train a young horse to wear a bridle and saddle, carry a rider and respond to a rider's commands.

BREAK DOWN: Become unable to race because of lameness or injury.

BREAK MAIDEN: A horse (or rider) winning the first race of its career.

BREATHER: Restraining or easing off for a short distance to allow the horse to conserve energy.

BREEZING: Running a moderate speed.

BRIDGE JUMPER: A person who wagers large amounts of money, usually on short-priced horses, hoping to realize a small but certain profit.

BROODMARE: Mare kept at stud for breeding, and not usually raced, although likely to have done so when younger.

BUMPING AND BORING: Interference in which one horse is intentionally forced by the jockey to collide with another.

BY THE NECK: The third-shortest winning distance, after short head and head.

CALL: Running position of horses in a race at various points.

CANTER: A slow gallop or a lope.

CAR PARK NO. 1: The premier car park at Royal Ascot with direct access to the Royal Enclosure, Car Park No. 1 is traditionally the lawn where the grandest picnics are hosted and the smartest chauffeur-driven cars displayed.

CARD: A fixture or race meeting.

CARPET: Odds of 3 to 1.

CENTURY (OR TON): £100 bet.

CHALK PLAYER: A bettor who bets on the favourite in a race.

CHAMPAGNE: Just as Pimm's is the traditional drink at Wimbledon, so champagne is drink of choice in the Royal Enclosure. In 2010, 60,000 bottles of champagne were sold at Royal Ascot.

CHAMPION NATIONAL HUNT JOCKEY: Jockey with the greatest number of NH wins in a season.

CHAMPION OWNER: Owner whose horses have won the most prize-money.

CHAMPION SIRE: The animal who has sired horses earning the most prize money in a season. Has sometimes been calculated in terms of number of wins.

CHAMPION TRAINER: Trainer whose horses have won the most prize money.

CHECK: Interference suffered by a horse during a race.

CHIEF APPRENTICE: The apprentice jockey with the greatest number of wins in a season.

CHOKING DOWN: When a driver tries to get a horse to run at a slowed rate, he or she will sometimes pull the head back, unintentionally cutting off its breathing. This can cause the horse to lose consciousness and collapse on the track.

CHOPPY: Describes a horse's short stride.

CLASSIC: A Classic race is one of the five tests for three-year-olds on the flat – the One Thousand Guineas, the Two Thousand Guineas, the Derby, the Oaks and the St Leger.

CLERK OF SCALES: A racing official responsible for weighing all riders out and in at races.

CLIENT: Purchaser of betting information from horseman or other tipster.

CLOSER: A horse that runs best in the latter part of the race.

COASTING: A horse running easily or without pressure, usually from the front.

COLOURS: Racing silks worn by the jockey.

COLT: An unaltered male thoroughbred between two and four years old.

COMBINATION BET: Selecting any number of teams/horses to finish first and second in either order.

CONFORMATION: The shape and relative proportion of a horse.

CONTRACT RIDER: Jockey on whose services an owner or trainer has first call by contract.

COOLING OUT: Restoring a horse to normal temperature, usually by walking.

CRACK: Top-notch horse.

CRACK AMATEUR: A non-professional, top-class jockey.

CRACKING PACE: When the leader of a race runs at a very quick speed, often in the early stages of a race.

CROPPER: When a horse or rider falls, as in 'coming a cropper'.

CROW'S NEST: The area at the top of the Grandstand where the announcer, stewards, judges and others watch the race from the highest vantage point.

CROWD: To race too close to another horse, forcing its rider to take up or change course.

CUT DOWN: Horse injured from being struck by another horse's shoes.

DAILY DOUBLE: A wager on two races, selecting the winner of each race on one ticket purchased prior to the first race.

DAM: The mother of a foal.

DARK: A day when no races are run.

DARK HORSE: An underrated animal that wins or has good prospects of a win.

DEAD HEAT: To come equal first. This was much more common before the days of photo-finishes. A horse that has won 10½ races has won 10 and dead-heated one.

DEAD TRACK: A racing surface that lacks resilience.

DEATH (THE): Also known as the death seat, this position is outside the leader with one horse off the rails or fence. The death is usually the toughest run in a race because the horse will have to cover more ground than the inside competitors, as well as bearing the brunt of the wind resistance.

DECLARATION (SCRATCH): A horse withdrawn from a race.

DEEP STRETCH: A position very close to the finish line in a race.

DEVELOPED PRINT (PHOTO-FINISH): A judge calls for a developed print when he has not been able to determine who won the race. A camera fitted into the finishing post takes a photograph the second a horse crosses its infrared beam.

DICTATE TERMS: A driver whose horse is in the lead and running at a pace that suits its ability without pressure from other runners is said to be dictating terms.

DISQUALIFICATION: To officially lower a horse's finishing position, deciding it interfered with others during the race, carried improper weight or was drugged.

DISTAFF RACE: A race for fillies, mares or both.

DISTANCE (A): Officially, a measure in excess of 30 lengths.

DISTANCE (THE): An unidentified spot 240 yards (just over a furlong) from the winning post. This derives from match races, where a horse finishing more than 240 yards behind the horse in front was disqualified from further heats, so that riders were discouraged from giving their horse an easy race in order to keep it fresh for later heats; a 'distance judge' was placed 240 yards from the finish.

DISTANCE OF GROUND: A route race, or a race greater than one mile.

DISTANCED: A horse out of touch with the rest of the field at the end of the race.

DOG: The underdog in any betting proposition.

DOG PLAYER: A bettor who mainly wagers on long odds.

DOPE: Slang for past performances.

DRAW: Refers to a horse's placing in the starting stalls for flat racing only.

DRIFT: Odds that lengthen are said to be on the drift.

DRIVE: All-out exertion under heavy punishment, especially in the home stretch.

DROP-DOWN: A horse moving down in class or claiming price.

DUAL FORECAST: A tote bet operating in races of three or more declared runners, in which the punter has to pick the first two to finish in either order.

DWELT: A horse that is late leaving the starting gate.

EACH WAY: Term for betting on a horse to win and/or place.

EARLY FOOT: Good speed at the start of the race.

EASE UP: To slow a horse's stride, reducing exertion.

ENTIRE HORSE: An ungelded horse.

EVEN MONEY: A bet of £1 to win £1.

EWE NECK: Where the horse's neck looks as if it has been put on upside-down.

EXCUSED: Withdrawn from a race with the consent of stewards.

EXOTIC WAGERS (GIMMICK BETS): Any bets other than straight win, place and show bets.

EXPOSURE: The amount of money one actually stands to lose on a race.

EXTEND: To force a horse to go all out.

FALSE START: The race starter will declare a false start and order a restart if one of the barrier tapes fails to release or if a runner has been denied a fair start.

FAST: A racing surface that is dry and hard, on which the footing is even and the race animals can run their best.

FAVOURITE: The horse on which most money has been wagered.

FEATHERWEIGHT: The lightest weight a horse can carry in a handicap race, or a jockey able to do this weight.

FEATURE: The best race on the card.

FETLOCK: Ankle of the horse.

FIELD: The number of horses in a race; in betting, all of them except the favourite.

FILLY: A female thoroughbred two to four years old.

FIRE: A burst of acceleration by a horse.

FIRED FORELEGS: Legs to which hot irons have been applied, to increase the blood flow and healing. No longer allowed in England.

FIRM: Optimum condition for the turn course (corresponds to fast on a dirt track).

FIRST JOCKEY: The stable's first choice; usually paid a retainer to ensure availability.

FIXED ODDS: Your dividend is fixed at the odds when you placed your bet.

FLAK JACKET: Worn to protect a jockey's ribs, kidney and back.

FLASH: The change or updating of odds information on the tote board.

FLAT RACE: A race on level ground, as opposed to a steeplechase. Often used in the term 'on the flat'.

FLATTEN OUT: A tired horse slowing considerably and dropping its head on a straight line with the body. Some horses do like to run with heads lowered, however.

FOAL: A baby horse.

FOOTING: Condition of the track surface.

FORCED WIDE: A horse forced to move wide on the track away from the inside running rail because of the action of another runner.

FORM: Performance history of a horse.

FOUL: An action by any horse or jockey that hinders or interferes with another horse or jockey during a race.

FRACTIOUS: A horse that kicks, resists being saddled or fights its handler.

FRESHENED: A rested horse.

FROG: V-shaped area found on the bottom of horses' hooves.

FRONT RUNNER: The horse that is winning the race.

FURLONG: 220 yards (one eighth of a mile). The numbered posts on British racecourses count the furlongs back from the winning post.

FALSE FAVOURITE: Horses run as favourite that the punter doesn't consider to merit its place in the betting.

GAIT: The manner in which a horse moves its legs when running.

GALLOP: A horse's fairest gait. A slang term for an easy race.

GARRISON FINISH: A fine finish on a winner, usually coming from off the pace.

GASSY: Highly-strung horse and 'silly' with it.

GELDING: A male that has been castrated to correct behaviour that would make him difficult to train for racing.

GENERAL STUD BOOK: Register of all genuine thoroughbred horses, maintained by Weatherbys.

GETAWAY DAY: Last day of a race meeting.

GIMPY: A horse that is slightly lame.

GODOLPHIN: The Al Maktoum family's private horseracing stable, named in honour of the Godolphin Arabian, which came from the desert to become one of the three founding stallions of the modern thoroughbred.

GOING: The condition of a racing surface.

GOING AWAY: Winning while increasing the lead.

GOLD CUP: The feature race of the third day of Royal Ascot (traditionally the busiest day of the week). The Queen traditionally presents the Gold Cup.

GONE: A horse that has lost all chances of winning a race.

GOOD: Condition between fast and slow; generally a bit wet.

GOOD BOTTOM: Track that is firm under the surface, which may be sloppy or wet.

GRAB A QUARTER: Injury to the back of the hoof or foot caused by a horse stepping on itself.

GRADUATE: First-time winning horse or rider.

GRAND (BIG'UN): A £1,000 bet.

GRASS SLIP: Permission to exercise a horse on the turf course.

GREY: A horse colour: the majority of the coat is a mixture of black and white hairs.

GROOM: A stable employee who cares for

horses and performs the daily chores such as grooming, bedding stall, bandaging, feeding, tacking and preparing for a race.

GUINEAS: Either the One Thousand Guineas or the Two Thousand Guineas; a guinea was one pound and one shilling (£1.05) and the name reflects the prize money irrespective of the number of subscribers. Bloodstock sales at Tattersalls are still conducted in guineas.

GYPSY: An itinerant owner or trainer.

HALF: The half-mile position.

HAND: The equivalent of four inches. A horse is measured in hands and inches from the top of the shoulder (withers) to the ground. Thoroughbreds typically range from 15 to 17 hands.

HANDICAP: In a handicap race, each horse carries weight dependent on the handicapper's assessment of its ability, usually based on previous form.

HAND RIDE: Urging a horse towards a longer, faster, rhythmic stride by rolling one's hands on a horse's neck and lifting its head at the beginning of the stride.

HANDLE: The total sum bet on a race.

HANGING: Veering to one side in a race rather than keeping in a straight line; probably used because the horse's head tends to hang to one side. Some courses (famously Epsom) have a camber (arched surface) that causes horses to hang towards the rails, or it can be caused by tiredness.

HARD: A condition of a turf course where there is no resilience to the surface.

HARD-MOUTHED: With little sensitivity in the mouth, so hard to restrain.

HEAVY: condition of track similar to, but even slower than, muddy.

HER MAJESTY'S REPRESENTATIVE: Crown-appointed administrator of Royal Ascot, responsible for running the course and determining entrance to the Royal Enclosure.

HOCK: The joint in the horse's leg between the knee and the fetlock, corresponding to the human ankle.

HOME STRAIGHT: The straight length of the track, nearest to the spectators, where the finish line is situated.

HOMEBRED: A horse bred by its owner.

HONEST: A kind, reliable horse.

HOPPED: A horse that has been illegally stimulated.

HOT WALKER: A stable hand who walks a horse while it cools out after a race.

HUNG: A horse that does not advance its position in a race when called upon by its jockey.

HURDLER: A horse that races over hurdles, which are lighter and lower than fences. Many former flat racers take to hurdling, but they do not have to be thus bred to excel.

IN TOUGH: A horse entered into a race with horses it is unlikely to beat.

INDIAN FILE: When a field of horses race in single file.

INQUIRY: Stewards may conduct an inquiry as a result of any incident that might have occurred during the race that suggests malpractice.

INSIDE RAIL: The fence or structure separating racing strip from infield.

INTRACTABLE: A horse that does things wrong, e.g. breaking, pulling or hanging during a race, or is difficult to control.

JOCKED OFF: When a fashionable jockey takes the already booked mount of a lesser rider.

JOCKEY: A race rider. As a verb, to jockey for a position during a race.

JOCKEY AGENT: A person who helps a rider obtain mounts in return for 20 per cent or more of the rider's earnings.

JOCKEY CLUB: The governing body of British racing.

JOCKEY'S RACE: A race whose outcome will hinge largely on strategic thinking by the rider.

JOG: A slow, easy gait, usually a trot, used primarily to warm up horses before a race.

JOSTLE: To bump another horse.

JOURNEYMAN: A professional jockey.

JUMP UP: When a horse wins in a surprising reversal of form.

JUVENILE: A two-year-old racehorse.

LADIES' DAY: Though never formally named as such, Ladies' Day is the colloquial title for the Thursday of Royal Ascot.

LAME: A horse that is limping or has difficulty walking.

LAST HALF: The time recorded by a horse during the last half of the final mile travelled in the race.

LATE MONEY: Money that has been bet within five minutes to post.

LATE SCRATCH: A horse withdrawn from a race after the official programme has been printed.

LATHERED UP: A horse with sweat that foams along the neck and flanks before a race. Too much sweat signifies nervousness.

LAY: To occupy a certain running position deliberately while waiting to make a strategic move.

LAYOFF: An extended period of time during which a horse is stopped from racing and shipped to a farm for rest, breeding or rehabilitation.

LEAD: Weights carried to make up the difference when a rider weighs less than the poundage a horse is assigned to carry.

LEAD PONY: The horse or pony who heads the parade of the field, from paddock to starting gate.

LEAD TIME: The time it takes for a horse to travel from the start of the race to the beginning of the last mile.

LEAKY-ROOF CIRCUIT: Refers to minor racecourses.

LEG LOCK: When a jockey illegally hooks legs with another rider, impeding the other horse.

LEG UP: To help a jockey mount his horse.

LENGTH: A unit of measurement. In horse racing it is theoretically the distance from the horse's nose to the tip of its flying tail.

LEVEL WEIGHTS, AT: All carrying the same weight.

LINE: Pedigree.

LIVE WEIGHT: The weight of a jockey that a horse carries, as opposed to dead weight.

LOCK: A sure thing.

LONG END OF THE PURSE: Winner's share.

LONG SHOT: The opposite of a favourite.

LOOSE HORSE: A horse that continues running after losing its rider. Also a slang term for a person with inconsistent mannerisms.

LOOSE REIN: A horse on a loose rein is one allowed to run freely, without any pressure from the driver to speed up or slow down.

LOP-EARED: With long ears, which sometimes flop sideways. Horses with lop ears are usually honest and good-natured.

LUG (IN OR OUT): The action of a horse that is becoming tired, bearing in or out, failing to keep a straight course.

MAIDEN: A horse that has never won a race; maiden races are run by these horses.

MAGNETIC FIELD: Physical therapy technique for horses that causes dilation of blood vessels and tissue stimulation.

MAGNIFICENT SEVEN: On 28 September 1996, jockey Frankie Dettori won seven consecutive races at Ascot. He was said to have cost the bookmakers £30 million.

MAKE A RUN: When a horse turns on the speed and makes a move in a bid to win the race.

MARE: Female horse aged five years or older.

MASTER OF THE BUCKHOUNDS: Administrator of Ascot on behalf of the Crown, appointed by the Monarch. The title endured from 1711 to 1901, when the Master was retitled His Majesty's Representative.

MATURITY: A race for four-year-olds, for which entries are made before their birth.

MEDICATION LIST: A list kept by the track veterinarian and published by the track and daily racing form showing which horses have been treated.

MEET: Race meeting.

MONEY RIDER: A rider who excels in races with high-stakes prize money.

MONKEY-ON-A-STICK: Type of riding with short stirrups popularized by jockey Ted Sloan.

MORNING GLORY: A horse that performs well in morning workouts but fails to reproduce form in races.

MOVE UP: Gain ground, or run in a higher-class race.

MUDDER: Horse that races well on muddy tracks. Also known as a mudlark.

NAME: Names of thoroughbreds registered by the Jockey Club must be no longer than eighteen characters, including punctuation and spelling.

NAVICULAR DISEASE: Degeneration of the bone behind the horse's heel causing acute lameness. Incurable.

NEAR SIDE: The left side of a horse on which a jockey is mounted.

NEW GRANDSTAND: In 2004, Ascot Racecourse closed for a period of twenty months for a £200 million redevelopment. As owner of the Crown Estate, the Queen reopened the racecourse on Tuesday, 20 June 2006. The Grandstand now has 255 private boxes including the Ascot Authority box for Her Majesty's Representative and his guests.

NIFTY: A £50 stake.

NIGHTCAP: The final race on a programme.

NOM DE COURSE: Name adopted by an owner or group of owners for racing purposes, such as Godolphin.

NOMINATION FEE: A fee paid by an owner to keep his horse eligible for an upcoming horse race.

NON-STARTER: A horse that fails to come within reasonable distance of the barrier.

NOSE (ALSO 'SHORT HEAD'): Smallest advantage by which a horse can win.

NOSE BAND: A leather strap that goes over the bridge of the horse's nose to help secure the bridle and keep the tongue from sliding up over the bit.

OBJECTION: Verbal or written statement against the eligibility of a horse for a race, or against the judge's placings after the all clear has been signalled.

ODDS: The amount of profit per pound to be paid on a winning bet.

ODDS AGAINST: The backer wins more than their stake, eg 6 to 4.

ODDS ON: A bet where you have to outlay more than you win.

OFF SIDE: The right side of a horse on which a jockey is mounted.

OFF THE BOARD: When the odds against a horse are more than 99 to 1.

OFF THE PACE: To run behind the early leaders.

ON THE BIT: When a horse is eager to run. Also known as 'in the bridle'.

ON THE MUSCLE: A fit horse.

ON THE NOSE: Betting a horse to win only.

ON THE PACE: A horse keeping up with another runner who sets the speed.

ON THE PAINT: A horse racing very close to the inside running rail.

OPEN CLASS: Horses that compete in races open to the most successful horses. Generally aged four years or older.

OUT OF LINE: Price not consistent with a horse's ability.

OUTRIDER: The person who leads the post parade and gets the horses and jockeys to the starting gate on time.

OVERALL TIME: The time taken to complete the distance of the race as opposed to the mile rate.

OVERLAND: Racing wide, outside the other horses.

OVERLAY: When the odds of betting on a horse are higher than past performance would suggest.

OVERPAY: A case where the price paid to winning ticket-holders is more than the correct price due to a bookie error.

OWNERS/TRAINERS: Royal Ascot owners', trainers' and jockeys' badges are handwritten, named and non-transferrable, prepared in advance by the Clerk of the Course. A further pass is mandatory for access to the Royal Enclosure lawns.

PACE: The speed of the leaders at each stage of the race.

PACEMAKER: A stable companion put into the contest to set the pace for another.

PADDOCK: Approximately twenty-five minutes before the race, horses are brought from the barn area to the Paddock and led to a row of stalls, where they are inspected and identified by track officials, ensuring the correct horses run the race.

PADDOCK JUDGE: Racing officials responsible for getting jockeys and horses in order to go to the starting gate.

PARKED OUT: A horse racing on the outside with at least one horse between it and the inside rail or barrier.

PARROT MOUTH: A horse with an extreme overbite.

PASTERN: Part of a horse's leg between the fetlock and just above the hoof.

PEEP: A horse finishing third.

PICK UP THE BIT: Take an interest in the race.

PINCHED BACK: A horse forced back due to racing in close quarters.

PINHOOKER: A person who buys a racehorse with specific intention of reselling it at a profit.

PLACE: A horse runs a place if it finishes in the first three in fields of eight or more horses.

PLACE BET: Betting a horse will finish second against straight or show.

PLODDING: A horse not racing as quickly as its ability allows.

PONY PERSON: A person on horseback who accompanies a horse and jockey to the starting gate.

POST POSITION: A race animal's position in the starting gate/box from the inside rail out; decided by a draw before the race.

PRINCE OF WALES STAKES: First run in 1862, this Group One race was named after the future King Edward VII, one of Royal Ascot's most successful royal owners.

PRIZE MONEY: Royal Ascot is the most valuable race meeting in Europe, with £4 million in prize money on offer in 2010, and featuring seven Group One races and seventeen group races in total.

PULLED: A horse that is pulled is deliberately restrained, either to fool the handicapper or to avoid winning as a result of a bribe. Results in horrible recriminations from the Jockey Club.

PUTTING UP OVERWEIGHT: Carrying more weight than that allocated by the handicapper.

PULLING: Some horses get fired-up during a race and try to run faster than the other runners. These horses are pulling, leaving little energy for the finish.

PULLING OUT: A horse pulling out in a race is one that comes from the rails or running-line position to head out wider on the track in an effort to secure a clear run.

PUNTER: An investor or person who places bets on the outcome of a race.

PURPLE PATCH: Return to form or performance.

PURSE: The total monetary amount distributed after a race to the owners of the entrants who have finished in the top four or five positions.

QUARTERS: The hind parts of a horse, specifically between flank and tail.

QUEEN ANNE STAKES: Race at Royal Ascot run in memory of the monarch who founded the course in 1711. The Queen Anne Stakes was first run in 1840 as the Trial Stakes and was renamed in 1930 in honour of the founder.

QUEEN'S RACING COLOURS: Her Majesty's jockeys always wear distinctive silks first registered by King George IV: purple body with gold braid, scarlet sleeves and black velvet cap with gold fringe.

RABBIT: A horse considered to have little chance of winning but is entered purely to ensure a fast pace and tire out the front runners, softening up the competition for the benefit of an entry mate.

RACE CARD: The signature cream, Royal-crested booklet listing the runners, riders, form and racing colours produced for each of the five days of the Royal Meeting.

RACING PLATE: A lightweight horseshoe used for racing, as opposed to the heavier iron plate. Now made of aluminium.

RACING POST: The Bible of the British horse racing fraternity.

RANK: A horse that refuses to settle under a jockey's handling, running in a headstrong manner without respect to pace.

REFUSE: When a horse will not break from the gate.

RETURN TO SCALE: The period between the finish of the race and the signalling of the all clear. This term refers to the jockeys having to return to the scale to check their weight before the all clear can be given.

RINGER: A horse racing under the name and identity of another.

ROARER: A horse that makes a noise when it gallops because of a problem with its wind or breathing; a tracheotomy may cure the problem.

RACING SOUND: A horse able to race and pass all veterinarian tests, but not 100 per cent.

ROGUE: An ill-tempered horse.

ROMP: Running and winning with ease.

ROYAL ASCOT: The annual five-day race meeting at Ascot traditionally held in the third week of June, beginning on Thursday. Until the Queen's Golden Jubilee in 2002, the Royal Procession only rode out from Tuesday to Friday. Since 2002, Saturday has also become a royal day, with the Queen in attendance and morning coats and formal day dress mandatory in the Royal Enclosure.

ROYAL ASCOT GATEMEN: Ex-servicemen who greet the Queen as she walks from the Parade Ring to the Royal Box, who wear a distinctive forest-green livery derived from that of the Yeoman Prickers.

ROYAL BOX: Box on the first tier of the Grandstand with fine views of the Winning Post for Her Majesty, the Royal Household and her invited guests. The doors to the Royal Box have handles in the shape of riding whips and are flanked by large medallion coins depicting the profile of every monarch from Queen Anne to Queen Elizabeth II.

ROYAL ENCLOSURE: The Royal Enclosure is the heart of Royal Ascot. Entry to the Enclosure is through sponsorship by an existing badgeholder who has attended for four previous years, though not necessarily consecutive.

ROYAL PROCESSION: At precisely 2 p.m. on every day of the Royal Meeting, the Royal Procession of four carriages rides out from the Golden Gates and processes down the racetrack and into the Parade Ring, where the Queen and her guests alight and are led to the Royal Box. The Queen's carriage is pulled by Windsor Grey horses and her coachmen wear a livery tailored solely for use at Windsor Castle and at Royal Ascot.

RULED OFF: When the stewards forbid a person to enter the grounds of the racetrack; also known as an 'exclusion'.

RUN DOWN: A change of odds in a bookmaking establishment caused by heavy betting on a horse or horses.

RUNNER: A messenger who makes bets and cashes winning tickets for a patron of the track.

RUNNING DOUBLE: When a punter has correctly selected the winner in two consecutive races.

SADDLE: A thoroughbred racing saddle is the lightest, weighing less than two pounds.

SALIVA TEST: Lab test to determine if a horse has been drugged or overdosed with permitted medication.

SAVAGE: When a horse bites another horse or person.

SAVE GROUND: To cover the shortest possible distance in a race.

SECOND STRING: The stable's second choice from two runners in a race; a string is the trainer's horse.

SELLING PLATER: A horse entered in a selling plate because it is not expected to win in any higher grade, or because it can do well against moderate opposition, which may result in a betting coup.

SELLING PLATE: A race in which the winner is offered at auction afterwards; other horses in the race may be claimed for a fixed sum. If the winning stable buys back its own horse it is said to be 'bought in'. Racecourses put on these races because they receive a percentage of the selling price of each horse.

SET: A group of horses exercised together.

SET DOWN: A suspension, when a jockey is set down for five days for careless riding. Also refers to when a jockey assumes a lower crouch in the saddle while urging the horse to pick up speed.

SHELLY FEET: Slightly concave and brittle hooves.

SHIP-IN: A horse that has to travel to race.

SHORT-FILED: A race with seven or fewer horses in the race.

SHORT-PRICED: The favourite will be short-priced, e.g. 3 to 1 or 2 to 1.

SHUT OFF: A horse that is unable to improve its position in a race due to being surrounded by other horses.

SIRE: The male parent of a horse.

SIT: To race in a trailing position.

SLEEPER: An underrated horse.

SLOW: A racing strip that is wet on both the surface and the base.

SMART MONEY: Insider's bet.

SNUG: Mild restraining hold by the rider.

SOFT RUN: An easy run.

SOLID HORSE: A contender.

SPELL: The resting period between preparations or racing. Horses cannot remain in peak form and hard training all year round.

SPIT THE BIT: A term referring to a tired horse that begins to run less aggressively.

SPRINT: A race around one turn less than a mile long.

SPRINTER: A race horse that shows a preference for short distances.

STAKE: A race for which the owner must pay a fee to run a horse.

STALL WALKER: A horse that moves about its stall constantly and frets rather than rests.

STALLION: A male horse retired from racing that stands as stud and is used for breeding purposes.

STANDING STARTS: Race start in which the horses are stationary at time of release.

STAYER: A horse that has the endurance to race well over long distances.

STEADIED: A horse being taken in hand by his rider, usually because of being in close quarters.

STEP UP: A horse moving up in class to meet better competition.

STEWARD: An official who presides over a race meeting.

STIRRUPS (IRONS): Metal D-shaped rings into which a jockey places his feet. They can be raised or lowered depending on the jockey's preference.

STRAIGHT AS A STRING: Description of a horse running at top speed.

STRIDE: A horse's way of running, or the ground it covers after each foot has been in contact with the track once.

STUD: A farm or stable where registered stallions and mares are located for breeding purposes.

SUCKLING: A foal in its first year of life.

SWAY BACK: Long, weak back.

SWEEPERS: Those horses racing at the rear of the field but moved out to race wide on the track by the drivers in order to get a clear run down the home straight towards the finish line.

SWINLEY BOTTOM: The lowest point of the course, with a 73-foot climb to the highest point at the Winning Post, making Royal Ascot a notoriously tough course to race.

TAP ROOT MARE: The ancestor on the female side of many winners.

TAILED OFF: A horse that drops so far back during a race that it is out of touch with the rest of the field.

TATTERSALLS: Dating from 1766 and operating from Park Paddocks in Newmarket, Tattersalls is Europe's largest bloodstock auctioneers and the world's oldest, offering more than 5,000 thoroughbreds every year.

THOROUGHBRED: A horse whose parentage traces back to any of the three founding sires – the Darley Arabian, Byerly Turk and Godolphin Barb – who has satisfied the rules and requirements of the Jockey Club.

TIGHT: Ready to race.

TOTE: Established in 1928 by Winston Churchill, the Tote (Totalisator Board) is the only British bookmaker allowed to run pool betting on horseracing. It was created to provide a safe, state-controlled alternative to illegal off-course bookmaking and channelled gambling revenues back into horse racing rather than into the pockets of the on- and off-course bookmakers.

TOUT: A person who gives tips on a race for profit.

TRACK RECORD: Fastest time at various distances recorded at a particular track.

TRAINER: The person who conditions and prepares a race horse for racing, with the absolute responsibility of ensuring the physical condition and eligibility of the horse.

TRIPLE CROWN: For colts, the Two Thousand Guineas, the Derby and the St Leger; for fillies, the One Thousand or Two Thousand Guineas, the Oaks or Derby and the St Leger. A winner of the appropriate three Classic races for three-year-olds is a hero or heroine of the turf.

TUCKED UP: A horse that is tightly drawn up around the abdomen; possibly having passed its peak for the season.

TURF: The grass upon which the horses race at Royal Ascot. For flat racing it is cut to a regulation four inches in height.

UNDER WRAPS: A horse racing exceptionally well and under restraint.

UNDER PUNISHMENT: A horse being whipped or driven.

UP: When riders mount their horses in the paddock.

USED UP: An exhausted horse.

VALET: An employee who takes care of the jockey's equipment and ensures that the correct silks are at the jockey's locker.

WAGER: Bet.

WASHED OUT: A horse that becomes so nervous that it sweats profusely.

WEAKENED: A horse that started well and was in position to win, but could not keep up the pace.

WEATHERBYS: From 1770 to the present day, the Weatherby family and firm has serviced horseracing and thoroughbred breeding as the sport's administrative service, financial agency and founding register of the racehorse breed and racing colours.

WEAVING: A swaying motion in the stall, or the act of threading a horse through the field in a race.

WEIGH IN: At a racetrack, the procedure where the Clerk of Scales checks the weight of the jockey and his riding equipment prior to the race.

WELL TRIED: A horse that has been well supported by punters.

WIRE: Another term for the finish line.

WORK RIDER: An employee, not necessarily a licensed jockey but good enough to ride a horse being tested or prepared on the gallops.

WRONG IN THE WIND: A horse with breathing difficulties.

YEARLING: A horse in its second calendar year of life, beginning 1 January

YIELDING: Condition of a turf course with a great deal of moisture.

With thanks to Royal Ascot, the National Horseracing Museum, Newmarket, and www.dictionaryofgambling.com

ASCOT IN PICTURES: MILLINERS & DESIGNERS

All images listed from left to right, unless otherwise indicated.

Page 46
Top: Stephen Jones; Philip Treacy; Stephen Jones; *Middle*: Not known; Philip Treacy; Luella; Rachel Trevor-Morgan; *Bottom*: Jasmine Guinness wears Stephen Jones; Philip Treacy; Philip Treacy.

Page 47
Top: Philip Treacy; William Chambers; Philip Treacy; Philip Treacy; *Middle*: Lisa Snowdon wears Philip Treacy and dress by Luella; Aishwarya Rai wears Ilda DiVico; Stephen Jones; *Bottom*: Rachel Trevor-Morgan; Rachel Trevor-Morgan; Philip Treacy; Stephen Jones.

Page 143
Middle row, left: Grace Jones wears Philip Treacy. Bottom row, right: James Lock & Co. Other designers not known.

Page 144
Top: Philip Treacy; James Lock & Co.; Stephen Jones for the Dorchester Collection; Philip Treacy; *Middle*: James Lock & Co.; Philip Treacy; not known; James Lock & Co.; *Bottom*: Chi Ling Lin wears Ilda DiVico; James Lock & Co.; Ilda DiVico.

Page 145
Top: James Lock & Co.; Isabell Kristensen wears Louis Mariette; not known; *Middle*: Ilda DiVico; Philip Treacy; James Lock & Co.; Stephen Jones for the Dorchester Collection; *Bottom*: James Lock & Co.; James Lock & Co.; Lady Martha Sitwell wears Philip Treacy; James Lock & Co.

Page 193
Top: Philip Treacy 2008 (both images); *Middle*: Vivienne Westwood S/S 2009; Philip Treacy 2008; Philip Treacy 2008; *Bottom*: Philip Treacy 2008; Philip Treacy 2007; Philip Treacy 2007.

Page 194
Top: Philip Treacy 2007; Philip Treacy 2008; Amanda Wakeley 2008; Philip Treacy 2007; *Middle*: Philip Treacy 2008; Philip Treacy 2007; Amanda Wakeley S/S 2010; *Bottom*: Philip Treacy 2008; Philip Treacy 2007; Stephen Jones 2010; Philip Treacy 2007.

Page 195
Top: Philip Treacy 2007; Philip Treacy 2007; Stephen Jones 2010; Philip Treacy 2007; *Middle*: Stephen Jones 2009; Stephen Jones 2010; Stephen Jones 2010 (millinery), Vivienne Westwood 2010 (attire); *Bottom*: Luella S/S 2009; Matthew Williamson 2008; Stephen Jones 2010.

Page 196
Top: Gieves & Hawkes S/S 2011; Kenzo S/S 2007; Vivienne Westwood Man Collection S/S 2010; Gieves & Hawkes S/S 2011; *Middle*: Vivienne Westwood Man Collection S/S 2010; Gieves & Hawkes S/S 2011; Gieves & Hawkes S/S 2011; Gieves & Hawkes S/S 2011. Bottom: (all images) Gieves & Hawkes S/S 2011.

Page 197
Top: Gieves & Hawkes S/S 2011; Gieves & Hawkes S/S 2011; Kenzo S/S 2007; Gieves & Hawkes S/S 2011. *Middle*: (all images) Gieves & Hawkes S/S 2011; *Bottom*: (all images) Gieves & Hawkes S/S 2011.

Page 198
Top: Vivienne Westwood Gold Label S/S 2010; Vivienne Westwood Gold Label S/S 2009; Amanda Wakeley S/S 2008; *Middle*: Amanda Wakeley S/S 2008; Vivienne Westwood Bridal 2008; *Bottom*: Vivienne Westwood Gold Label S/S 2010; Mary Katranzou S/S 2010; Vivienne Westwood Gold Label S/S 2010.

Page 199
Top: Vivienne Westwood Gold Label S/S 2010; Matthew Williamson S/S 2008; *Middle*: Vivienne Westwood Gold Label S/S 2010; Vivienne Westwood Gold Label S/S 2010; Vivienne Westwood Gold Label S/S 2010; *Bottom*: Vivienne Westwood Gold Label S/S 2010 (attire), Stephen Jones 2010 (millinery); Vivienne Westwood Gold Label S/S 2008.

PICTURE CREDITS

p. 2: Courtesy of Ascot Racecourse; p. 3: Courtesy of Ascot Racecourse; p. 4–5: Tim Clayton/CORBIS; p. 6: Popperfoto/Getty Images; p. 7: Toby Melville/Reuters/Corbis; p. 8: Courtesy of Ascot Racecourse; p. 12: Courtesy of Ascot Racecourse; p. 15: Courtesy of Amanda Wakeley; p. 16: Courtesy of Philip Treacy; p. 18: Courtesy of Ascot Racecourse; p. 19: Courtesy of Ascot Racecourse; p. 21: Courtesy of Ascot Racecourse

p. 22: Courtesy of Grosvenor Prints/Author's collection; p. 24: Courtesy of Ascot Racecourse; p. 25: Courtesy of Grosvenor Prints/Author's collection; pp. 26–27: Courtesy of Kerry Taylor Auctions; p. 29: Getty Images; p. 30: Columbia/American Zoetrope/Sony/The Kobal Collection; p. 32: (all) Courtesy of Ascot Racecourse; p. 33 Pathé/BBC Films/The Kobal Collection; p. 35: Courtesy of Andrew Edmunds/Author's collection; p. 37: (top) Courtesy of Ascot Racecourse; (bottom, left and right) Author's collection; pp. 39–43: (all) Courtesy of Ascot Racecourse; p. 45: Photography by Philippe Kerlo/Courtesy of Philip Treacy; p. 46: (top, left to right) Courtesy of Ascot Racecourse; Courtesy of Philip Treacy; Courtesy of Ascot Racecourse; (middle, left to right) Courtesy of Ascot Racecourse; Courtesy of Philip Treacy; Courtesy of Ascot Racecourse; Courtesy of Ascot Racecourse; (bottom, left to right) Courtesy of Ascot Racecourse; Courtesy of Ascot Racecourse; Courtesy of Philip Treacy; p. 47: (top, left to right) Courtesy of Philip Treacy; Courtesy of William Chambers; Courtesy of Philip Treacy; Courtesy of Philip Treacy; (middle, all images) Courtesy of Ascot Racecourse; (bottom, left to right) Courtesy of Ascot Racecourse; Courtesy of Ascot Racecourse; Courtesy of Philip Treacy; Courtesy of Ascot Racecourse.

p. 49: GK Films/The Kobal Collection; p. 50: Courtesy of Ascot Racecourse; p. 51: Courtesy of Ascot Racecourse/Photography by Simon Procter, art direction by Gary England, millinery by Stephen Jones, attire by Vivienne Westwood, styling by Brigitte Stepputis; p. 52: (top) Courtesy of T. Alana Brett/Author's Collection; (bottom) Courtesy of Kerry Taylor Auctions; p. 53: Courtesy of Ascot Racecourse; p. 54: The Royal Collection © 2011 Her Majesty Queen Elizabeth II/The Bridgeman Art Library; p. 55: Author's collection; p. 56: Courtesy of Storey's Limited/Author's collection; p. 57: Courtesy of Kerry Taylor Auctions; pp. 58–59: Courtesy of Ascot Racecourse; pp. 60–61: Courtesy of Storey's Ltd/Author's collection; p. 62: Author's collection; p. 63: Courtesy of Ascot Racecourse; p. 64: Author's collection; p. 65: Courtesy of Ascot Racecourse; p. 66: Getty Images; p. 67: Courtesy of Ascot Racecourse;

pp. 68–69: Getty Images; pp. 71–75: (all) Courtesy of Ascot Racecourse; p. 76: Everett Collection/Rex Features; p. 77: Sunset Boulevard/Corbis; pp. 79–81: (all) Courtesy of Ascot Racecourse.

p. 82: Getty Images; p. 85: (top left) Courtesy of Ascot Racecourse; (top right) Courtesy of Kerry Taylor Auctions; (bottom) Courtesy of Ascot Racecourse; pp. 86–87: Getty Images; p. 88: Hulton-Deutsch Collection/CORBIS; p. 89: (both) Courtesy of Kerry Taylor Auctions; p. 90: Author's collection; p. 91: Courtesy of Ascot Racecourse; p. 92: Author's collection; p. 93: Courtesy of Kerry Taylor Auctions; p. 94: Getty Images; p. 95: Courtesy of Ascot Racecourse; p. 96: (top) Everett Collection/Rex Features; (bottom) ITV/Rex Features; p. 97: Author's collection; p. 98: Courtesy of Kerry Taylor Auctions; p. 99: Author's collection; p. 100: SSPL via Getty Images; p. 102: Courtesy of Ascot Racecourse; p. 103: Courtesy of the Dowager Duchess of Devonshire's private collection; pp. 104–5: SSPL via Getty Images; pp. 107–9: Courtesy of Ascot Racecourse; pp. 111–13: Courtesy of Ascot Racecourse.

p. 114: Gieves & Hawkes Archive; p. 116: (all) Courtesy of Wartski; p. 117: Time & Life Pictures/Getty Images; p. 118: Courtesy of Kerry Taylor Auctions; p. 119: (all) Author's collection; p. 120: Getty Images; p. 121: Courtesy of Kerry Taylor Auctions; pp. 122–23: Popperfoto/Getty Images; p. 124: Courtesy of Ascot Racecourse; p. 125: Courtesy of Ascot Racecourse; p. 126: Courtesy of Ascot Racecourse; p. 127: Getty Images; p. 128: AFP/Getty Images; p. 129: Courtesy of Kerry Taylor Archive; pp. 130–31: Courtesy of Ascot Racecourse; p. 132: Courtesy of Ascot Racecourse; p. 133: Courtesy of Ascot Racecourse; p. 134: Courtesy of Ascot Racecourse; p. 135: Courtesy of Ascot Racecourse; pp. 137–41: (all) Courtesy of Ascot Racecourse; p. 143: (all) Courtesy of Ascot Racecourse; p. 144: (top, left to right) Courtesy of Philip Treacy; Courtesy of Ascot Racecourse; Courtesy of Coworth Park, part of the Dorchester Collection, www.coworthpark.com; Courtesy of Philip Treacy; (middle, left to right) Courtesy of Ascot Racecourse; Courtesy of Philip Treacy; Courtesy of Ascot Racecourse; Courtesy of Ascot Racecourse; (bottom, all images) Courtesy of Ascot Racecourse; p. 145: (top, all images) Courtesy of Ascot Racecourse; (middle, left to right) Courtesy of Ascot Racecourse; Courtesy of Philip Treacy; Courtesy of Ascot Racecourse; Courtesy of Coworth Park, part of the Dorchester Collection, www.coworthpark.com; (bottom, all images) Courtesy of Ascot Racecourse.

p. 146: Getty Images; pp. 148–49: (all) Courtesy of Hardy Amies Archive; p. 150: (both) Courtesy of Kerry Taylor Auctions; p. 151: Getty Images; p. 152: (top) Courtesy of Ascot Racecourse; (bottom) Courtesy of Kerry Taylor Auctions; pp. 154–155: Warner Br/Everett/Rex Features; p. 155: Courtesy of Kerry Taylor Auctions; p. 156: Getty Images; p. 158: Courtesy of Jasper Conran; p. 159: Tessa Traeger ©; p. 160: Courtesy of Kerry Taylor Auctions; p. 161: Getty Images; p. 162: Courtesy of Ascot Racecourse; p. 163: Courtesy of Kerry Taylor Auctions; p. 164: Selwyn Tait/Sygma/Corbis; p. 165: Courtesy of Ascot Racecourse; p. 166: Courtesy of Ascot Racecourse; p. 167: (left) Courtesy of Kerry Taylor Auctions; (right) Getty Images; p. 168: Courtesy of Kerry Taylor Auctions; p. 169: Getty Images; p. 170: Getty Images; p. 171: Courtesy of Ascot Racecourse; p. 172: Courtesy of Kerry Taylor Auctions; p. 173: Courtesy of Ascot Racecourse/photography by Finlay Mackay, art direction by Brigitte Stepputtis, millinery by Stephen Jones, attire by Vivienne Westwood; p. 174: (top) Courtesy of Hardy Amies; (bottom) Courtesy of Ascot Racecourse; p. 175: Getty Images; p. 177: Photography by Kevin Davies/Courtesy of Philip Treacy; p. 178: Courtesy of Hardy Amies; p. 179: Courtesy of Hardy Amies; p. 180: (both): Courtesy of Ascot Racecourse; p. 181: Courtesy of Ascot Racecourse; pp. 182–83: Courtesy of Ascot Racecourse; p. 184: WireImage; p. 185: WireImage; p. 186: Getty Images; p. 187: Michael Dunlea/Rex Features; p. 189: Courtesy of Ascot Racecourse; p. 191: Courtesy of Ascot Racecourse/Photography by Finlay Mackay, art direction by Gary England, millinery by Stephen Jones, attire by Vivienne Westwood and Gieves & Hawkes, styling by Brigitte Stepputis; pp. 193–99: (all) Courtesy of Ascot Racecourse; p. 200: (top) Courtesy of David Shilling; (bottom) Courtesy of Ascot Racecourse; p. 201: Tim Graham/Getty Images; pp. 203–205: (all) Courtesy of Ascot Racecourse.

p. 208: (all) Courtesy of Ascot Racecourse; p. 209: Photography by Aaron Hayden/Courtesy of Henry Poole & Co.; p. 211: Courtesy of Henry Poole & Co.; p. 212: Courtesy of Ede & Ravenscroft; p. 213: Courtesy of Ascot Racecourse.

Jacket photograph courtesy of Ascot Racecourse/Photography by Simon Procter, art direction by Gary England, millinery by Stephen Jones, attire by Vivienne Westwood, styling by Brigitte Stepputis. Endpaper photographs courtesy of Ascot Racecourse.

Ascot Racecourse photography by Lee Farrant, Patch Dolan and Andy Parish from RPM Ltd.

BIBLIOGRAPHY

ARISTOCRACY

Balsan, Consuelo Vanderbilt. *The Glitter and the Gold.* Maidstone: George Mann, 1973.

Dalley, Jan. *Diana Mosley: A Life.* London: Faber & Faber, 1999.

Davenport-Hines, Richard. *Ettie: The Intimate Life and Dauntless Spirit of Lady Desborough.* London: Weidenfeld & Nicolson, 2008.

Devonshire, Deborah, Dowager Duchess of. *Wait for Me! Memoirs of the Youngest Mitford Sister.* London: John Murray, 2010.

Devonshire, Deborah, Dowager Duchess and Leigh Fermor, Patrick. *In Tearing Haste: Letters between Deborah Devonshire and Patrick Leigh Fermor.* London: John Murray, 2008.

Foreman, Amanda. *Georgiana: Duchess of Devonshire.* London: Harper Collins, 1998.

Jennings, Charles. *Them and Us: The American Invasion of British High Society.* Stroud: Sutton Publishing, 2007.

Mosley, Charlotte (ed.). *The Mitfords: Letters Between Six Sisters.* London: Fourth Estate, 2007.

Mosley, Charlotte (ed.). *The Letters of Nancy Mitford and Evelyn Waugh.* New York: Houghton Mifflin, 1996.

Osborne, Frances. *The Bolter.* London: Virago Press, 2008.

Taylor, D. J. *Bright Young People: The Rise and Fall of a Generation 1918–1940.* London: Chatto & Windus, 2007.

FASHION HISTORY

Amies, Hardy. *ABC of Men's Fashion.* New York: Abrams, 2007.

Chrisman-Campbell, Kimberly (ed.). *Fashioning Fashion: European Dress in Detail 1700–1915.* New York: Delmonico Books, 2010.

de la Haye, Amy. *The Cutting Edge: 50 Years of British Fashion.* London: V&A, 1996.

Demornex, Jacqueline. *Lucien Lelong.* London: Thames & Hudson, 2008.

Kelly, Ian. *Beau Brummell: The Ultimate Dandy.* London: Hodder & Stoughton, 2005.

Dior, Christian. *Dior by Dior.* London: Penguin, 1958.

Laver, James. *Costume & Fashion: A Concise History.* London: Thames & Hudson, 1969.

McDowell, Colin. *Forties Fashion and the New Look.* London: Bloomsbury, 1997.

Packer, William. *Fashion Drawings in Vogue: Carl Erickson.* Exeter: Webb & Bower, 1989.

Picardie, Justine. *Coco Chanel: The Legend and the Life.* London: Harper Collins, 2010.

Ross, Josephine. *Beaton in Vogue.* London: Thames & Hudson, 1986.

Vreeland, Diana with Christopher Hemphill. *Allure.* San Francisco: Chronicle Books, 2010.

Webber, Caroline. *Queen of Fashion: What Marie Antoinette Wore to the Revolution.* London: Arum, 2006.

HATS & ACCESSORIES

Corson, Richard & James Sherwood. *Fashions in Makeup: From Ancient to Modern Times.* London: Peter Owen, 2003.

Jones, Stephen. *Hats: An Anthology.* London: V&A Publishing, 2009.

JEWELS

Menkes, Suzy. *The Royal Jewels.* London: Grafton Books, 1985.

Meylan, Vincent. *Queen's Jewels.* New York: Assouline, 2008.

RACING

Cope, Alfred. *Cope's Royal Cavalcade of the Turf.* London: David Cope Ltd, 1953.

Laird, Dorothy, with the Jockey's Association of Great Britain. *The Benson & Hedges Book of Racing Colours.* Birmingham: Weather Oak Press Ltd, 1973.

ROYALTY

Bradford, Sarah. *Elizabeth: A Biography of Her Majesty the Queen.* London: Penguin Books, 2002.

Carter, Miranda. *The Three Emperors: Three Cousins, Three Empires and the Road to World War One.* New York: Penguin Group, 2009.

Gelardi, Julia. *Born to Rule: Granddaughters of Victoria, Queens of Europe.* London: Hodder Headline, 2004.

Haslip, Joan. *The Lonely Empress: A Biography of Elizabeth of Austria.* London: Weidenfeld & Nicolson, 2004.

Heald, Tim. *Princess Margaret: A Life Unravelled.* London: Weidenfeld & Nicolson, 2007.

Longford, Elizabeth. *The Royal House of Windsor.* London: Weidenfeld & Nicolson, 1974.

Mackenzie, Sabrina & Jane Roberts. *Five Gold Rings: A Royal Wedding Souvenir Album From Queen Victoria to Queen Elizabeth II.* London: Royal Collection Publications, 2007.

Pope-Hennessy, James. *Queen Mary 1867–1953.* London: Orion, 2003.

Ross, Josephine. *Royalty in Vogue.* London: Chatto & Windus, 1989.

Seward, Desmond. *Eugenie: The Empress and her Empire.* Stroud: Sutton Publishing, 2004.

Vickers, Hugo. *Alice: Princess Andrew of Greece.* New York: St Martin's Griffin, 2000.

Vickers, Hugo. *Elizabeth: The Queen Mother.* London: Hutchinson, 2005.

Waller, Maureen. *Ungrateful Daughters: The Stuart Princesses who Stole their Father's Crown.* London: Hodder & Stoughton, 2002.

Waller, Maureen. *Sovereign Ladies: The Six Reigning Queens of England.* London: John Murray, 2006.

Williams, Kate. *Becoming Queen.* London: Hutchinson, 2008.

Windsor, Duke of. *A Family Album.* London: Cassell, 1960.

ROYAL ASCOT

Cawthorne, George James. *Royal Ascot: Its History and its Associations.* London: Longmans, 1900.

Laird, Dorothy. *Royal Ascot.* London: Hodder & Stoughton, 1976.

Magee, Sean with Sally Aird. *Ascot: The History.* London: Methuen, 2002.

SOCIETY DIARIES & BIOGRAPHIES

Beaton, Cecil & Richard Buckle (eds.). *Self Portrait with Friends: The Selected Diaries of Cecil Beaton.* London: Pimlico, 1979.

Beaton, Cecil. *The Unexpurgated Beaton: The Cecil Beaton Diaries as they Were Written.* London: Weidenfeld & Nicolson, 2002.

King, Greg. *A Season of Splendor: The Court of Mrs Astor in Gilded Age New York.* New Jersey: John Wiley & Sons, 2009.

Melville, Joy. *Diaghilev and Friends.* London: Haus Publishing, 2009.

Norwich, John Julius (ed.). *The Duff Cooper Diaries 1915–1951.* London: Weidenfeld and Nicolson, 2006.

Payne, Graham with Barry Day. *My Life with Noel Coward.* New York: Applause, 1994.

Payne, Graham with Sheridan Morley. *The Noel Coward Diaries.* London: Weidenfeld & Nicolson, 1982.

Vickers, Hugo. *Cecil Beaton: The Authorized Biography.* London: Weidenfeld & Nicolson, 1985.

INDEX

Page numbers in *italic* refer to illustrations.

201
QUILT BLOCKS

201
QUILT BLOCKS

Motifs, projects and ideas

Louise Bell

CICO BOOKS
LONDON NEW YORK

Contents

Published in 2008 by CICO Books
an imprint of Ryland Peters & Small
20–21 Jockey's Fields,
London WC1R 4BW

www.cicobooks.co.uk

10 9 8 7 6 5 4 3 2 1

Text copyright © Louise Bell 2008
Design and photography
copyright © CICO Books 2008

A CIP catalogue record for this book
is available from the British Library

ISBN-13: 978 1 906094 88 1

Printed in China

Editors: Sarah Hoggett, Marion Paull
Designer: Ian Midson
Photographer: Geoff Dann
Illustrator: Stephen Dew

Introduction

Becoming a quilt maker was an accident just waiting to happen. I made a patchwork quilt as I waited for my University results, thudding the patches together on an old manual sewing machine and then quilting by hand. It was an awful lot of sewing. A neighbour asked if I would make another to sell in her craft shop: What else did I make? Well, I decided I would make anything she asked for – just as soon as I could get my hands on an electric sewing machine.

I had never thought of quilt making as a job – careers advisors had not suggested it and I had never met any craftspeople who earned a living through their work. I did, however, know people (most of my family, in fact) who were passionate about making things, building things, and drawing or painting things, and I spent most of my spare time doing the same. As I seemed to have an irresistible urge to create, doing it for a living seemed not only to be my perfect occupation, but something of a privilege.

My first quilt, Grandmother's Fan, was the same design as a quilt we had at home. My Canadian great grandmother had made it as a wedding gift for my parents. As a child, I had spent hours looking at the fabrics, tracing the design with my finger, counting the colours and patches, trying to make sense of this busy, lively pattern. When I later compared mine with hers I realized I had not remembered it quite right. I had made an impression of the quilt, based on hazy

The Pineapple block (see page 116) is Log Cabin with a twist. For this pattern strips are pieced diagonally, as well as horizontally and vertically.

memories. There are hundreds of traditional American block designs and I suspect that some of this proliferation is due to faulty memories like mine. As I looked at other quilts and learnt how to draft blocks, I discovered how knowing just a few simple rules could help jog my memory and make sense of a puzzling quilt. Four-patch is a block divided in four, while seven-patch has seven patches; draw a square and divide it up to make your templates. Simple. Rotate some of the patches or subdivide them to produce new patterns then alter colour placements and scale to change the effect yet again. One of the hardest things to achieve is an exact copy of someone else's quilt, and that's the best part of it: whatever you make will be unique and personal to you.

Most of the other quilts we had at home were traditional geometric block designs. Some of the best ones had fabric repeats while some, the everyday ones, seemed more and more confusing the closer I looked. From a distance, the design appeared

Gentleman's Fancy (see page 34) looks at first glance like the foundation block Snail Trail, with its central square and triangles pieced around the middle. It is in fact a nine-patch block. To draft accurate templates, you must divide the grid into nine rather than four.

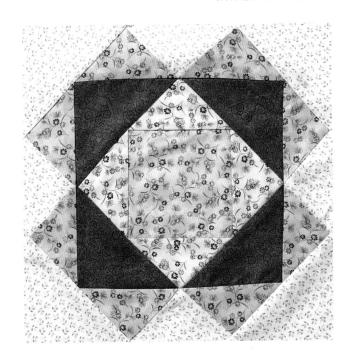

clear, but close up the patches seemed random and some of the smallest patches were themselves patched. These scrap quilts were a way of making something useful and beautiful out of not very much at all – the main ingredients being the quilter's need for economy combined with a desire to make sense and order from a scrap bag. When you start making quilts you discover that those little bags of irresistible fabrics soon become stacks. They fill shelves, sometimes whole rooms, and the box of leftovers grows and grows. Quilts like the Nine Patch framed

in Liberty lawns (see page 118) and the Bird and tulip ring (page 150) are ideal for keeping the fabric stash tamed, while the Child's counting quilt (page 130) and Tumbling Blocks (page 122) are the perfect way to use favourite leftovers and memory snippets.

I enjoy using highly patterned lawns that blur and soften geometric shapes. I also love plain fabrics – rich and vibrant silks that shout the block designs. And then there are the appliqué designs. Doves, hearts and tulips feature on many vintage quilts, their simple shapes are so easily recognizable. But iris and bluebell, roosters and hens, seahorses and shells can all be just as striking.

When working to commission I take notes of the likes and dislikes of my customers and try to make an impression of the quilt they will enjoy. I like working out how to appliqué favourite plants – thistles and

Grandmother's Fan (see page 124) is traditionally pieced with blocks edge to edge, or with alternating plain squares between each one. The project quilt has sashing strips and the blocks have been rotated to give a central flower design.

dandelions will push me a bit harder as the plants don't naturally lend themselves to the stylized shapes of appliqué.

I love pattern, shape and colours that blend and can rarely resist filling my work up with all three elements. Inspiration comes from anywhere and everywhere – the second quilt I made was, I thought, entirely original, until I looked down and saw a similar pattern on a Victorian tiled floor. I once put some pea pod shapes in a quilt. A while later I opened a book I had read some time before and there it was, a tiny design at the start of every chapter. I would like to acknowledge everyone whose ideas and designs have inspired me, but I am rarely aware of where the ideas come from. Patterns, motifs and arrangements seem to seek me out, hiding in my subconscious until the perfect project comes along.

Monogrammed cushions (see page 140) make the perfect gift for a loved one and are straightforward to make. Use the alphabet templates on page 90 to personalize your block.

I had spent hours and weeks making my first quilt and an electric machine was essential when I decided to turn play into work. Quilt making is my job – so what of my spare time? I stitch by hand. I think up ever more complex appliqué designs for beds and walls. I sew and make quilts, taking as long as I want, because I just like doing it.

I hope this book will inspire you to start that quilt, make that memory cushion, use up that tantalizing fabric you've been saving, try out something new or adapt a design to suit your taste.

Louise Bell

Bird and leaf ring cushion (see page 143). As an alternative, try using the Butterfly or Dragonfly motifs (see page 65).

PATCHWORK BLOCKS

To draft blocks accurately, draw a square the size you want the stitched block to be and divide it into patches – four, five, seven, nine, or even hexagon and star shapes. Next, subdivide the patches to make the individual block design. The sizes given are suggestions – you can create larger or smaller finished pieces simply by redrafting the block.

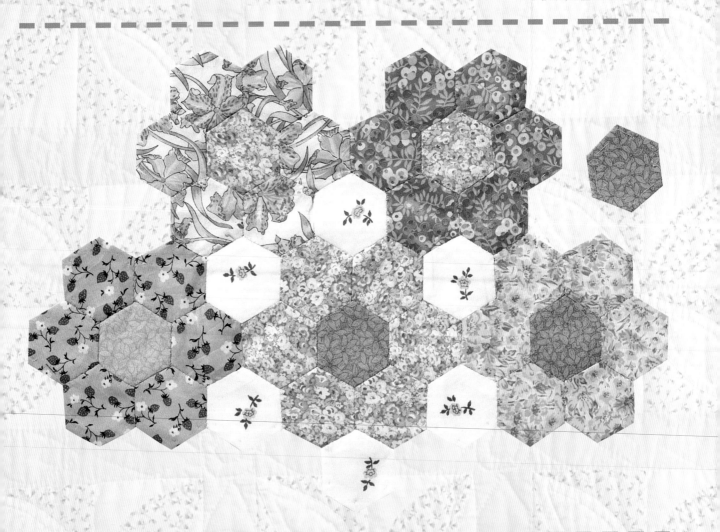

Four-patch blocks

Patchwork blocks that have two equal sections across the top, or a multiple of two sections, are called four-patch blocks. Some blocks, such as Fly, have four patches that are identical and are rotated to form the design. Others, such as Broken Dishes, have identical design patches in two colour variations. Ann and Andy has two different design patches, while in Flower Basket each quarter is different.

Four Patch

Size of finished block: 15 cm (6 in.) square

Size of each finished patch: 7.5 cm (3 in.) square

When it is pieced in two colours only, Four Patch looks like a checkerboard. Using three colours and piecing them uniformly together with the same colour top right and bottom left each time creates a diagonal chain effect, while using a different colour for each patch gives the block a jewel-like effect.

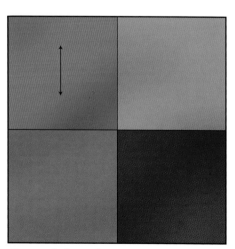

One patch, four colours

■ Draft the template (see page 160) and cut four squares in two, three or four colours.

■ First, piece the upper and lower patches together to form two vertical strips, and press the seams in opposite directions.

■ Pin the two strips together, carefully aligning the seams, and stitch slowly to prevent the patches from slipping out of position. Press the vertical seam; it does not matter which way you press it, but for a whole quilt, press all the vertical seams the same way.

Broken Dishes

Size of finished block: 15 cm (6 in.) square

Size of each finished patch: 7.5 cm (3 in.) square

In two contrasting colours, this design looks dramatic, like ceramic tiles, and using four contrasting colours (as here) creates a chain effect when rotated across the quilt.

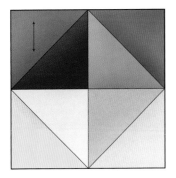

One patch, rotated repeat

■ Draft the template (see page 160) and cut two triangles each in red, blue, pale green and dark green. The fabric grain on all pieces must run either vertically or horizontally.

■ Piece the triangle squares – red/pale green, blue/dark green – and press the seams towards the darker fabric.

■ Lay the patches out in sequence and piece as for Four Patch, pinning before stitching to ensure that the seams align and the points meet at the centre.

Windmill

Size of finished block: 15 cm (6 in.) square

Size of each finished patch: 7.5 cm (3 in.) square

Windmill has diagonally quartered patches, with the grain line running in a different direction on the large and small triangles. Paler outer triangles increase the pinwheel effect.

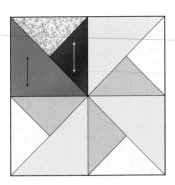

One patch, rotated repeat

■ Draft the templates (see page 160) and cut four large triangles in red and four small triangles each in green and a sprigged white.

■ Assemble the small triangles first. Lay pale on dark and machine stitch along one short side to make four identical large triangles. Press the seams towards the darker fabric.

■ Join these triangles to the red triangles along the long edge to make triangle squares, then press the seams towards the large triangles.

■ Lay the patches out in sequence and piece as for Four Patch, pinning before stitching to ensure that the seams align and the points meet at the centre.

Fly

Size of finished block: 15 cm (6 in.) square

Size of each finished patch: 7.5 cm (3 in.) square

If this block is worked in just two colours and the blocks are joined without sashing, the effect will be the same as two-tone Broken Dishes. The design works best with alternating blocks in two colourways.

■ Draft the template (see page 160) and cut four triangles in each of two colours. The fabric grain on all pieces must run either vertically or horizontally, otherwise the block will stretch out of shape; always mark the direction of grain on the templates.

■ Piece the triangle squares and press the seams towards the darker fabric.

■ Lay the patches out in sequence and piece as for Four Patch, pinning before stitching to ensure that the seams align and the points meet at the centre.

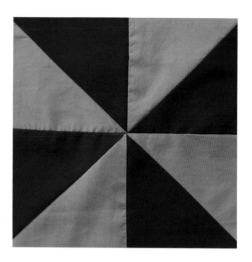

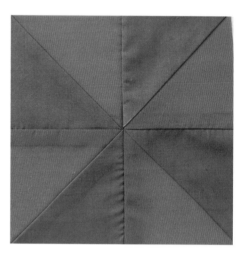

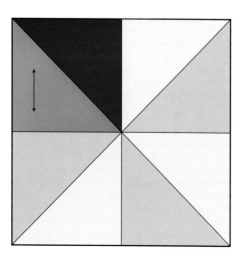

One patch, rotated repeat

Fly in two colourways, alternating blocks

Big Dipper

Size of finished block: 15 cm (6 in.) square

Size of each finished patch: 7.5 cm (3 in.) square

For the most dramatic effect, use contrasting tones on the inner and outer triangles.

■ Draft the template (see page 160) and cut four triangles in each of four contrasting colours, with the grain line running along the long edge of each triangle.

■ Lay pale green on dark green and blue on red, and stitch along one short side to make four identical large triangles in each colourway. Press the seams towards the darker fabric.

■ Lay out the triangles in sequence and piece them into triangle squares, being careful to match up the seams at the centres. Press the seams in alternate directions.

■ Continue as for Four Patch, pinning before stitching to ensure that the seams align and the points meet at the centre.

BIG DIPPER BLOCKS SET EDGE TO EDGE

If Big Dipper blocks are set edge to edge, they resemble Fly in two colourways (see facing page) but with a diagonal set.

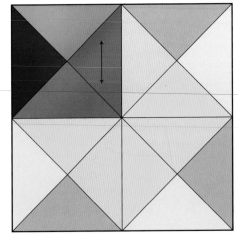

One patch, rotated repeat

Big Dipper quilt, four strips of four blocks each

FOUR-PATCH BLOCKS OF MULTIPLE PATCHES

The four-patch blocks on pages 14–20 each have four patches across and four patches down, and the last four-patch block on page 21 has eight patches across and eight patches down. Most of the blocks are first pieced into patches, then into vertical strips. The individual patches – squares or triangle squares – are assembled in different sequences to make a variety of blocks. You can restrict yourself to just two colours per block or choose up to five to change the look of each block even more.

Ann and Andy

Size of finished block: 30 cm (12 in.) square

Size of each finished patch: 7.5 cm (3 in.) square

In this design, the top left and lower right quarters are all made up of triangle squares, while the top right and lower left quarters are a combination of triangle squares and squares. If blocks are placed edge to edge on a quilt top, without blank squares or sashing in between, the diagonal string of squares takes prominence and gives a diagonal chain effect across a quilt. In a strong or bright shade, this can look really striking.

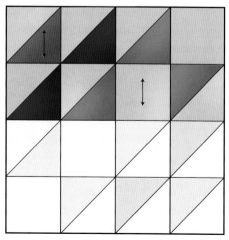

Two quarter blocks, mirrored

■ Draft the templates (see page 160) and cut four pale squares and 12 matching pale triangles. Cut six triangles in one dark shade, four in another and two in a third.

■ Piece the 12 triangle squares (pale/dark) and press the seams towards the darker colour.

■ Lay the patches out in sequence, piece into four vertical strips and press the seams in alternate directions. Join the strips and press all the vertical seams in the same direction across the block.

Triangle Squares

Size of finished block: 30 cm (12 in.) square

Size of each finished patch: 7.5 cm (3 in.) square

This is a repeating patch block, so you only need to draft one quarter; however, there are two different colour sequences and the quarters are rotated through 90° to create the pattern. The design works best with triangles in strongly contrasting tones.

■ Draft the templates (see page 160) and cut two squares each in navy and mauve. Cut 12 triangles in yellow, and six each in blue and green.

■ Piece the triangle squares (yellow/green, yellow/blue) and press the seams towards the darker fabrics.

■ Lay the patches out in sequence and piece into four vertical strips, pinning near the seams to keep the points aligned. Press the seams in opposite directions. Join the strips and press all the vertical seams in the same direction across the block.

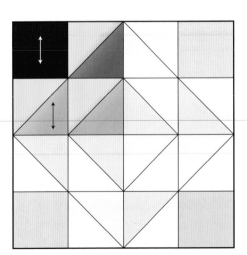

One quarter block, rotated repeat

TRIANGLE SQUARES BLOCKS SET EDGE TO EDGE
If the blocks are assembled without sashing, alternating the colour of the corner squares adds interest as little Four Patch blocks appear between the diamonds. Here, nine Triangle Squares blocks have been pieced together in three strips of three.

Double X

Size of finished block: 30 cm (12 in.) square

Size of each finished patch: 7.5 cm (3 in.) square

This block works well when the centre squares are in a different tone or colour to the outer squares and triangle squares, as the Four Patch centre stands out.

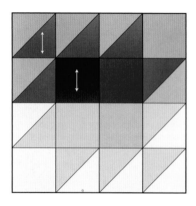

■ Draft the templates (see page 160) and cut two squares each in lilac, purple and navy, and ten triangles each in lilac and mauve.

■ Piece the triangle squares (pale/dark) and press the seams towards the darker colour.

■ Lay the patches out in sequence. Pin near the seams to keep the points aligned, piece into four vertical strips and press the seams in alternate directions. Join the strips and press all the vertical seams in the same direction across the block.

Indian Star

Size of finished block: 30 cm (12 in.) square

Size of each finished patch: 7.5 cm (3 in.) square

This is a repeating patch block, but it has two different sets of colour – so it is important to lay the block out before you piece it in order to get the colour sequence right.

■ Draft the templates (see page 160) and cut two squares each in lilac, yellow, green and blue, and eight triangles each in navy and pale green.

■ Piece the triangle squares (navy/pale green) and press the seams towards the darker colour.

■ Lay the patches out in sequence. Piece into vertical strips, pinning near the seams to keep the points aligned, and press the seams in alternate directions. Join the strips and press all the vertical seams in the same direction across the block.

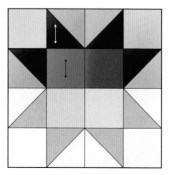

One quarter block, rotated repeat

Diamond Star and Crystal Star

Size of finished block: 30 cm (12 in.) square

Size of each finished patch: 7.5 cm (3 in.) square

The only difference between these blocks is the positioning of the central triangle squares. Both are repeating patch blocks in which the patch is rotated to create the pattern, with alternating colours on the corners.

■ For either block, draft the templates (see page 160) and cut two mid-mauve and two green squares, eight navy and eight pale green triangles and four triangles each in dark mauve and yellow for the centres.

■ Piece the triangle squares (navy/pale green and yellow/dark mauve) and press the seams towards the darker fabric.

■ Lay the patches out in sequence. Piece into four vertical strips, pinning near the seams to keep the points aligned, and press the seams in alternate directions. Join the strips and press all the vertical seams in the same direction across the block.

DIAMOND STAR

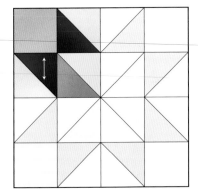

One quarter block, rotated repeat

CRYSTAL STAR

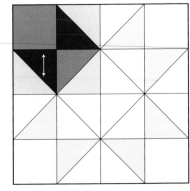

One quarter block, rotated repeat

Chevron

Size of finished block: 30 cm (12 in.) square

Size of each finished patch: 7.5 cm (3 in.) wide

Chevron can be confusing to assemble as the patches repeat left to right, with different colours top and bottom.

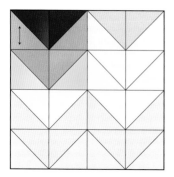

One quarter block, straight repeat

■ Draft the template (see page 160) and cut eight triangles each in lilac, yellow and mauve, and four each in green and dark mauve.

■ Lay the pieces out in sequence. Piece into triangle squares and press the seams towards the darker fabric.

■ Lay the patches out in sequence again. Piece into four vertical strips, pinning near the seams to keep the points aligned. Press the seams in alternate directions. Join the strips and press all vertical seams in the same direction across the block.

Flying Geese

Size of finished block: 30 cm (12 in.) square

Size of each finished patch: 7.5 cm (3 in.) wide

Using a pale tone for the small triangles on the right-hand side of each quarter and a mid-tone on the left creates a pin-wheel effect.

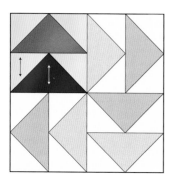

One quarter block, rotated repeat

■ Draft the templates (see page 160) and cut four large triangles in navy and four in purple, and 16 small triangles in yellow. The grain direction is very important, so make sure you mark it on the templates.

■ Piece the long side of a small triangle to the short side of a large triangle. Press the seam away from the large triangle. Piece a second small triangle to the remaining short side. To keep the point true, it is best to stitch towards the seam. Press the seam away from the large triangle.

■ Piece two triangle rectangles together to form a quarter of the block, with a purple/yellow rectangle at the top of the quarter and a navy/yellow rectangle at the base. Press the seam towards the purple. Make another identical quarter block and then make two more quarters, reversing the colours so that purple/yellow rectangles are at the base.

■ Arrange the patches and piece as for Four Patch (see page 10).

Batchelor's Puzzle

Size of finished block: 30 cm (12 in.) square

Size of each finished patch: 7.5 cm (3 in.) square

To achieve the effect of rectangular boxes, use the darkest tone for the squares, the lightest for the centre and corner triangles, and a mid-tone for the other triangles.

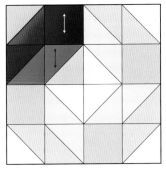

One quarter block, rotated repeat

■ Draft the templates (see page 160) and cut four blue squares and eight triangles each in yellow, green and purple.

■ Piece the triangle squares (four yellow/green, four yellow/purple, four purple/green) and press the seams towards the darker fabric.

■ Lay the patches out in sequence; even though the quarters are identical, this is a confusing block to assemble. Piece into four vertical strips, and press the seams in alternate directions. Join the strips together and press all the vertical seams in the same direction across the block.

Mosaic

Size of finished block: 30 cm (12 in.) square

Size of each finished patch: 7.5 cm (3 in.) square

This block works best pieced edge to edge, without sashing or alternating plain squares. The red-based designs will stand out when repeated across a quilt. Alternating the colours on the outer triangles will give even more interest.

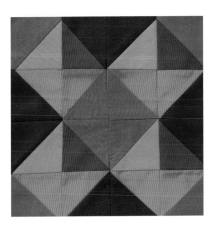

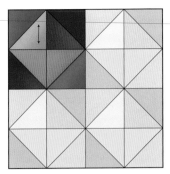

One quarter block, straight repeat

■ Draft the template (see page 160) and cut eight triangles each in red, blue and dark green, and four each in pale green and purple.

■ Piece the triangle squares – four blue/red, two blue/pale green, two blue/purple, four dark green/red, two dark green/pale green and two dark green/purple.

■ Lay the patches out in sequence. Piece the four vertical strips and press the seams in alternate directions. Join the strips together and press all the vertical seams in the same direction across the block.

Old Maid's Puzzle

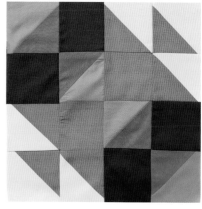

Size of finished block: 30 cm (12 in.) square

Size of each finished patch: 7.5 cm (3 in.) square

This block has two different quarters to draft – top left (repeated lower right) and top right (repeated lower left). All the triangles have the grain line running along a short edge.

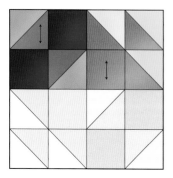

Two quarter blocks, mirrored

■ Draft the templates (see page 160) and cut two red squares and six red triangles, four navy squares, six yellow triangles, four green triangles and four blue triangles.

■ Piece the triangle squares (red/yellow and blue/green) and press the seams towards the darker fabrics.

■ Lay the patches out in sequence. Piece into four vertical strips and press the seams in alternate directions. Join the strips together and press all the vertical seams in the same direction across the block.

Flower Basket

Size of finished block: 30 cm (12 in.) square

Size of each finished patch: 7.5 cm (3 in.) square

This design works best with sashing or alternating plain squares, so that the stylized basket is not lost.

■ Draft the templates (see page 160) and cut one red square and four red triangles, five yellow squares and five yellow triangles, five green triangles, three navy triangles, two purple triangles and one mid-blue triangle.

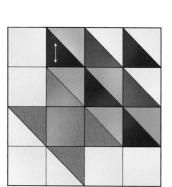

Four quarter blocks, all different

■ Piece the triangle squares (two yellow/red, two yellow/purple, one yellow/ mid blue, three green/navy and two green/red). Press the seams towards the darker fabrics.

■ Lay the patches out in sequence before piecing. Pin near the seams to keep all the seams aligned and piece into four vertical strips.

■ Press the seams in alternate directions. Join the strips together, again pinning carefully, and press all the vertical seams in the same direction across the block.

Odd Fellow's Chain

Size of finished block: 60 cm (24 in.) square

Size of finished quarter block: 30 cm (12 in.) square

Size of each finished patch: 7.5 cm (3 in.) square

Odd Fellow's Chain is a four-patch block, but it has eight patches across and down, making 64 squares or triangle squares to piece. A non-slip board is essential for laying out the pieces before assembling. It is best not to attempt to make this block too small. I made this one twice the size of the others, in order to place it in the centre of the Four-patch Sampler Quilt (page 117).

Although it is hard to make out, you'll see that each quarter of this block is a Double X (see page 16) and an Indian Star (see page 16) has appeared in the centre.

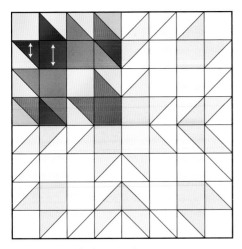

One quarter block, rotated repeat

■ Draft the templates (see page 160) and cut eight squares and 24 triangles in yellow, eight squares and 16 triangles in mid-blue, two squares and eight triangles in navy, four squares and eight triangles in dark green, two squares in purple, 16 triangles in red and eight triangles in pale green.

■ Make sure that the grain line (running along a short side) is maintained on all the triangles and cut the pieces very accurately.

■ Piece all the triangle squares – eight green/mid blue, eight red/pale green and all the others pieced to a yellow. Press the seams towards the darker fabrics and lay the patches out in sequence on a design board.

■ Piece vertical strips of eight patches. Press all the seams of each strip in alternating directions across the block. Join the strips and press all the vertical seams in the same direction.

Five-patch blocks

Five-patch blocks are more difficult to draft and piece than four- and nine-patch blocks, since they are not always put together in strips of equal width. The diagrams show the easiest ways to assemble them. Some blocks with borders show how they would look with sashing.

Lady of the Lake

Size of finished block: 32.5 cm (12½ in.)
Size of each finished small triangle-square patch:
6.5 cm (2½ in.)

This block is assembled diagonally. One half is made up of triangle squares around two edges of a triangle, while the other is a large plain triangle. The block works best without sashing or alternating plain squares, and in contrasting colours.

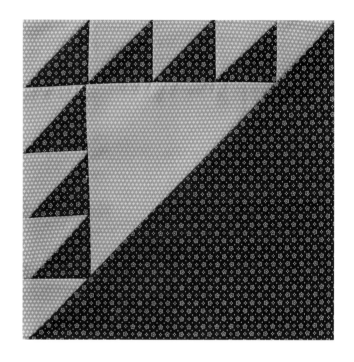

■ Draft the templates (see page 160) and cut seven small dark triangles and nine small pale triangles, one medium pale triangle and one large triangle in dark fabric. The grain lines must run along the short side of all triangles.

■ Piece seven dark/pale triangle squares and press the seams towards the darker fabric. If the fabric has a pattern direction it should be constant across the block, so make sure you assemble each one the same way (lay dark fabric over pale and always stitch on the same side).

■ Join together three triangle squares with an extra pale triangle at the bottom, and press the seams towards the darker fabric.

■ Join four triangle squares with an extra pale triangle on the right and press the seams towards the darker fabric.

■ Join the first triangle squares strip to one short edge of the medium-sized pale triangle, so that all the pale triangles point the same way, and press the seam towards the large triangle.

■ Join the second triangle squares strip to the remaining short edge of the medium triangle, and press the seam away from the small triangles.

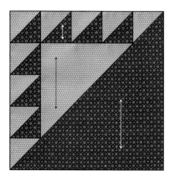

Triangle squares, straight repeat

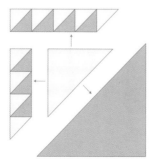

left-hand strip = 1, top strip = 2, small triangle = 3.

■ Join this triangle to the large dark triangle.

Grape Basket

Size of finished block without border: 32.5 cm (12½ in.)

Size of each finished triangle-square patch: 6.5 cm (2½ in.)

This block works best alternating with plain squares on a quilt or as a single block with a border around, so the stylized basket shape is not lost.

■ Draft the templates (see page 160) and cut 13 small triangles and eight squares in grey, six small tan triangles, five small mid-green floral triangles, two small dark green triangles, and one large triangle each in grey and dark green.

■ Piece the small triangle squares – six grey/tan, five grey/mid-green and two grey/dark green – and one large grey/dark green triangle square.

■ Lay the patches out in sequence; note that the triangle squares do not follow the same direction. Piece vertical strips 1, 2 and 5 and press the seams in alternate directions.

■ For strips 3 and 4, piece the tan/grey, green/grey and dark green/grey triangle squares into horizontal pairs and then assemble the wide vertical strip, pressing the horizontal seams in a different direction from the seams in strips 2 and 5.

■ Join these four strips together.

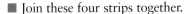

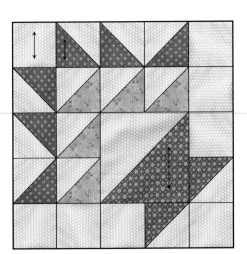

Triangle squares, rotated repeat

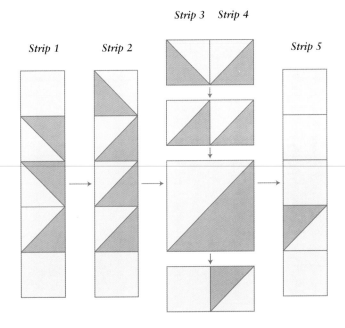

Strip 1   Strip 2   Strip 3   Strip 4   Strip 5

Goose Tracks

Size of finished block without border: 32.5 cm (12½ in.)

Size of each finished small three-triangle patch: 6.5 cm (2½ in.)

The block is shown with a border. Omitting the border and placing the blocks side by side changes Goose Tracks' appearance dramatically.

■ Draft the templates (see page 160) and cut eight tiny triangles each in cream and green, eight larger triangles in tan, four squares each in cream and tan, one green square for the centre and four rectangles in bright green. The fabric grain runs along the long edge of the tiny triangles and along the short edges of the larger triangles.

■ First, piece the tiny triangles to make larger triangles. The pairs are mirror images, so place half the green triangles on cream and half the cream triangles on green and stitch along the right-hand short side. Press the seams towards the darker fabric.

■ Join the cream and green triangles to the tan triangles to make eight triangle squares, and press the seams towards the tan fabric.

■ Lay out in sequence and piece four identical patches: cream square above triangle square and mirror image triangle square above tan square. Piece upper to lower patch, then piece left side to right side. Pin either side of the cross seam so that the seams and points in the centre align, and stitch slowly.

■ Lay these pieced squares out in sequence along with the remaining patches and piece into three vertical strips. Press the seams in alternate directions and join the strips.

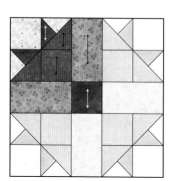

One corner section, rotated around centre square and strip

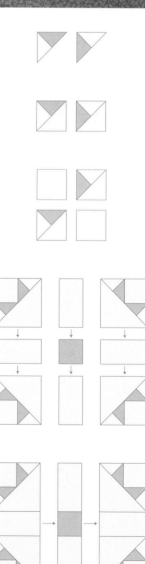

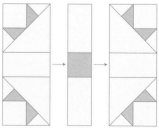

Pin Wheel

Size of finished block without border: 32.5 cm (12½ in.)

Size of each finished corner-square patch: 6.5 cm (2½ in.)

Pin Wheel has triangles with different grain directions, plus some acute angles to match up, but only one design patch, which is rotated around a central square.

■ Draft the templates (see page 160) and cut four tall triangles each in cream and red, four squares in red, four tiny triangles each in mid green and cream, four larger triangles each in spotted and dark green, and one dark green square.

■ Piece the tall (red/cream) triangle rectangles and press the seams towards the darker colour.

■ Piece the large triangles (dark green/spotted) along a short edge to form larger triangles, laying the pale fabric over the dark and stitching down the right-hand edge each time so that the patches are identical. Press the seams towards the darker colour.

■ Place a tiny cream triangle on a red square and join the short edge of the triangle to the right-hand edge of the square. Press the seam away from the square. Piece a mid-green triangle to the top edge of the red. Make three more of these new triangles. Press the seams towards the darker fabric.

■ Lay the pieces out in sequence and make the four corner triangle squares, pinning near the cross seams to align the seams and ensure that the points meet in the centre.

■ Assemble into three vertical strips, pressing the seams in alternate directions strip by strip, and finally join the strips together.

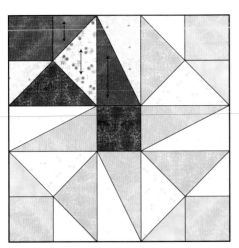

One corner section, rotated repeat

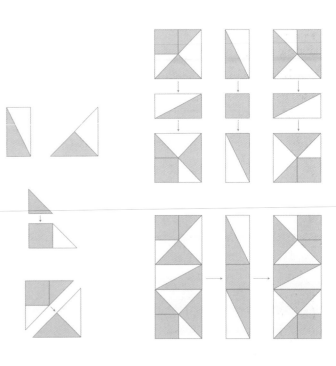

Double Irish Chain

Size of finished block: 32.5 cm (12½ in.)

Size of each finished small square patch: 6.5 cm (2½ in.)

This is a two-block design. It is best to use either a patterned pale fabric or one that is fairly opaque; otherwise, you will have to trim dark fabrics at the seams to prevent them from showing through. You need at least nine blocks in total to see the chain effect.

BLOCK A

■ Draft the template (see page 160) and cut 12 red, nine mid-green and four pale squares.

■ Lay the squares out in sequence and piece into five vertical strips. Press each seam towards the darker fabric.

■ Join the strips and press all the vertical seams in the same direction.

BLOCK B

■ Draft the templates (see page 160) and cut four small red squares, four rectangles and one large central square in the pale fabric.

■ Join a rectangle to each side of the central square. Join a red square to each end of the remaining rectangles and join these to the top and lower edges of the square. Press the seams towards the darker fabric.

BLOCK A

BLOCK B

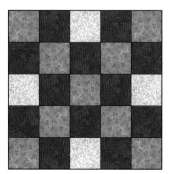

Block A

Block B

Flying Birds

Size of finished block without border: 32.5 cm (12½ in.)

Size of each finished patch: 6.5 cm (2½ in.)

The block is shown with a dark border to show how it would look assembled on a quilt with sashing or with alternating plain blocks. Placing the blocks side by side changes the appearance dramatically, as hexagonal shapes with intersecting squares appear.

■ Draft the templates (see page 160) and cut eight tan triangles and four tan squares, eight grey triangles and eight grey squares, four mid-green squares and one dark green square.

■ Piece the tan/grey triangle squares; if the fabrics have a pattern direction, then the second four need to be mirror images of the first four. Press the seams towards the darker fabric.

■ Lay the patches out in sequence and piece into five vertical strips. Press the seams in alternate directions and join the five strips together.

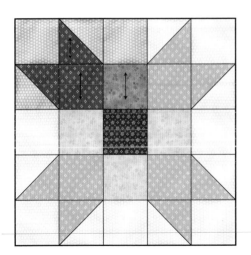

One corner section, rotated repeat

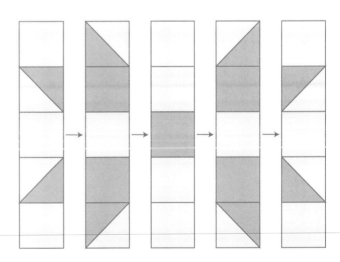

Nine-patch blocks

At its simplest, a nine-patch block consists of nine square patches – three across and three down – but it can also be made up of any number across and down that is a multiple of three. When the central square is left plain and the surrounding ones are halved or quartered diagonally, you get Star designs. Some blocks such as Grandma's Star and Flagstones have two entirely different patches to draft.

Sawtooth

Size of finished block: 30 cm (12 in.) square

The central diamond squares become very prominent as a chain on a quilt when the blocks are joined edge to edge. The grain on all the triangles should run along a short edge and on the squares from point to point.

■ Draft the templates (see page 160) and cut four large triangles each in red and yellow, four red squares, 16 green and four yellow small triangles.

■ Piece the yellow/red triangle squares for the corners and press the seams towards the darker fabric.

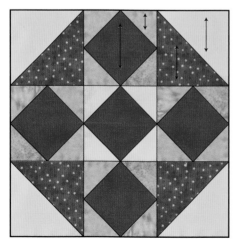

Two patches, alternating as shown

■ Join the long edges of two small triangles to opposite sides of a square and press the seams away from the square. Repeat on the remaining two edges and press the seams outwards. Do this on all five diamond squares.

■ Lay the patches out in sequence and join into three vertical strips. Press the seams in alternate directions from strip to strip to avoid bulk at the seams. Join the strips together and press all the vertical seams in the same direction across the block.

Nine Patch

Size of finished block: 30 cm (12 in.) square

When simple Nine Patch blocks are joined without sashing or alternating plain squares and with three diagonal squares in contrasting tones from the others, a diagonal chain will appear across the quilt.

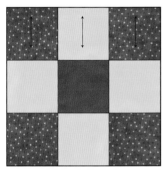

Four mirror-image corner patches, alternating with plain squares

■ Draft the template (see page 160) and cut four yellow squares, four patterned red squares and one plain red square.

■ Lay the patches out in sequence and piece into three vertical strips. Press the seams in alternate directions. Join the strips together and press all the vertical seams in the same direction across the block.

Shoo-fly

Size of finished block: 30 cm (12 in.) square

The corner patches of Shoo-fly are triangle squares. If blocks are joined edge to edge, an alternating colour sequence of the squares and triangles from block to block will give a checked vertical/horizontal chain.

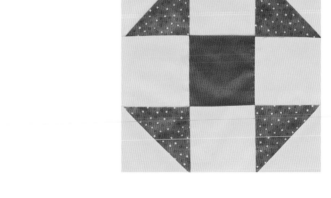

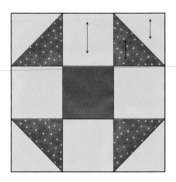

Four mirror-image corner patches, alternating with plain squares

■ Draft the templates (see page 160) and cut four triangles each in yellow and red, four yellow squares and one red square.

■ Piece the yellow/red triangle squares and press the seams towards the darker fabric.

■ Lay the pieces out in sequence and piece into three vertical strips. Press the seams in alternate directions. Join the strips together and press all the vertical seams in the same direction across the block.

Ohio Star, Swamp Patch

Size of finished block: 30 cm (12 in.) square

The corner patches – square on Ohio Star, triangle squares on Swamp Patch – turn into Broken Dishes when the blocks are joined without sashing, as on the cushion on page 109.

OHIO STAR

■ Draft the templates (see page 160) and cut eight red, four pale yellow and four striped yellow triangles. (The grain line should run base to point on two of the inner small triangles and along the long edge of the other two.) Also cut four pale yellow squares and one checked yellow centre square.

■ Lay pale yellow triangles on red triangles, and the remaining red triangles on striped triangles, and stitch along one short edge to make eight larger triangles. Press the seams towards the darker fabric. Piece into four triangle squares, being careful to match the centres.

■ Lay the patches out in sequence. Piece into three vertical strips and press the seams in alternate directions. Join the strips and press all the vertical seams in the same direction across the block.

SWAMP PATCH

■ There are two sizes of triangles on Swamp Patch, with the grain lines running in different directions. If you are using a striped fabric, then the grain line should run from base to point on two of the inner small triangles and along the long edge of the other two.

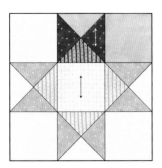
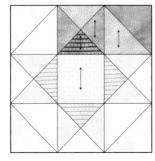

One patch rotated, with plain corner squares

One patch rotated, with triangle squares in the corners

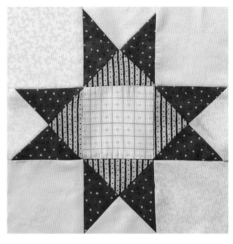

OHIO STAR

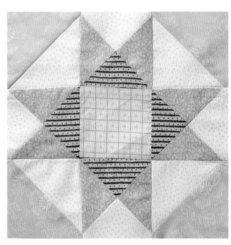

SWAMP PATCH

■ Draft the templates (see page 160) and cut eight yellow, four dotted cream and four striped small triangles, two large triangles each in dotted cream and beige and one checked centre square.

■ Piece the large dotted cream/beige triangles into triangle squares. Press the seams towards the darker fabric.

■ Piece the small yellow/striped and yellow/dotted cream triangles into larger triangles as for Ohio Star, and press the seams towards the darker colour. Piece into four triangle squares, being careful to match the centres.

■ Lay the patches out in sequence. Piece into three vertical strips, and press the seams in alternate directions. Join the strips and press all the vertical seams in the same direction across the block.

Grandma's Star

Size of finished block: 30 cm (12 in.) square

This block requires careful drafting, because there are two sizes of tall triangles to piece.

■ Draft the templates (see page 160) and cut eight thin white triangles (mirror image), four large green triangles and 10 squares each in two contrasting colours.

■ Piece the squares into five Four Patch blocks (see page 10).

■ Lay a thin white triangle along one long edge of each large green triangle and stitch together. Press the seam towards the darker fabric. Join a mirror-image thin triangle to the other long edge and press the seam towards the darker fabric again.

■ Lay the patches out in sequence. Piece into three vertical strips and press the seams in alternate directions. Join the strips, being careful to match the points in the centre, and press all the vertical seams in the same direction across the block.

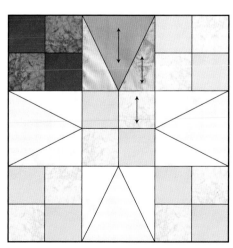

Two patches, alternating as shown

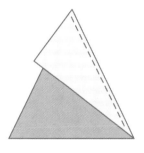
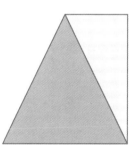
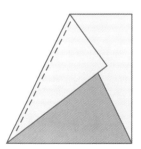
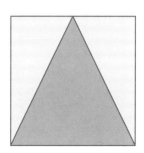

Cat's Cradle

Size of finished block: 30 cm (12 in.) square

The six identical triangle patches are rotated to make the design, with the large squares forming a diagonal through the block.

■ Draft the templates (see page 160) and cut six large triangles and three squares in patterned red, six small red triangles and 18 small yellow triangles.

■ Piece six small red/yellow triangle squares and press the seams towards the red fabric. Place one short edge of a small yellow triangle on one red edge of each triangle square and stitch together. Attach another yellow triangle to the remaining red edge of the triangle square. Press the seams towards the long edge of the new large triangle.

■ Join each pieced large triangle to a red patterned triangle to make six triangle squares, being careful not to lose the points.

■ Lay the patches out in sequence. Piece into three vertical strips and press the seams in alternate directions. Join the strips and press all the vertical seams in the same direction across the block.

One patch rotated, with plain squares forming a diagonal chain

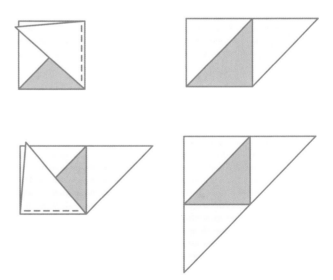

Air Castle

Size of finished block: 30 cm (12 in.) square

This block has four identical triangle squares and four split triangle squares rotated around a central diamond square. Grain lines vary but it is important to cut the centre square with the grain line running vertically to avoid distortion and stretch.

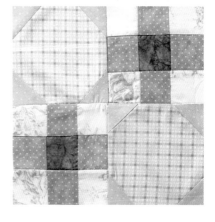

■ Draft the templates (see page 160) and cut four large triangles each in plum, pink and white sprigged fabric, four medium-sized triangles each in white sprig and pink floral fabric, four small triangles in white sprigged fabric and one plum square.

■ Piece together the small white-sprigged triangles and the plum square. Press the seams on all pieces towards the darker fabric. Piece the medium-sized triangles in pairs to make four large triangles and sew these to the pink fabric triangles to make triangle squares. Piece the large plum/white sprigged triangle squares.

■ Piece the patches into three vertical strips and sew the strips together.

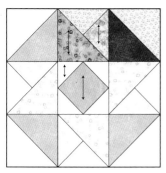

Two patches, alternating as shown, around a central diamond square

---

Flagstones

Size of finished block: 30 cm (12 in.) square

Flagstones consists of a simple Nine Patch and an octagon, which is made into a square by filling in each corner with a triangle. Although this block is easy to draft, it can be difficult to match the octagon seams to the Nine-patch squares.

■ Draft the templates (see page 160). For the two Nine-patch squares, cut eight green, eight cream and two mauve squares. For the two octagon patches, cut two checked fabric octagons and eight pale triangles.

■ Piece the two Nine-patch quarters (see page 29).

■ Piece the long edge of the triangles to the cut edges of the octagons (so that the grain matches) and press the seams away from the octagons.

■ Join each Nine-patch quarter to an octagon patch. Press the seams in alternate directions. Join the two strips and press all the vertical seams in the same direction across the quilt.

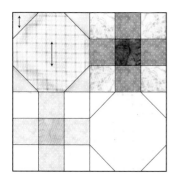

Two quarter blocks, alternating as shown

Gentleman's Fancy

Size of finished block: 30 cm (12 in.)

This block is drafted as a Nine Patch (page 29), but it is built up from the centre, around the central square, and not in strips. The small triangles have the grain line along their long edge, while on the larger ones the grain line follows a short edge.

■ Draft the templates (see page 160) and cut four small triangles each in cream sprigged and dotted cream fabric, eight small pink sprigged triangles, four large triangles each in plum and cream dot, and one pink sprigged centre square.

■ Join the long side of one small cream sprigged triangle to each side of the centre square to form a square 'on point' and press the seams outwards. Join the long side of each large plum triangle to one side of the square on point and press the seams outwards.

■ Join a small pink sprigged triangle to each short side of a small dotted cream triangle and press the seams towards the darker fabric. Join these pieces to the square, being careful to keep the points matched, and press the seams outwards. Finally, join in the large dotted cream corner triangles.

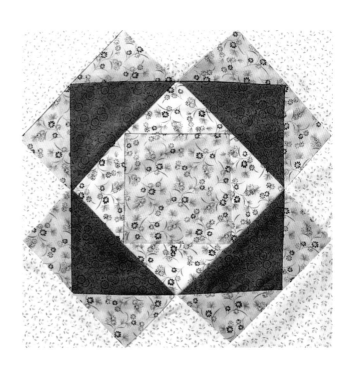

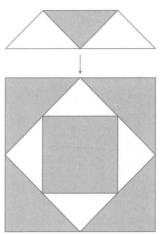

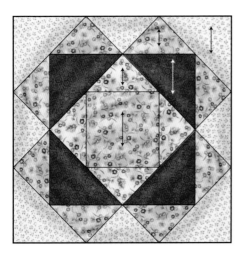

Bright Star

Size of finished block: 30 cm (12 in.) square

Bright Star looks like a four-patch block, as it has four identical patches rotated to make the design, but each quarter is drafted as a nine-patch block.

◼ Draft the templates (see page 160) and cut eight blue and 12 yellow small triangles, four medium-sized mid-mauve triangles and four large lilac triangles.

◼ Piece eight blue/yellow triangle squares and assemble in pairs. Attach one short edge of a small yellow triangle to one end of each pair. Press the seams towards the darker fabric to avoid show-through.

◼ Piece to one short edge of a mid-mauve triangle to make a large triangle. Join each large pieced triangle to a large lilac triangle to make four triangle squares.

◼ Lay the patches out in sequence. Piece into two vertical strips and press the seams in alternate directions. Join the strips together, being careful to match up the centre points.

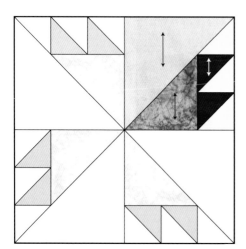

One quarter block, rotated

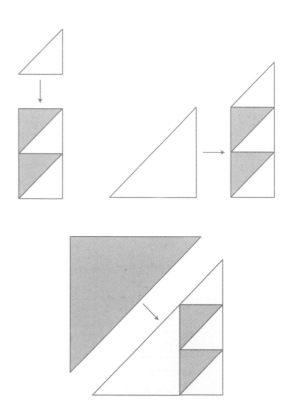

Barn Fence

Size of finished block: 30 cm (12 in.) square

Barn Fence is a simple Nine Patch with patches made up of strips. The strips do not have to be of even width, so this is a good design for using up scraps. Blocks are generally joined edge to edge without sashing, to give a woven effect.

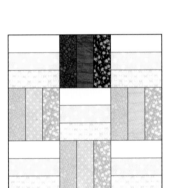

One patch, rotated

■ Draft the templates (see page 160). Piece strips together to make nine patches – four in one colourway and five in another. Press the seams towards the darker fabric.

■ Join the patches in three vertical strips, and press the seams in alternate directions. Join the strips together and press all the vertical seams in the same direction across the block.

London Roads

Size of finished block: 30 cm (12 in.) square

London Roads has four patches made of strips (as Barn Fence). Corner patches are quartered diagonally, and the centre square is plain. The strips can be random widths. Here, the central bars are a similar colour to the adjoining dark corner triangles, so vertical arrows have appeared.

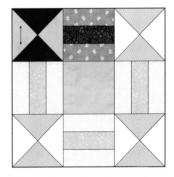

Two patches, alternating as shown, around a plain centre square

■ Draft the templates (see page 160) and cut one green centre square. Cut eight small triangles each in blue and green and piece into eight identical large blue/green triangles. Join in pairs to make four triangle squares. Press the seams towards the darker fabric. Piece four patches from strips, as for Barn Fence.

■ Lay out the patches in sequence. Join into three vertical strips and press the seams in alternate directions. Join the strips and press the vertical seams in the same direction across the block.

Pine Tree

Size of finished block: 39 cm (15 in.) square

When Pine Tree is combined with alternating plain squares, the tree shape is retained. If joining blocks edge to edge, make the trunk thinner, so that the pines look separated by intricate triangle-square sashing across the quilt top.

■ Draft the templates (see page 160) and cut 18 small triangles each in cream and green, two green squares, one large green triangle, two smaller blue triangles, and a fawn trunk.

■ Join each blue triangle to the trunk along one short edge to make a triangle, and piece into a triangle square with the large green triangle.

■ Piece the small cream/green triangles into 18 triangle squares. Join eight triangle squares together into vertical pairs and press the seams towards the darker fabric. Piece the pairs into a strip and join to the top of the large triangle square. Press the seams towards the trunk.

■ Join the remaining small triangle squares into two vertical strips for the right-hand edge of the block with a green square as the second patch down on the left-hand strip and as the top patch on right-hand strip.

■ Attach the two vertical strips to the block and press the seams towards the trunk.

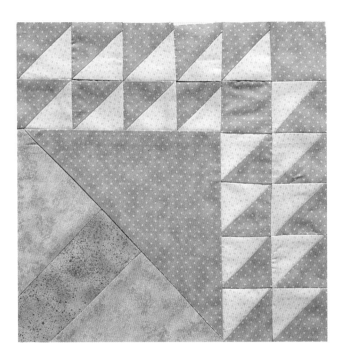

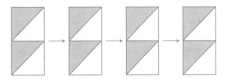

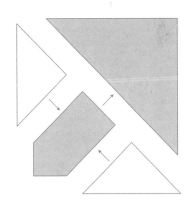

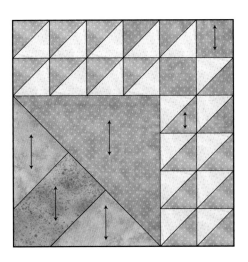

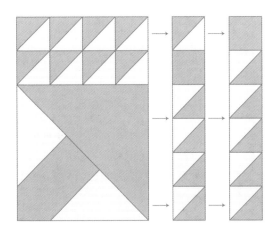

Seven-patch blocks

Seven-patch blocks have seven patches across and down, so it is best not make them too small. Some, such as Bear's Paw, have very distinctive shapes and look better with sashing, while others, such as Checkers, can be pieced edge to edge.

Bear's Paw

Size of finished block: 35 cm (14 in.) square

Four identical patches are separated by a central cross. All triangles point outwards, so must be even. Separate blocks with sashing to preserve the distinctive shape.

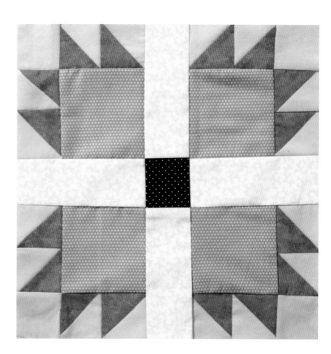

■ Draft the templates (see page 160) and cut 16 small triangles each in bright red and pale green, four small pale green squares for the corners, one small black square for the centre, four large squares in grey and four oblongs in yellow.

■ Piece the 16 red/pale green triangles into triangle squares and press the seams towards the darker fabric. Assemble into four sets of mirror-image pairs.

■ Lay the patches out in sequence and piece the red edge of one of each pair of triangle squares to one edge of a large grey square. Press the seams towards the square. Join a small pale green square to the red edge of each of the remaining pairs. Press the seams towards the darker fabric.

■ Join these strips to an adjacent edge, so that the pale green square at the end of the strip forms the corner. Press the seams towards the grey square.

■ Lay out in sequence and join into vertical strips, with the yellow oblongs in between. Press the seams towards the oblongs and trim the seams to avoid show-through. Piece the central strip with the black square in its centre. Join the three vertical strips and press the seams towards the centre.

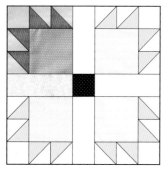
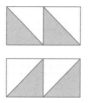

One patch, rotated around centre square and strip

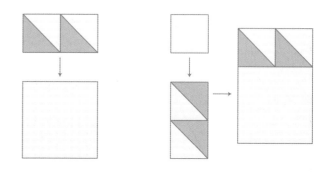

Checkers

Size of finished block: 42 cm (15¾ in.) square

Alternate the sequence of small squares to avoid piecing the same colours next to each other, or use different colours.

■ Draft the templates (see page 160) and cut 16 red and 17 yellow small squares, and four large grey squares.

■ Piece six yellow/red squares into pairs and the rest into strips of seven squares; two of the seven-square strips should have a yellow patch at each end, one should have red at each end. Press the seams towards the dark colour.

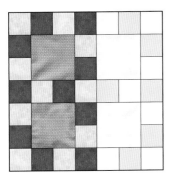

■ Lay out in sequence and join the pairs of squares to the grey squares to make two broad strips.

■ Assemble these five strips and press seams in the same direction across the block.

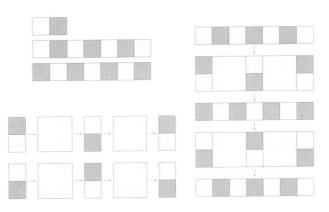

Prickly Pear

Size of finished block: 42 cm (15¾ in.)

This block is best made quite large with the outer triangles in strong colours. It is simple to piece, but can be confusing so it is essential to lay the pieces on a board before assembling.

■ Draft the templates (see page 160) and cut 28 grey, 20 black and eight yellow triangles, and four squares each in black, red and yellow, one in grey, eight in white.

■ Make eight yellow/grey and 20 black/grey triangle squares.

■ Lay out the patches in sequence and assemble them into seven vertical strips. Press the seams in alternate directions strip by strip and join the strips together. Press the vertical seams in the same direction across the block.

Hexagons, diamonds and stars

Hexagons and diamonds are traditionally pieced by hand over light paper templates so are perfect for using scraps. They must be made with even-weave cottons or silks, because synthetics will stretch out of shape and will not lie flat. Star blocks can either be pieced by hand over papers or machine stitched. They are pieced from the centre outwards – first the stars are pieced and then the triangles and squares are added to the edges to make the blocks square.

Grandmother's Flower Garden

Size of finished rosette: 14 cm (5½ in.)

In this pattern, individual rosettes are made up of a central hexagon with six matching or random petal hexagons around it. You will also need extra hexagons (white with pink flowers in the example shown here) to fill in the gaps when the rosettes are joined together. Alternatively, make large rosettes with six inner and 12 outer petals.

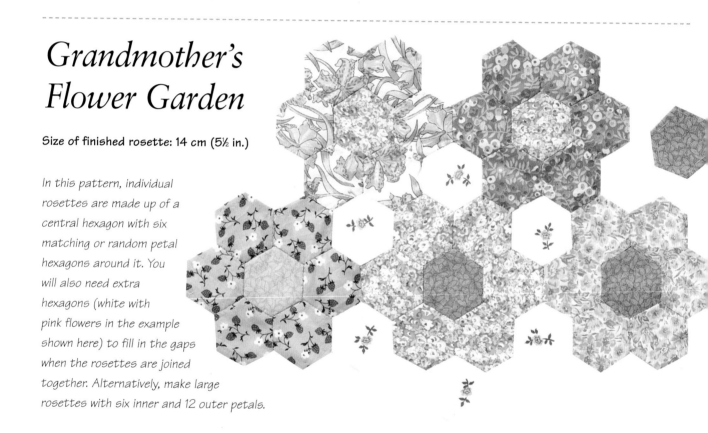

■ To make a template, draw a circle with a 2.5-cm (1-in.) radius and mark the edge at 60° intervals. Draw a line between these marks. This is the template for the backing papers. Now add a 6-mm (¼-in.) turning allowance to each edge and make a second template for fabric cutting. It is best to make templates from card or plastic, because a quilt project requires hundreds of hexagons.

■ For each rosette, cut seven backing papers from the first template, and six fabric shapes in one colour and one fabric shape in a contrasting colour for the centre from the second template.

■ Pin the papers to the wrong side of the fabric hexagons, turn the edges over and tack; try not to knot the thread, but if you do, leave the knots on the right side of the fabric to make the tacking easier to remove.

■ Take the centre hexagon and place right sides together with a rosette hexagon. Overstitch along one edge and then flatten. Take a second rosette and again, right sides together, overstitch it to an adjacent edge of the centre hexagon. Flatten and then pinch together the two rosette hexagons to stitch the adjoining seam. Continue until the rosette is complete.

■ You will need extra hexagons (white on the example shown here) to fill in the spaces between the rosettes when you come to join them together.

■ Leave all the backing papers in place until the whole project is complete. There is no need to press the patchwork as the tacking will have made a good crease over the time it takes to work a quilt top.

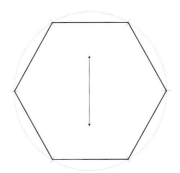

■ When finished, remove the tacking stitches and backing papers; you may find that you have caught the edges of the papers in your stitching, so be gentle when removing them.

Pentagon Rosette

Size of finished rosette: 14 cm (5½ in.)

Pentagon Rosettes can be used in conjunction with Grandmother's Flower Garden rosettes, since the outside edges are the same shape.

■ Draft a hexagon template in the same way as for Grandmother's Flower Garden, but extend two edges to twice the length of the other sides.

■ Piece with papers, joining the shapes one by one along their long edges.

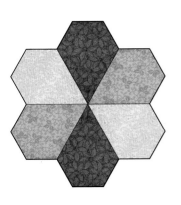

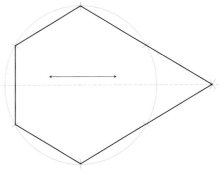

Six-Pointed Star

Size of finished block: 20 cm (8 in.)

Length of finished diamond: 10 cm (4 in.)

This design can be worked by hand over papers and the resulting hexagons joined into large rosettes. However, it is quite straightforward to piece by machine, as described here.

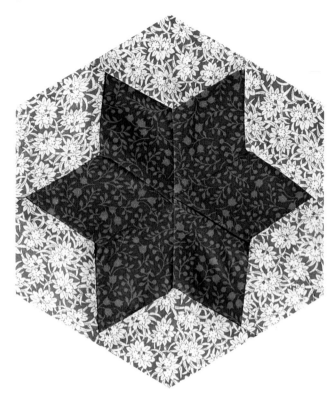

■ Draw a circle with a radius of 10 cm (4 in.) and mark the edge at 60° intervals. Draw lines radiating from the centre to each of the marked points. Divide one segment in half and draw lines at 60° from the circle edge to the segment lines. All four sides will be the same length. Make a template, adding a 6-mm (¼-in.) seam allowance all around.

■ Cut six diamonds in each of two colours. Place two diamonds of the same colour right sides together and stitch along one edge – but do not secure the ends of the seam, as you will need to undo the stitching at one end by about 6 mm (¼ in.) later. Press the seam. Take a third diamond in the same colour and stitch it to the second edge of the first diamond.

■ Make another set of three diamonds in the same colour, and press the seams in the same direction as the first set. Pin at the centre and piece the two halves together, stitching slowly over the seams to keep the points true.

■ Place an outer diamond (in the second colour) in position and stitch from the outside towards the seam of the star. Stop stitching when you reach the seam, and break off. Undo about 6 mm (¼ in.) of the star seam and bring the edge of the diamonds level. Stitch from the seam to the outer edge of the diamond. Press the seams outwards, away from the star – you'll find that the tenting will flatten. Repeat all the way around.

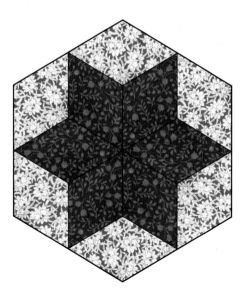

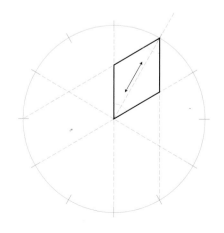

Tumbling Blocks

Size of finished block: 10 cm (4 in.) wide

Length of finished diamond: 10 cm (4 in.)

This design could be worked by hand over papers or machine stitched, as described here. To create the 3-D effect, choose fabrics with strong light, mid and dark tones.

The templates are drafted in the same way as for Six-Pointed Star, but the diamonds are pieced in threes, with mid and dark diamonds pieced to adjacent edges of a light diamond. The resulting hexagon blocks are then joined first into rows, and then row upon row.

■ Make a diamond template in the same way as for Six-Pointed Star and cut three diamonds – one light, one mid-tone and one dark. Stitch the pale diamond to the mid-toned diamond along one edge, starting and stopping the seam about 6 mm (¼ in.) from the ends.

■ Place the dark diamond above the first two and stitch the dark diamond to the pale one from the outside towards the seam of the pale and mid diamonds, starting and stopping about 6 mm (¼ in.) from the ends. Bring the dark diamond edge level with the mid-toned one and stitch towards the point, again starting and stopping about 6 mm (¼ in.) from the ends. Once several blocks have been pieced together, press the seams towards the darker fabrics. You'll find that the tenting will flatten.

■ To join several tumbling blocks together, first piece two together, mid-toned to pale edge, starting and stopping about 6 mm (¼ in.) from the ends. Next, add a third block above these two, right sides together, stitching a pale edge to a dark edge, and starting and stopping 6 mm (¼ in.) from the ends as before. Add a fourth block and continue, always with just two edges to stitch.

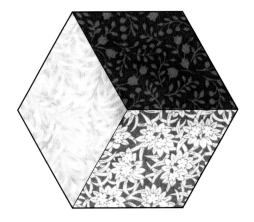

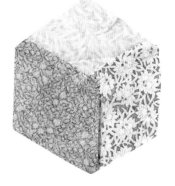

Back

Front

Eight-Pointed Star

Size of finished block: 33 cm (13 in.)

Length of finished diamond: 18 cm (7 in.)

This design can be worked by hand over papers or by machine, as described here. The Star is pieced first, and then the edge triangles and corner squares are added.

■ Draw a circle with a 15-cm (5¾-in.) radius and mark the edge at 45° intervals. Draw lines radiating from the centre to each of the marked points. Divide one segment in half and draw lines at 45° to the segment lines. You can now draw in the block edges so they are level with the tips of the star. The grain line should be along the long edge of the triangles. On the diamonds it can run along the length so any pattern direction on the fabric looks even. Add a 6-mm (¼-in.) seam allowance to all templates.

■ Cut four diamonds in each of two colours and four triangles and squares in cream.

■ Piece the diamonds in contrasting pairs, and join the pairs in groups of two to make the two halves of the star. Don't secure the seam ends as you will need to undo the stitching at one end by about 6 mm (¼ in.). To avoid bulk at the centre, press the seams so they lie in opposite directions at the centre. Lay the two halves of the star right sides together and stitch, being careful to match the centre points.

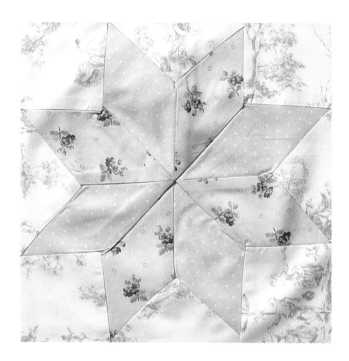

■ With right sides together, and working with the star uppermost, stitch a corner square along one edge of a diamond to the seam, stopping the seam 6 mm (¼ in.) from the end near the star seam. Undo about 6 mm (¼ in.) of the star seam and bring the edge of the next diamond and square level. Stitch from the seam to the outer edge of the square. Press the seams outwards, away from the star – you'll find that the tenting will flatten. Repeat all the way around.

■ Insert the triangles in the same way. Press the seams away from the star.

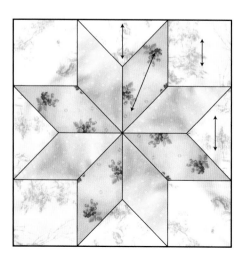

Star of the East

Size of finished block: 33 cm (13 in.) square

Length of finished diamond: 18 cm (7 in.)

This block has split diamonds in contrasting colours, and works best with sashing or as a central medallion.

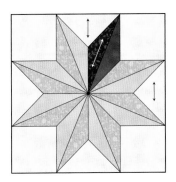

■ Draft a star within an 15-cm (5¼-in.) radius circle, as for Eight-pointed Star (see page 44), then divide the diamond shape in half, from point to point to make the split diamond template. Piece the diamond halves together first and press the seams towards the darker fabric. Then piece the remainder of the block in the same way as for Eight-Pointed Star. There will be a lot of bulk in the centre, so take extra care to keep the points true.

Star upon Stars

Size of finished block: 33 cm (13 in.) square

Length of finished diamond: 9 cm (3½ in.)

Each point is made of four, nine or 16 diamonds. The cushion project on page 108 has nine diamonds per point.

■ Draft a star within an 15-cm (5¼-in.) radius circle, as for Eight-Pointed Star (see page 44) and then quarter the diamond to make the small diamond templates. Draft the corner squares and triangles in the centre of each side as for Eight-Pointed Star.

■ Cut eight dark blue, eight cream sprig and 16 mid-blue diamonds, four yellow triangles and four yellow squares.

■ Piece eight cream/mid blue and eight mid blue/dark blue diamonds in identical pairs and press the seams towards the darker fabric. With right sides together, stitch alternate pairs together to make eight identical large diamonds. Pin at the seam intersections to keep the points true and stitch together to make the central eight-point star.

■ Assemble the block with the squares at the corners and triangles along edges in the same way as for Eight-Pointed Star (see page 44).

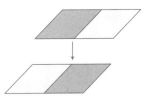

Kaleidoscope

Size of finished block: 29 cm (11½ in.) square

This block is divided into eight segments like Eight-Pointed Star, but it is much easier to piece as the segments fill the block.

■ Divide the block through the centre into 45° angles, as for Eight-Pointed Star, and draw lines to the edges of the block. Draw a straight line across each corner between the marked points. The cones have the grain line running along their length; on the corner triangles, the grain line is parallel to the edges of the block. Add a 6-mm (¼-in.) seam allowance to each template.

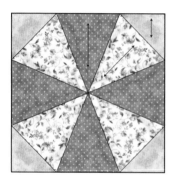

■ Cut four cone shapes each in blue dots and white sprig, and four pale blue corner triangles.

■ Piece each triangle to a white sprig cone and press the seams outwards. Piece this to a blue dot cone to make quarter blocks. Join two quarter blocks, and then join the two halves across the centre, being careful to match the points. The seams should be in alternate directions to avoid bulk at the centre.

Spider's Web

Size of finished block: 29 cm (11½ in.) square

This can be made with alternating striped and plain cones. The stripes do not have to be of even width. The diagonal cones are single pieces of fabric, without corner triangles.

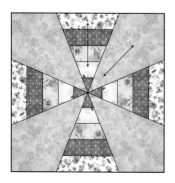

■ Cut four solid fabric blue cones and four striped ones made up of 4-cm (1½-in.) strips.

■ Assemble as for Kaleidoscope.

Attic Windows

Size of finished block: 24 cm (9½ in.) square

To achieve the 3-D effect, use fabrics that contrast strongly in tone for the 'frames'. The 'window panes' could all be made from different fabrics or even from small appliquéd blocks.

■ To draft templates, draw a 12-cm (4¾-in.) square for one quarter block. The frame is 3 cm (1¼ in.) wide with a 45° angle. Add a 6-mm (¼-in.) seam allowance to each template.

■ Cut four patterned squares and four rectangles each of pale and dark fabric. The pale rectangles are mirror image of the dark ones.

■ With right sides together, stitch a pale rectangle to a square, stopping 6 mm (¼ in.) before the angle. Next, stitch a dark rectangle, again stopping 6 mm (¼ in.) before the angle. Pull the angle edges level and mitre the corner (see page 171). Press the seams outwards, away from the central squares.

■ Join the patches in vertical pairs and press the seams in alternate directions. Join these pairs together and press all the vertical seams in the same direction across the quilt.

Curved blocks

Curved patches can form part of any block. The ones shown are all four-patch blocks (Drunkard's Path is subdivided into 16 patches), apart from the Fan blocks, which are one-patch blocks. The curves are pieced first and the resulting patches assembled into vertical strips. If there are several curved pieces in a patch, the smallest, inner curves should be pieced first.

Robbing Peter to Pay Paul

Size of finished block: 36 cm (14 in.) square

This design is similar to Drunkard's Path (see page 50), but is trickier to piece as all the patches have curves to match up on every side.

■ Draw an 18-cm (7-in.) square on graph paper. Using a compass, draw a quarter circle halfway along one edge, using a 9-cm (3½-in.) radius. Add a 6-mm (¼-in.) seam allowance all around each template.

■ Cut two of each shape in two different colours.

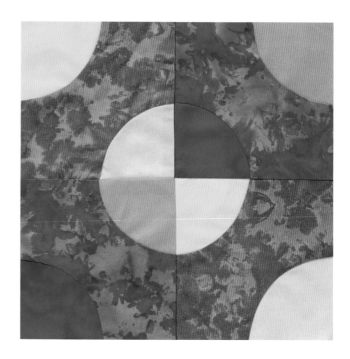

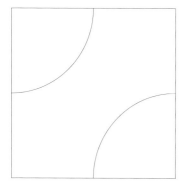

Four-patch block in two colourways

■ In the same way as for Drunkard's Path (see page 50), fold each piece in half diagonally along its curve and crease the centre mark to make it easier to match up. Pin and piece one side of a patch, press the seam away from the quarter circle and then piece the second quarter circle.

■ Pin and piece the upper and lower patches together and press the seams in alternate directions. Join the two sections and press all the vertical seams in the same direction across the quilt.

Fair Play

Size of finished block: 36 cm (14 in.) square

Although the individual patches are similar to Drunkard's Path (see page 50), the design is much less forgiving as the two curves need to be cut and pieced very accurately so that they meet exactly when joined.

■ Draw an 18-cm (7-in.) square on graph paper. Using a compass, draw a quarter circle halfway along one edge, using a 9-cm (3½-in.) radius. Mark a second ring 4.5 cm (1¾ in.) further along. Add a 6-mm (¼-in.) seam allowance all around each template.

■ Cut two of each shape in two different colours.

■ In the same way as for Drunkard's Path (see page 50), fold each piece in half diagonally along its curve and crease the centre mark to make it easier to match up. Pin and piece the centre segments first and press the seams away from the centre. Repeat with the outer rings. If a dark fabric is being pressed towards a paler one, you may need to trim the darker seam allowance so that it doesn't show through on the front.

■ Pin and piece the upper and lower patches together and press the seams in alternate directions. Join the two sections and press all the vertical seams in the same direction across the quilt top.

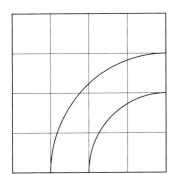

Four-patch block in two colourways

Drunkard's Path

Size of finished block: 48 cm (19 in.) square

This is a repeating block of 16 patches, with only two shapes and three colours. Since a double-bed quilt would need five blocks across and five down, making 400 of each shape, it is best to make sturdy templates that won't get damaged with so much use.

■ Draw a 12-cm (4¾-in.) square on graph paper. Using a compass, draw a quarter circle two-thirds of the way along one edge, using a radius of 8 cm (3⅛ in.). Cut out and glue the pieces to card, adding a seam allowance of 6 mm (¼ in.) all the way around each piece.

■ Cut eight blue and eight yellow squares with concave curves, and eight blue and eight cream quarter circles.

■ If the fabric has a directional pattern, as shown here, cut half the shapes with the right side of the fabric facing you and half with the wrong side facing. The shapes are simple but the pattern repeats can be very confusing, so lay the 32 pieces out in sequence, alternating lights and darks, before piecing, keeping the fabric direction uniform across the block.

■ Fold each square and quarter circle in half diagonally and crease mid curve as a matching guide. Place a quarter circle on a square, right sides together, and pin along the crease with the pin head facing outwards so that you can remove it easily as you stitch.

Pull the straight edges of each side level and pin. Add just a couple more pins to the curve. Turn over, as it is easier to stitch the stretchy concave curve to the quarter circle curve. As you stitch (slowly), tug gently at the top fabric to keep the fabric edges level and make the curves fit.

■ Press, gently ironing the quarter circle flat. You can nudge the curve into shape with the tip of the iron from the front.

■ When all the patches are pieced and pressed lay them out in sequence again and join in vertical strips. Alternate the seam directions from strip to strip to avoid bulk at the seams. Join the strips together and press all the vertical seams in the same direction across the quilt.

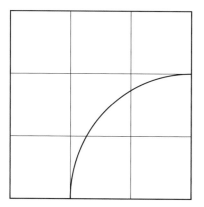

One patch, rotated repeat

Mary's Fan

Size of finished block: 25.5 cm (10 in.) square

This is a one-patch block. Traditionally, it was made into a quilt top with alternating plain blocks, giving scope for hand-quilted designs in each. It could also be assembled with sashing strips.

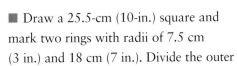

■ Draw a 25.5-cm (10-in.) square and mark two rings with radii of 7.5 cm (3 in.) and 18 cm (7 in.). Divide the outer ring into six segments at 15° intervals. Make templates, adding a 6-mm (¼-in.) seam allowance all around. The segments have grain lines running lengthways.

■ Piece the segments and press the seams towards the darker fabric. Fold the pieces to mark the centre points and piece as for Drunkard's Path (see page 50), working the small curve first and pressing the seams outwards.

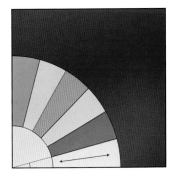

Broken Circles

Size of finished block: 36 cm (14 in.) square

Size of each finished patch: 18 cm (7 in.) square

This is a four-patch block, with two different patches to draft. The top left and lower right quarter blocks have rings with radii of 4 cm (1½ in.) and 10 cm (4 in.). On the top right and lower left quarter blocks, the radii of the rings are 7 cm (2¾ in.) and 15 cm (6 in.). Make templates, adding a 6-mm (¼-in.) seam allowance all around.

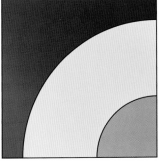

Two patches, mirror images

■ Cut two of each shape in different colours.

■ Fold, pin, piece and press the inner rings first, as for Drunkard's Path (see page 50), then piece the outer rings.

■ Pin and piece the upper and lower patches together, pressing the seams in opposite directions. Join the two sections to complete the block and press all the vertical seams in the same direction across the quilt.

Grandmother's Fan

Size of finished block: 25.5 cm (10 in.) square

This is a one-patch block, similar to Mary's Fan but put together differently. The fans are assembled and stitched onto a backing, and then the centres are applied. This makes it a sturdy, hardwearing block, and one suitable for using different weights and recycled fabrics because the strain is taken by the backing fabric, not the piecing.

■ Cut a 28-cm (11-in.) backing square. (You can trim it to size once finished.)

■ Draw a 25.5-cm (10-in.) square and mark two rings with radii of 9 cm (3½ in.) and 21 cm (8¼ in.). Divide the outer ring into five segments at 18° intervals. Make templates, adding a 6-mm (¼-in.) seam allowance all around (unless you are working by machine, in which case the quarter circle does not need a seam allowance on the curved edge).

■ Cut the segments with the grain lines running lengthways. Piece the segments and press the seams towards the darker fabric. Pin onto the backing square.

■ If you are working by hand, turn the curved edges under and slipstitch to the backing fabric, gently undoing the seams a little to tuck the turning allowance under. Stitch the quarter circle in place.

Hand finished

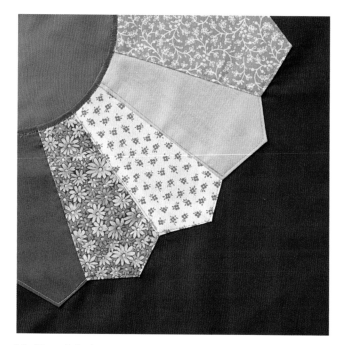

Machine stitched

■ If you are machine stitching, turn the segment edges under straight to form a point and topstitch, gently undoing the seams a little to tuck the turning allowance under. Topstitch the segment seams, too. Pin and satin stitch the curved edge of the quarter circle (stitch width 4).

Dresden Plate

Size of finished block: 40 cm (15¾ in.) square

This particular design has 20 segments, so it has the same angles (18°) as Grandmother's Fan (see page 52). You can use the same template, reducing the radii to 4 cm (1½ in.) and 17.5 cm (7 in.). Dresden Plate can, however, be made with any number of segments. For 24 divisions, use the template for Mary's Fan (page 51), with the segments having an angle of 15°; for 16 divisions, the angle would be 22.5°. The 'Plate' is stitched onto a backing fabric and the central circle applied last.

◼ Cut a 43-cm (17-in.) backing square. (You can trim it to size once finished.)

◼ To make the template, draw a 20-cm (8-in.) square (one-quarter of the block) and mark two rings with radii of 4 cm (1½in.) and 17.5 cm (7 in.). Divide the outer ring into five segments at 18° intervals. Make a

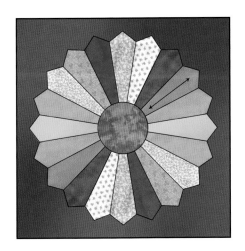

segment template, adding a 6-mm (¼-in.) seam allowance all around. The segments have the grain lines running lengthways. The centre circle has a 4.5-cm (1¾-in.) radius; no seam allowance is added if it is satin stitched in place, but if you are working by hand it will need a 6-mm (¼-in.) turning allowance.

◼ Cut and piece all the segments to form a ring and, pressing from the back, press all the seams in the same direction. Pin this big ring to the backing fabric and topstitch it in place, turning the curves under to form points. Then topstitch the segment seams.

◼ Pin and satin stitch the centre circle in place (stitch length 4) or turn the allowance under and slipstitch by hand.

Foundation blocks

Foundation blocks are stitched onto a backing fabric to keep the lines true. They have a centre patch which is pieced around and around. They are good blocks to choose if you are using recycled fabrics of different strengths, as the strain will be taken by the backing fabric rather than the seams. These blocks can be worked without a backing fabric, but if they are made any larger than 33 cm (13 in.) there is a risk of 'tenting', which means that the centres will bulge and distort.

Log Cabin and Courthouse Steps

Size of finished block: 30.2 cm (11½ in.) square

Size of each finished strip: 3.3 cm (1¼ in.) wide

These two blocks are constructed in a very similar way – the difference being that in Log Cabin adjacent sides of the central square are in light or dark tones, while in Courthouse Steps opposite sides of the central square are light or dark.

Vary the fabric of the outer strips of the blocks, so that dark can be placed next to dark without the risk of the same fabric being on the edge of the neighbouring block.

For a large double-sized quilt, you will need about eight blocks across and down.

■ Cut the centre square 5 cm (2 in.) square and the strips 4.5 cm (1¾ in.) wide – this includes the 6-mm (¼-in.) seam allowance. The longest strip required is 72 cm (28 in.).

■ Cut a piece of backing cotton about 35 cm (13½ in.) square, fold it in quarters and then diagonally, and press. The crease lines will act as a piecing guide to keep the block square. Pin the centre square (which is traditionally red to represent the hearth in the Log Cabin) in place.

Log Cabin

Courthouse Steps

Log Cabin

■ With right sides together, piece the palest strip to one side of the centre square, trimming to length as you go. When you flip the strip over, it will be right side up. Press flat, turn the block clockwise and add the second pale strip. Press, turn the piece clockwise again, add a dark fabric, and then repeat. It is best to iron the block as you piece. Continue building the block by adding pale and dark strips around and around.

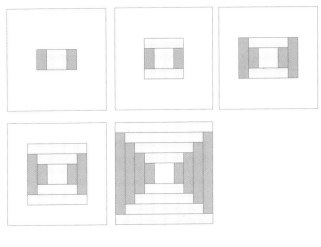

Courthouse Steps

■ With right sides together, piece two dark strips to opposite sides of the centre square. Then piece two pale strips to the top and lower edges. Continue adding dark strips to the sides and light strips to the top and bottom, until the block is the required size.

Log Cabin settings

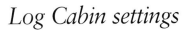

■ Different patterns become apparent with different placements and rotations of the blocks.

■ Light and Dark has the blocks all in the same direction across the quilt.

■ In Straight Furrow, the neighbouring block is rotated 180°. It is best to make two sets of blocks with different fabrics on the outside edges to avoid identical fabrics being pieced together.

■ Barn Raising needs an even number of blocks across and down to make it symmetrical. It is best to make two sets of blocks with different fabrics on the outside edges to avoid identical fabrics being pieced together. Lay out in sequence from the centre, with all the darks together, then continue as Straight Furrow.

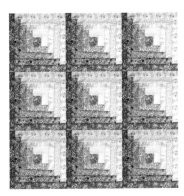

Light and Dark

Straight Furrow

Barn Raising

Pineapple

Size of finished block: 28.3 cm (12 in.) square

Size of finished strip: 2.3 cm (1 in.) wide

Working around a central square, piece four pale and then four dark strips, the pales horizontally and vertically, the darks across the diagonals. Cut the strip lengths as you go. You may need to trim away excess fabric from the dark strips to avoid show-through. You could draft the design on paper and cut templates (adding a 6-mm/¼-in. seam allowance all around) for each of the strips.

■ Cut the centre square 6.5 cm (2½ in.) square and the strips 3.5 cm (1½ in.) wide – this includes the 6-mm (¼-in.) seam allowances. The longest pale and dark strips required (two of each) are 132 cm (52 in.).

■ Cut a piece of backing cotton about 32 cm (14 in.) square, fold it in quarters and then diagonally, and press. The crease lines will act as a piecing guide to keep the block true. Pin the centre square in place.

■ With right sides together, piece four pale strips to the edges of the centre square, trimming to length as you go. The strips should overlap by about 6 mm (¼ in.) at the

ends. Flip over the strips as you proceed, so they are right side up, and press flat.

■ Piece four dark fabrics diagonally, again overlapping the ends by about 6 mm (¼ in.). Press.

■ The next four pale strips do not need to overlap, but should just reach the outer edges of the dark fabric. They are placed horizontally and vertically.

■ Continue by piecing four dark fabrics diagonally.

■ Continue around and around, alternating light and dark. A further two dark strips will be needed on the corners. Finally, trim the block square.

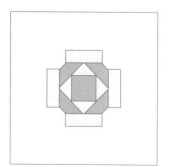

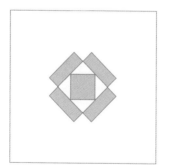

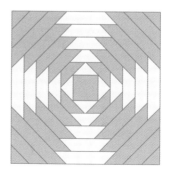

Snail Trail

Size of finished block: 33 cm (13 in.) square

This block requires templates for the triangles, with the grain directions marked. The grain must run vertically to avoid distortion and stretch, and the grain is different from one size of triangle to the next. Using striped fabrics will increase the swirling effect when the blocks are joined together.

■ Draw a 33-cm (13-in.) square, with an 8-cm (3⅛-in.) square in the centre, quartered. Draw a square on point around this, touching the corners of the centre patch, then a square, and so on. Add a 6-mm (¼-in.) seam allowance around each template.

■ Cut a piece of backing cotton about 38 cm (15 in.) square, fold it in quarters and then diagonally, and press. These crease lines will act as a piecing guide to keep the block true.

■ Piece the centre Four Patch, press it and pin it to the centre of the backing fabric.

■ With right sides together, piece the two smallest pale triangles to opposite sides of the centre Four Patch, then piece the two smallest dark triangles to the top and lower edges. Flip back the triangles and press flat.

■ Turn the block anticlockwise. Piece pale triangles to the sides and dark triangles to the top and bottom. Press. Repeat until the block is complete.

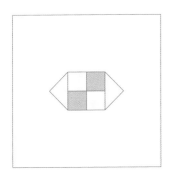
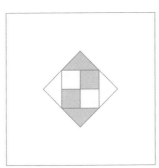

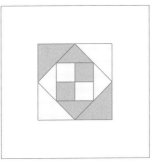
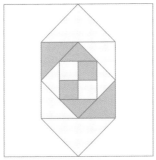
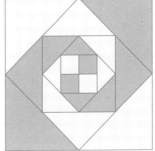

Patchwork borders

When the same blocks are repeated across an entire quilt, there is no need for a border pattern. If, however, your quilt would benefit from a border, there are several distinct patterns to choose from, as well as part blocks that can be used as borders – Bear's Paw, Goose Tracks and Bright Star work well, and Old Maid's Puzzle has two different quarter patches, either of which could be repeated around a quilt of that design. Draft the templates for borders as explained on page 160.

Sawtooth

Size of finished patch: 7.5 cm (3 in.)

Sawtooth has squares made up of two differently coloured triangles pieced in the same orientation, while for Reverse Sawtooth the squares are rotated. A double row of Sawtooth is effective since the triangles become split diamonds, while a double row of Reverse Sawtooth is, in fact, Fly or Broken Dishes. Using more than two colours can change the appearance of Sawtooth.

Sawtooth

Reverse Sawtooth

Sawtooth using more than one colour

Double row of Sawtooth

Chevron

Size of finished patch: 7.5 cm (3 in.) square

This uses two or more colours to divide squares into triangles, and two rows are arranged so that either the same colours or tones touch. A Chevron border can either be pieced as separate rows or into four-patch blocks and then assembled.

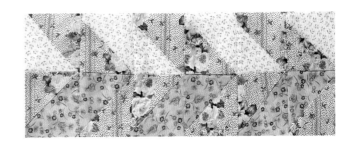

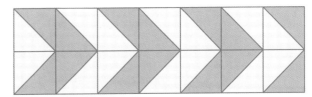

Air Castle

Size of finished patch: 10 cm (4 in.)

This pattern of triangle squares with one half split appears in many quilt blocks. The grain direction is different on the large and small triangles. First, piece identical triangles from the small ones, press seams to the dark side and then make up the squares and assemble in a row.

Mitred Stripes

Size of finished border: 15 cm (6 in.) wide

Width of strip: 2.5–6.5 cm (1–2½ in.)

Use the leftovers from the quilt top for this border so that the design of the matching coloured border will not clash with the block design. Cut the strips and piece together at random to form a long ribbon. Press all seams in the same direction. Fold and cut one end of the border at a right angle and stitch the length to one edge of the quilt top, starting and ending the seam about 6 mm (¼ in.) from each end. At the uncut end, fold the border at right angles and cut. Piece a second edge in the same way. Bring the two diagonals together and stitch from the quilt to the outside. Open the seam out and press. Repeat on all sides of the quilt.

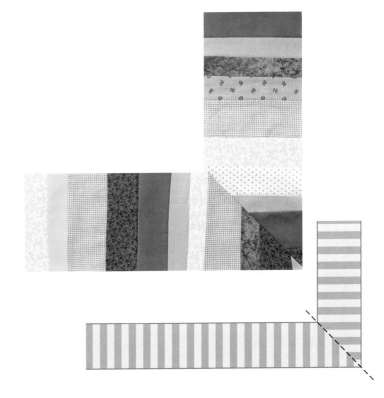

Nine Patch

Size of finished block: 15 cm (6 in.) square

Patches on this nine-patch block can be worked in many different colour combinations, although two is enough. Piece the blocks together to make a border ribbon.

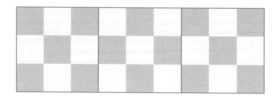

Diamond Squares

Size of finished patch: 10 cm (4 in.) square

Cut the triangles with the grain along a short edge, and the squares with the grain from point to point. Piece the long edge of the triangles to the squares and press seams outwards. Join patches to make a border ribbon. Keeping the colouring simple – four colours only – gives the border more impact.

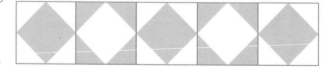

Dog Tooth

Size of finished triangle/border:
10 cm (4 in.) wide

The triangles are equilateral, each angle being 60°, and have the grain running from a point to the centre. Piece one triangle to another, press the seam to the darker side and then piece the next to make a continuous border ribbon.

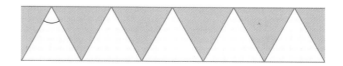

Dog Tooth Split

Size of finished border: 10 cm (4 in.) wide

First, piece the long edges of the half triangles together to make rectangles, press the seams to the dark side and then piece the rectangles together to make a continuous border ribbon.

Flying Geese

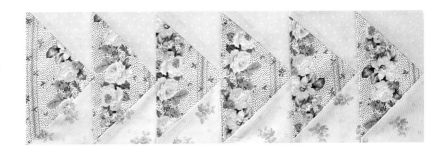

Size of finished border: 15 cm (6 in.) wide

For the small triangles, the grain runs along the short edge while for the large ones it runs point to base. Piece the long edge of the small triangles to the short edge of the large ones and press the seams towards the small triangles. Repeat on the opposite side and then piece these together, point to base, one after the other to make a continuous border ribbon. Be careful to keep the points intact.

Flying Geese 2

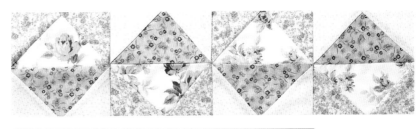

Size of finished border: 15 cm (6 in.) wide

Assemble large and small triangles in two colourways in the same way as for Flying Geese. Piece the Flying Geese base to base to form squares, and then piece these together, one after the other, to make a continuous border ribbon. Be careful to keep the points intact.

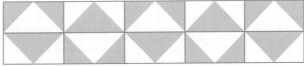

Ribbon

Size of finished border: 20 cm (8 in.) wide

This border is made up of two rows of triangle squares pieced above and below a row of squares. Piece the triangle squares and then assemble into rectangles by sandwiching a square of the same colour between by each vertical pair. To achieve a concertina effect for the ribbon, use contrasting tones and piece them mirror image. These are then pieced lengthways to make a continuous strip.

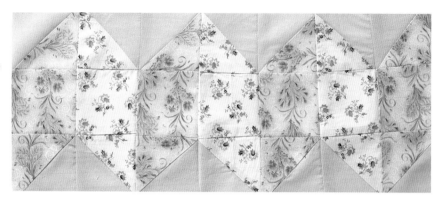

  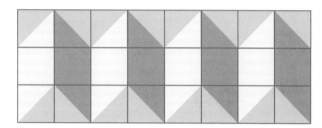

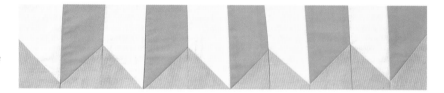

Nelson's Victory

Size of finished border: 12 cm (4¾ in.) wide

Despite its name, this border looks like Beach Huts upside down. Cut differently coloured four-sided shapes so that they make mirror images of each other. Piece the triangles to the diagonals of the four-sided shapes and press the seams towards the triangles. Then piece these one after the other to make a continuous border ribbon.

  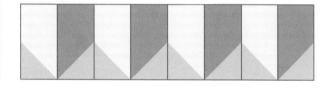

APPLIQUÉ BLOCKS

The appliqué blocks work equally well when stitched by hand or machine, although the finished effect will be very different. Hand-stitching will give a more traditional look with the edges appearing to blend in with the background, while machine-satin stitch outlines the motif. When hand-appliquéing, it's advisable to use plain or patterned fabrics with a small repeat design. If working by machine you can afford to use paler or less distinct fabrics.

Appliqué blocks

Scale the templates on pages 64–96 up or down to the size you require for your block. Cut backing squares larger than required and trim to size and shape once appliquéd and pressed. When cutting out the motifs, keep the line of symmetry to the line of the grain so that there will be the same amount of stretch on each side of the motif if it is slightly distorted with stitching. Stitch clockwise around motifs.

Single Tulip, Tulip Bunch, Butterfly, Dragonfly

Finished block with frame: 27 cm (10½ in.) square

Central appliqué: 19 cm (7½ in.) square

Cut the backing fabric to 25 cm (10 in.) square, make the templates and cut out the motifs. Pin the motifs in place, keeping them within an area of 18 cm (7 in.) square.

■ **Single Tulip** To start, lay the top thread along the line of stitching and stitch over it for about 3 cm (1 in.) before trimming it off. This will conceal and secure it. Satin stitch (stitch width 3) from the base of a leaf to its tip along the outside edge. With the needle down and on

the outside of the motif, turn the fabric and stitch the inner edge of the leaf. Without breaking off, stitch the second leaf and then the straight stem towards the tulip. Draw the threads to the front and tuck them under the tulip, to hide and secure them. (See page 66 for the stitching order when following the instructions).

■ Starting at the centre top of the tulip under the pinned petal, stitch up to the right hand point, spin the fabric round the needle again (the needle should always be on the side away from the motif), then stitch around the base and back up and around the other point. Draw threads to the front and tuck behind the petal.

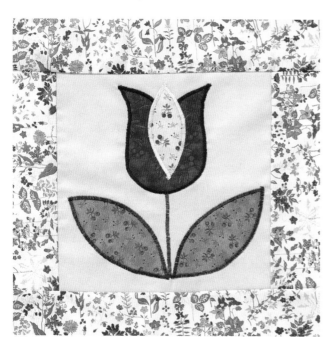

Tulip

Tulip bunch

■ Start stitching the petal midway along one edge, progress to a point, go along the other edge, to a point, and back to where you started. Draw the threads to the back, tie and trim. Trim the other thread ends on the back.

■ **Tulip Bunch** Work the leaves and one stem as for the Single Tulip. Work the remaining stems next by starting from just under a tulip and stitching towards the base. Turn and stitch back up the final stem. Work the tulips as for the Single Tulip.

Butterfly and Dragonfly Leave a small space between the wings to avoid a bulge under the body. Work the wings first. For the body, start on one antenna (reduce stitch width to 2) and stitch about 1 cm (½ in.) towards the body. Stop, lift the needle and pull back to stitch the second antenna (don't break off the thread). Increase the stitch width to 3 and stitch the body. Draw threads to the back, tie and trim.

Butterflies

Dragonflies

■ Press the appliquéd block on the wrong side and trim it to 21 cm (8½ in.).

■ Cut 6-cm (2½-in.) strips of fabric for the frame. Taking a 1-cm (½-in.) seam allowance, sew on the side strips first, then the top and bottom. (Each block will need a strip 102 cm (40 in.) long.) Press seams outwards, away from the centre square.

Sewing order

——— *First*

——— *Second*

——— *Third*

Leaf Ring and Bird and Bee blocks with Multi fabric frames

Finished block with frame: 33 cm (13 in.) square

Central appliqué: 25 cm (10 in.) square

Cut the backing fabric to 29 cm (11½ in.) square, make templates and cut out the motifs. Keep the line of symmetry to the line of the grain, especially on the bird. Pin the motifs in place, keeping them within an area of 23 cm (9 in.).

■ **Leaf Ring** Draw a 7.5 cm (3 in.) radius circle with a quilter's pencil on the backing fabric. Cut out 16 small leaves, a daisy and a 3-cm (1¼-in.) circle – no need for a template, just draw around a coin – in as many different fabrics as you wish.

■ Stitch the leaves, changing the thread to tone each time. Start stitching near the ring and stitch over the top thread to conceal it when you start. Draw threads to the back and trim as each leaf is finished. When you stitch the ring, all these threads will be secured as you stitch over the tips of the leaves. Tie the threads at the back when the patch is finished.

■ **Bird and Bee** Draw a short section of a 7.5 cm (3 in.) radius circle for the stem.

■ Stitch the bird's beak and legs first, then the body, starting and ending just under the wing, which will hide threads pulled to the front. The eye is a 6 mm (¼ in.) line of stitching on the widest setting. Tie threads at the back and trim.

■ Stitch the leaves in pairs and change the thread for the stem. The bud conceals the ends of the stem threads.

■ The bee wings should just touch, but not overlap, to avoid a bulge under the body. Two horizontal lines of brown stitching represent its markings.

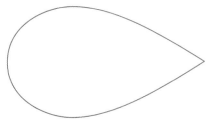

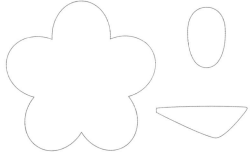

■ Press the block on the wrong side and trim it to 26.5 cm (10½ in.) square.

■ Cut frame strips 6 cm (2½ in.) wide and in varied lengths of 10–16 cm (4–6¼ in.). Stitch together at random. You will need a length of about 130 cm (51 in.) for each block. Taking a 1-cm (½-in.) seam allowance, sew a strip to each side and then to the top and bottom. Press seams outwards, away from the centre square.

Leaf ring and daisy

Bird and Bee

Hearts, Dove, Tulips and Flower

Hearts, doves and tulips are traditional quilt block themes and are here worked by hand in red-and-white gingham and plain red, reminiscent of the 'Turkey red' of vintage quilts. The motifs are shown on table linen and a pillowcase (see pages 138–139 and 145) but would also work well on a sampler quilt, where you could vary the direction of the dove and the number of tulips, and experiment with a different placement of hearts on each block.

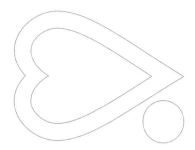

Size of finished block: 14 cm (9½ in.) square

■ Cut the backing fabric 21 cm (13 in.) square.

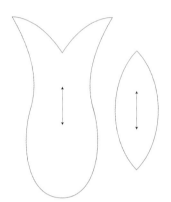

■ As all these motifs are fairly small, you do not need to match the direction of grain on the motif to that of the backing fabric, but you do need to keep the line of symmetry to the line of grain. Add 6 mm (¼ in.) extra around each template for turning under.

■ The diagrams show which layer to stitch first and the best starting point. Use threads in colours that match the darkest of the appliqué fabrics. You will need to snip into the sharp curves in the turn-under allowance at the top of the hearts. Leave the detail stitching of stems and bird eye until last and use three strands of embroidery thread and running stitch.

■ If you are stitching by machine, use stitch width 3, narrowing to 1 for the detailing.

Heart

Dove

Tulips

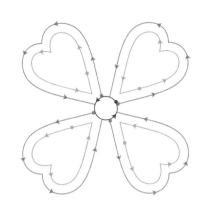

_____ First
_____ Second
_____ Third

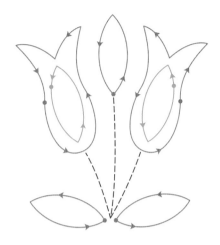

_____ First
_____ Second
_____ Third

_____ First
_____ Second
_____ Third

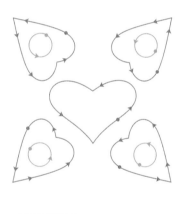

_____ First
_____ Second

Flower

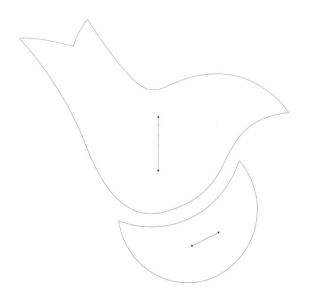

Leaf motifs

The ash, maple and oak motifs are used together on a cushion (page 144). Alternatively, you could work each block in a different colour, to indicate different seasons, and use them on a quilt top or hanging. The holly design could be applied to Christmas tablecloths, napkins or stockings or three leaves could be reduced in size for cards with beads or buttons for the berries.

Ash and holly width: 23 cm (9 in.) square

Maple and oak width: 30 cm (12 in.) square

Satin stitch width: 3, narrowing to 1 for detailing

■ Cut the backing fabric 4 cm (1½ in.) larger than required. You can trim it to size later.

■ Cut the motifs with the grain line running along the length of the leaf; this gives equal stretch around the motif and makes it less likely to stretch.

■ Draw the branches in chalk and then pin the leaves either side. Start stitching the leaves near the branches, as the branch satin stitching will conceal the thread ends. If you are working by hand, use stem stitch for the branches and running stitch for the veins.

Ash

■ As the ash keys are on top of the leaves, stitch these after you have appliquéd the leaves.

Holly

■ Leave the detail stitching of the veins on the holly and the branch until last. For the veins, work towards the branch, widening the satin stitch as you go.

Maple and oak

■ The maple and oak veins are best worked from a narrow to a wide satin stitch, with the central vein concealing all the other stitch endings and widening to form the branch.

Ash

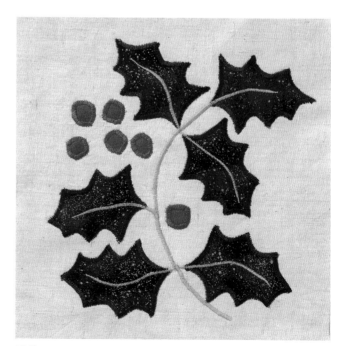

Holly

Maple

Oak

Flowers in bunches

*Use several different fabrics on the flower heads and
change the thread colour to give variety.*

Size of finished block: 20 x 28 cm (8 x 11 in.)

Satin stitch width: 3, narrowing to 1 on the points

■ For these two flowers, first stitch the stems, and then appliqué
the flower heads and leaves.

■ If you are working by hand, work the stems in stem or running
stitch. As the motifs are small, pin and turn the allowance under
with the point of the needle as you slipstitch. On the bluebells,
you will need to snip into the sharp angles.

Bluebells   *Hyacinth*

Flowers in vases

Highly patterned Liberty lawns are good here, with bold repeating designs on the vases, floral designs on the flower heads and leaves, and plain fabrics for the flower centres. Try to centre the vases so that they look symmetrical.

Cornflower: 33 x 53 cm (13 x 21 in.)

Daisy: 33 x 51 cm (13 x 20 in.)

Iris: 33 x 56 cm (13 x 22 in.)

Satin stitch width: 3, narrowing to 1 for detailing

■ Pin the motifs in place and draw the stems lightly in chalk.

■ First stitch the stems from vase to flower head. The start and finish of the stitching will then be concealed under the appliqué motifs. Use stitch width 3 if you are machine stitching, and stem stitch with stranded silk if working by hand.

■ Then stitch on the flower heads. If you are working by machine, start on an inside curve where it will show least; if working by hand, start on a smooth curve.

■ Stitch the daisy heads as if the petals were separate pieces, starting narrow (width 1) and widening the stitch to 3 as you go from just under the centre and around the petal tips. Stop and lift the needle and presser foot without breaking the thread and start from the centre again on the next petal, stitching over the loop of thread.

■ On the irises, stitch the pale petal first and then the three darker petals. Do the detailing last, starting narrow and widening the stitch towards the centre of the flower.

■ The cornflower has tight curves, so lift the presser foot with the needle still in the fabric of the motif and turn the panel around the needle.

■ Next, appliqué the flower centres.

■ Finally, appliqué the jug or vase. Stitch the inside of the jug and urn handles first, and then the outside edges.

Daisy in vase

Iris in a vase

Cornflower vase

Appliqué Rooster and Hen

The rooster is used on a wall-hanging project with a patchwork border (see page 133), but it would work equally well as the central panel on a cushion. These designs have several layers, which can put strain and distort the backing fabric, so use calico or a sturdy furnishing linen as the backing.

Size of finished block: 40 cm (16 in.) square

Motif height: 35.5 cm (14 in.)

Satin stitch width: 3, narrowing to 1 at the points

■ Cut the backing about 10 per cent larger than required and trim it to shape and size when the piece has been stitched and pressed. Use threads that match the darkest or brightest colour in the fabrics to make the design more vibrant.

■ Cut all the pieces on the straight of grain, with the larger pieces matching the grain line of the backing fabric to avoid distortion.

■ Pin all the pieces in place, one layer on another. The layers should all overlap a little.

■ The stitching diagram shows the order in which to work. The start and finish of many layers is concealed under an upper layer.

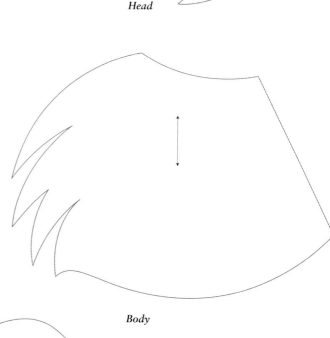

Head

Body

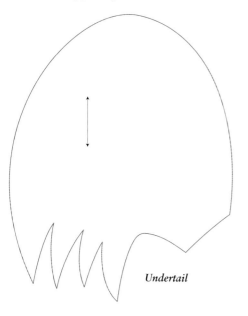

Undertail

Tail feathers

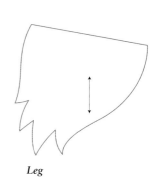

Leg

Rooster

■ For the rooster, first stitch the feet, comb and undertail, starting and finishing just under the overlapping layers and narrowing the stitch width as you approach the points.

■ Work the leg and then the body. Next, stitch the upper tail feathers, starting near the body. Then stitch the ruff, throat and beak, starting the beak nearest the eye.

■ Finally work the eye, on stitch width 3 or 4. Work a couple of stitches, stop with the needle in the fabric, spin the fabric a fraction and work another couple of stitches; continue until you have completed a circle.

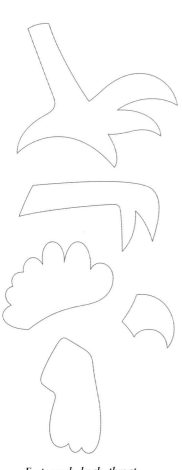

Feet, comb, beak, throat

Sewing order

First
Second
Third
Fourth
Fifth
Sixth

Hen

■ For the hen, first stitch the feet, comb and tail feathers, then the tail and body. Next stitch the upper wing and then the wing feather. Finally, stitch the ruff, throat and beak, and eye.

■ Bring the threads of both blocks to the back of the fabric, tie and trim.

■ Press on the wrong side and trim the blocks to shape and size.

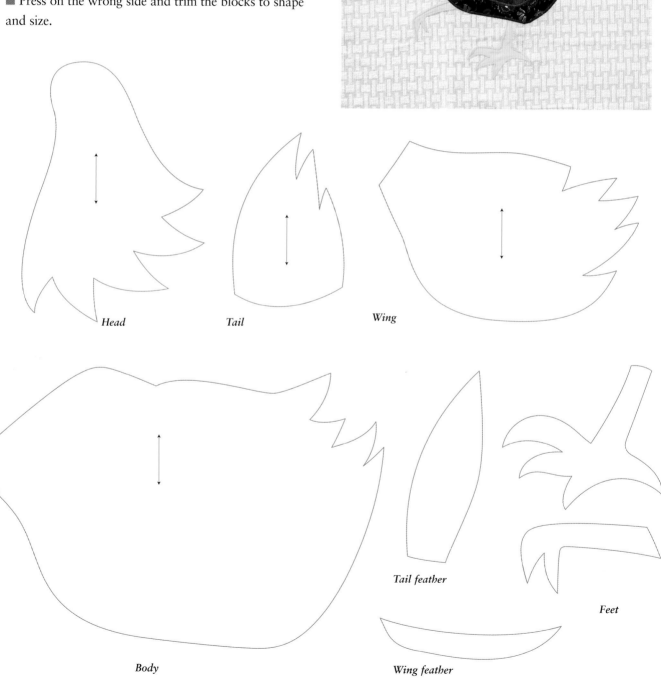

Head

Tail

Wing

Tail feather

Feet

Body

Wing feather

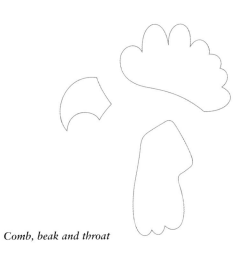

Comb, beak and throat

Sewing order

———	First
———	Second
———	Third
———	Fourth
———	Fifth
———	Sixth
———	Seventh
———	Eighth

Sleeping Cat

This block, with its simple, smooth outline and intricate detailing on the face, can be worked either by hand or machine. Use as the centre panel on a cushion or stitch cat blocks in different fabrics together to make a quilt.

Size of finished block: 31 cm (12 in.) square

Satin stitch width: 3, narrowing to 1 for detailing

■ The motif is large and liable to stretch out of shape, so cut it with the grain line running vertically and match to the grain of the backing fabric. Take care when pinning the cat in place on the backing fabric, as the legs and tail may distort.

■ Start stitching on the back leg that is furthest away, work round it and onto the belly, towards the front legs and so on. When you have finished, carry on stitching across the top of the first leg and onto the body a little way to detail the thigh.

■ Work the face detail stitching last, setting a very narrow stitch width for the whiskers and eyes and a slightly wider one for the mouth. The nose is a triangle worked in width 2 satin stitch and then filled in with more rows of satin stitch. If you are hand stitching, use stem stitch for the eyes and mouth, satin stitch for the nose and running stitch for the whiskers.

Farmyard motifs

These motifs are used on a child's cot quilt (see page 132), but could also be made into colourful wall hangings for a bedroom or playroom.

Size of finished blocks: 30 cm (12 in.) square

Satin stitch width: 3, narrowing to 1 for detailing

■ Many of these motifs are layered. The diagrams show the order in which to appliqué them to the background fabric. If you are working by machine, start stitching on an inside corner where it will show least, bring threads to the back, tie and trim. If you are working by hand, start on a smooth curve or straight area.

Pigs

■ Stitch the legs that are furthest away first, and then the rest of the pigs. Narrow the stitch to width 1 for the snout and tail details. It is easiest to stitch the tail from the tip. Leave the needle in the fabric, lift the presser foot and turn a little every few stitches to work the curl. If hand stitching, use chain stitch for the tail.

Sewing order

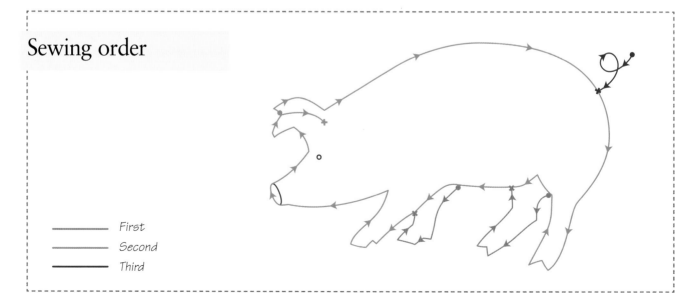

———— First

———— Second

———— Third

Tractor

■ First stitch the hay bales, then the cart and tractor, leaving the wheels until last.

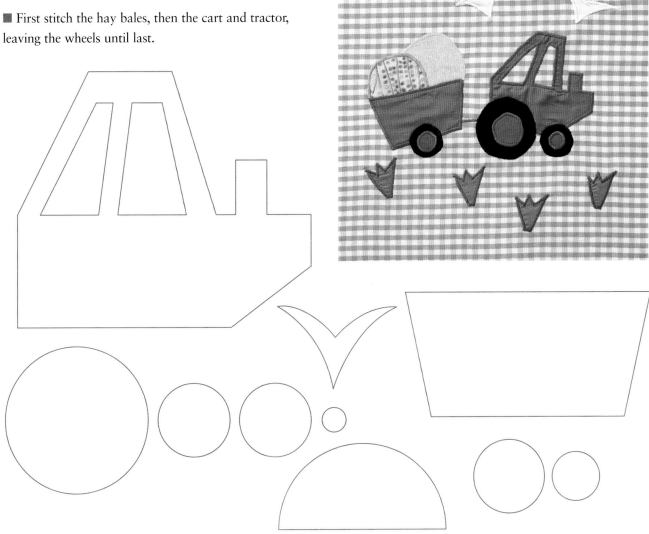

Sewing order

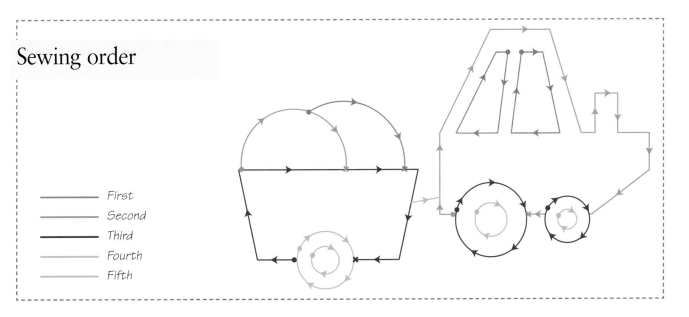

First
Second
Third
Fourth
Fifth

Sheep

■ Stitch the legs first (the body will conceal the stop and start of the stitching), then the bodies and finally the heads.

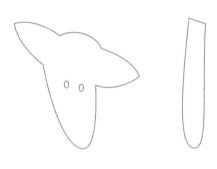

Sewing order

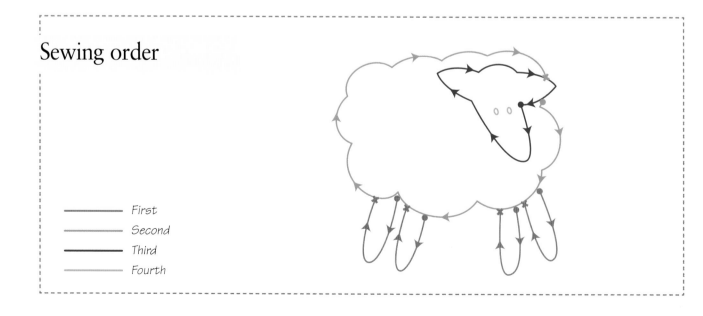

——— First
——— Second
——— Third
——— Fourth

Cows

■ Stitch the udders and then the legs that are farthest away first, before the rest of the cow bodies. Stitch the white patches and then the detailing. Note that the eyes are not round but tiny crescent shapes.

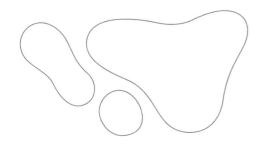

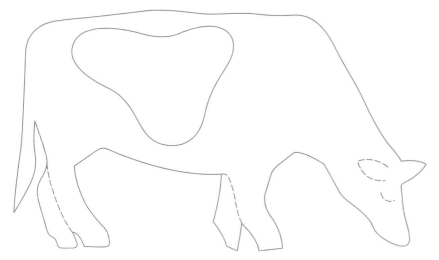

Sewing order

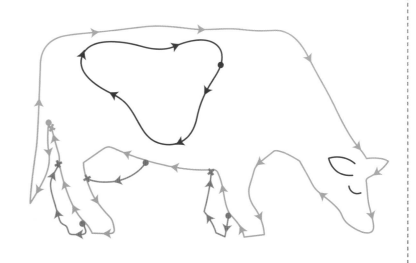

———— First
———— Second
———— Third

Christmas motifs

These motifs are used on Christmas cards but could also be appliquéd to Christmas stockings or sacks, table napkins and tablecloths. Add extra branches to make a taller tree.

Size of finished block: 23 cm (9 in.) square

Satin stitch width: 3, and 1 for detailing

Trees

■ Stitch the trunks first, so that the thread ends are concealed under the foliage, and if machine stitching, reduce the stitch width on the branches.

Snowman

■ Stitch the balls of snow first, starting with the lower one. Begin stitching just under the overlap of the smaller ball of snow to conceal the thread ends. Next, stitch the scarf and hat. Leave the detailing until last and stitch from the pointed ends to the wide, widening the stitch as you work. The eyes and buttons are in stitch width 2, working 12 stitches very close together.

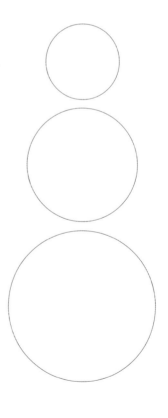

Watery motifs

The fish motifs are used on the Child's Counting Quilt (see page 130), as well as on the Fancy Fish Album Cover (see page 129). The designs on this page and on pages 84 and 85 could also be used on curtains, duvet covers, children's pockets, bibs or beach bags.

Size of finished block: 24 cm (9½ in.) square

Satin stitch width: 3, narrowing to 1 for detailing

■ Cut the motifs with the grain line running vertically; this gives equal stretch around the motif and makes the fabric less likely to distort. Cut the backing fabric larger than required – say 30 cm (12 in.) square – and trim it to size later. When you pin the motifs in place, remember to keep them well within a 23-cm (9-in.) central window.

■ Start stitching on an inside corner where the stitching will show least. When you have finished, bring the threads to the back, tie and trim.

■ Always leave detail stitching and the fishes' eyes until last and use a darker colour of thread.

Tips

● Narrow the stitch width on the spikes of the spiky fish, the palm and the gulls to make them more pointed.

● The eyes of the slender fish, fat fish, fancy fish and the seahorse are made of about six satin stitches very close together, with threads tied and trimmed at the back.

● Pin the seahorse well or it will be likely to distort as you stitch.

● Widen the stitch width as you sew the shell and starfish details. I find it easier to start narrow and end wide; the detail stitching on the starfish ends at its centre.

● Match the grain line of the sun and island to the backing fabric to avoid rippling. Appliqué these pieces first, then stitch the trunk and finally the leaves. Start stitching the trunk from the top, so that the start and finish are concealed by the leaves.

Spiky and slender fish

Fat and fancy fishes

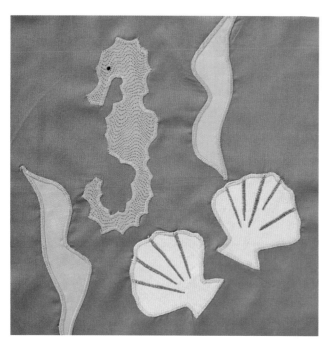

Seahorse and shells

Green fish and starfish

Palm tree island

Sailing boat

Fruit bowls

These blocks have been hand stitched, but you could make them just as well by machine. The blocks could be used as cushion panels. If joined with sashing across a wall hanging or quilt, they would be reminiscent of traditional Baltimore designs, with every block having a different set of fruit and placements.

Size of finished block: 37 cm (14½ in.) square

Satin stitch width: 3, narrowing to 1 for detailing

■ The diagrams show which pieces to stitch first, working up from layer to layer; always start stitching just under an overlap. You will need to snip into the turning allowance on inside curves, such as the foot of the bowl and the pineapple leaves, to achieve a smooth curve. Leave the detail stitching to last. If you are working by machine, use stitch width 3, narrowing to 1 on the pineapple leaf tips and all the detailing.

■ The oranges and lemons are slightly padded with wadding, giving a raised effect. The wadding is poked under the fruit through a gap in the stitching when the stitching is almost complete.

■ For detailing, the oranges and lemons have cross stitches, the grapes stem stitches and the cherries chain stitches; the apple and pear stalks are satin stitched.

Bowl with pineapple and watermelon slice

Basket with apples and pears

Basket with grapes and strawberries

Sewing orders

First
Second
Third

First
Second
Third
Fourth
Fifth

First
Second
Third

First
Second
Third

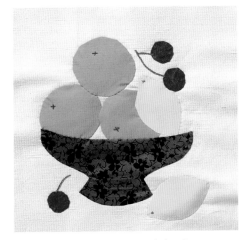

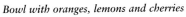

Bowl with oranges, lemons and cherries

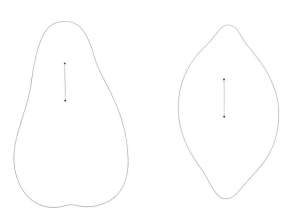

Hawaiian appliqué

Hawaiian motifs are very often worked in dark colours on a white background, although a patterned background fabric can make the quilt a little less stark. Use different motifs for each block.

Size of finished block: 36 cm (14 in.) square

Size of motif: 26 cm (10 in.)

■ To make the template, take a piece of paper the size you want the motif to be and fold it in quarters and then diagonally. Draw a spiky snowflake design radiating from the centre, cut through all the layers and unfold – much like a child's paper-people chain.

■ Pin the template to the motif fabric, making sure the grain is vertical, add a turning allowance of maximum 6 mm (¼ in.) – narrower is better if the design is spindly – and cut.

■ Tack the motif to the backing fabric along the spindles and start stitching on a straight area. If you have a cut-out in the centre of the motif, work this last. Press from on the wrong side.

Orange Peel

This is traditionally worked in just two colours, as in the project (see page 154). You could also vary the colour of the backing squares diagonally with white segments throughout. This block is best pieced by hand.

Size of finished block: 28 cm (11 in.) square

■ For the template, draw a 14 cm (5½ in.) square. Placing the compass point in one corner, trace a quarter circle with a 14 cm (5½ in.) radius. Repeat from the opposite corner. Cut out the resulting segment shape.

■ Pin the template to the motif fabric, with the grain running along the length of the shape. Add a 6 mm (¼ in.) turning allowance and cut out.

■ The backing fabric is best cut 17 cm (6½ in.) square and trimmed to size once appliquéd. Fold the square diagonally and use the crease line as a positioning guide for the segment. Hand appliqué the motifs in place.

■ Piece patches into vertical pairs and then assemble these strips to make the blocks.

Appliqué alphabet

These monograms can be used on many items, such as personalized cushions, scarves and pockets. They could even be worked intertwined on an appliqué wedding quilt block. The motifs are quite large and liable to stretch out of shape, so always cut with the grain line running vertically and match to the grain of the backing fabric.

Size of finished block: 24 cm (9½ in.) square

Motif height: 16.5 cm (6½ in.)

Satin stitch width: 3

■ Cut the backing fabric about 10 per cent larger than required. It will be trimmed to size once it has been stitched and pressed.

■ Pin the motifs carefully to the backing fabric – say, eight pins per motif – with the pins going across so that you can remove them easily as you machine stitch.

■ Some letters, such as M, V and S, are simple, with no cross-over stitching. By machine, start stitching these letters at an inside corner, where the stitching will show least. For the other letters, the diagrams (see pages 92–93) show the easiest direction in which to stitch, with the least number of threads to tie off at the beginning and end. The start and finish of the first line of stitching will be concealed by the subsequent stitch lines.

■ If you are hand stitching, start on a straight or smooth curve, not an inside corner, and work anticlockwise, using slipstitch. On the letters that have cross-overs (A, C, D, for example), hand embroider along the cross-over lines in stem, running or chain stitch using stranded embroidery silks.

■ The stitch directions shown on the diagrams are for machine stitching, which is best worked with the motif to the left of the needle, while hand stitching is worked anticlockwise.

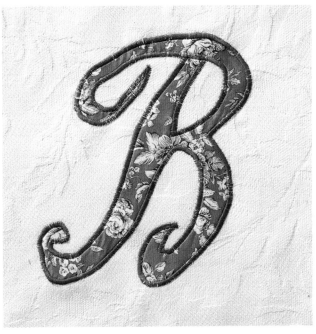

Templates

A B C

H I J K

O P Q

D E F G

L M N

R S T

Templates

Sewing order

●	Start
✕	Finish
———	First
———	Second
———	Third

Appliqué numbers

These numbers are used on the Child's Counting Quilt on page 130. You could also appliqué them onto children's pockets, bags or dungaree bibs, or scatter them on a plain curtain or duvet cover. Reduced to quarter size, they could be used on 'age' birthday cards.

Size of finished block: 11 cm (4¼ in.)

Motifs: 9 cm (3½ in.) tall

Satin stitch width: 3

■ Cut the motifs with the grain line running vertically. If you enlarge the numbers, it is best to match the grain of the motif to the grain of the backing fabric to avoid the risk of distortion and rippling.

■ The numbers 1, 2, 3, 5 and 7 can be stitched in one go. If you are machine stitching, start stitching at an inside corner, where the stitching will show the least. To manoeuvre around sharp corners, keep the needle in the fabric on the side of stitching away from the motif and spin the fabric around the needle before continuing.

■ On the numbers 4, 6, 8, 9 and 0, stitch the centre rings first and then work the outside of the motif, starting at an inside corner whenever possible.

■ If you are hand stitching, start on a straight or smooth curved area and work anticlockwise. Stitch the centre rings first.

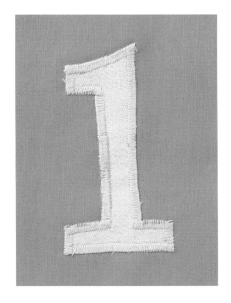

Templates

PROJECTS

Substitute any of the blocks used on the projects to make a
cushion, bag or quilt personal to you. The quantities given for
each project in the 'You will need' boxes are based on fabrics at
least 115 cm (45 in.) wide. 'Fat quarters' are great for appliqué,
but avoid them when buying material for patchwork projects as
you will be working with full-width fabric.

Four Patch silk scarf

The simple Four Patch block looks vibrant and jewel-like when isolated with plain borders. Silk is easy to sew because it holds a crease so well. This scarf has eight Four Patch windows, each measuring just 6 cm (2½ in.) square. As silk can fray easily, the seam allowances are all 1 cm (½ in.).

Size of scarf: 28 x 165 cm
(11 x 65 in.)
Size of finished block: 6 cm
(2½ in.) square

■ Cut a strip along the length of the fabric 30 cm (12 in.) wide x 167 cm (66 in.) long for the backing, and two strips 13 cm (5 in.) wide x 167 cm (66 in.) long for the sides of the scarf. From the remaining fabric, cut nine 8 x 15 cm (3½ x 6 in.) strips for the sashing between the blocks.

■ Referring to the Four Patch block (see page 10), draft and make eight multi-coloured blocks with bright silk squares, taking a 1-cm (½-in.) seam allowance throughout.

■ Join the blocks alternating with short strips of black silk to make the central band, with a strip of black at each end. Press the seams towards the black fabric.

■ Join the side strips to the patchwork panel and press the seams towards the side strips.

■ Lay the scarf on the backing fabric, with right sides together, and pin it in place. Silk frays easily, so use a small stitch. Machine stitch all around, leaving a gap of 10 cm (4 in.) near the centre of one long edge. Trim the corners and turn right side out. Hand stitch the gap closed and press.

You will need

● 1.7 m (2 yd) black silk
● 32 squares of bright silks, each 5 x 5 cm (2¼ x 2¼ in.)
● Matching thread

Courthouse Steps silk purse

Foundation blocks are easy to piece on a small scale – and the foundation fabric gives a slight stiffness to the work. This little purse is made up of three Courthouse Steps blocks – one each for the front, back and flap – and has a red silk lining. The vibrant scraps of silk catch and reflect the light, making it perfect for an evening purse.

Size of purse: 9 cm (3½ in.) square
Size of finished block: 9 cm (3½ in.) square

■ Referring to the Courthouse Steps block (see pages 54–55), draft and make three blocks as shown, using 2.5-cm (1-in.) silk strips and a 6-mm (¼-in.) seam allowance throughout. The blocks should each be 9 cm (3½ in.) square, plus the seam allowance.

■ Trim away the excess foundation fabric and then join the blocks together in a strip. Trim the lining to the same size as the patchwork. With right sides together, stitch the patchwork to the lining, leaving a 5-cm (2-in.) gap in one side. Trim the corners and turn right side out. Hand stitch the gap closed and press.

■ Fold the purse in thirds and hand stitch the two sides together. If desired, sew on a snap fastener or a Velcro patch to secure the flap.

You will need

- Silk scraps in seven colours, cut 2.5 cm (1 in.) wide and a maximum of 60 cm (24 in.) long
- Three 11.5-cm (4½-in.) foundation squares
- 11.5- x 32-cm (4½- x 12½-in.) piece of lining fabric in a colour to match the centre square
- Matching thread

Child's apron with patchwork pockets

Make the apron from sturdy, washable calico or fine canvas so that it's suitable for cooking, painting, craft and other messy activities. Three sizes are given – two for children and one adult size. For the blocks, I used plain, bright fabrics that stand out from the apron and chose Fly, Big Dipper and Broken Dishes for the pockets (see pages 11, 12 and 13). Any border strip would also work well, but complex blocks could look fussy on the big check of the apron fabric.

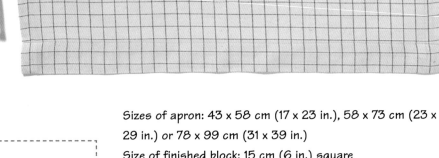

■ From the calico or canvas, cut a rectangle 53 x 68 cm, 68 x 83 cm or 88 x 109 cm (21 x 27, 27 x 33 or 35 x 43 in.) and cut away two quarter circles with a radius of 12.5, 18 or 35 cm (5, 7 or 13¾ in.) at the top corners.

You will need

- 70, 85 or 110 cm (27½, 33½ or 43¾ in.) calico or canvas
- Scraps of red, blue, pale and dark green for pockets, each 10 x 40 cm (4 x 16 in.)
- Large snap fastener
- Matching thread

Sizes of apron: 43 x 58 cm (17 x 23 in.), 58 x 73 cm (23 x 29 in.) or 78 x 99 cm (31 x 39 in.)
Size of finished block: 15 cm (6 in.) square

■ Also from the length of the calico or canvas, cut two 43- x 8-cm (17- x 3-in.) waist strips, and a 43- x 6-cm (17- x 2½-in.) neck strip. Fold all three strips in half lengthways, turn in raw edges and topstitch, folding under one short end also. Cut a 47- x 18-cm (18½- x 7-in.) piece of canvas or calico for the pocket lining.

■ Fold over 2.5 cm (1 in.) twice around the edge of the apron and topstitch.

■ Referring to the patchwork blocks, draft and piece three blocks – each 15-cm (6-in.) square, plus the seam allowance.

■ Join the blocks edge to edge and press the seams in the same direction along the strip. With right sides together, stitch the blocks to the lining along the top edge and press the seam away from blocks. Fold in half, so that the lower edges of the blocks and the lining are level, and 1 cm (½ in.) of lining folded over along the top edge. Stitch all the way round, leaving an 8-cm (3-in.) gap in one edge. Turn right side out, press flat

and topstitch the top edge; then pin and stitch to the apron. Stitch between the blocks to make compartments in the pocket strip.

■ Lay the apron wrong side up, pin the unfinished ends of the waist straps just below the arm curve, and the neck strap to the top edges of bib top (left of bib only for a child) so that they point towards the apron, and stitch along the turning seams. Turn the apron over and topstitch the straps close to the edges to secure.

■ Stitch the snap fastener to the inside of the top right side of the bib and to the neck strap end for a child's apron. If you are making an adult-sized apron, the neck strap can be stitched to the bib at both ends.

Patchwork bookmarks

Choose simple border blocks that are one patch deep or foundation blocks when working on a small scale. The foundation backings help to keep tiny blocks square. The designs are based on Sawtooth, Diamond Squares and Squares borders, with the backing of the bookmarks folded over to the front as the binding. The borders vary from 1–1.75 cm (½–⅝ in.) wide.

Size of bookmark: 6 x 21.5 cm (2½ x 8½ in.)

■ For Sawtooth, draft and make five 3.5-cm (1⅜-in.) triangle squares in random colours and piece edge to edge into a strip (see page 28). For Diamond Squares,

draft and make four finished size 5-cm (2-in.) blocks and piece edge to edge into a strip (see page 58). For Squares, cut and piece eight finished size 3-cm (1-in.) squares into a strip. Press the seams in the same direction along the strips.

■ Centre the patchwork on the backing fabric, with the interlining sandwiched in between, and pin the three layers together. Fold the top and bottom edges of the backing fabric to the front, folding under the raw edges, and topstitch. Repeat at the sides and press.

You will need

- Scraps of fabric for the patchwork
- 6- x 21.5-cm (2½- x 8½-in.) piece of cotton for the interlining
- 10- x 25.5-cm (4- x 10-in.) piece of fabric for backing
- Matching thread

Six-Point Christmas Star

Each of the diamonds is in a different pattern, so making this star is a good way of using up scraps of Christmas designs, ginghams, stripes and other small-patterned fabrics to match your Christmas decor. You could also use velvets, silks and sparkly fabrics.

Size of star: 22 cm (8½ in.) across
Length of finished diamond: 11 cm (4¼ in.)

■ Referring to the Six-Pointed Star block (see page 42), draft and cut 12 diamonds in different fabrics – each 11 cm (4¼ in.) long, plus the seam allowance. Piece into two six-point stars – but press all the seams open, not to the side, to avoid puckering at the seams when you pad it.

■ Place the two stars right sides together and stitch around the edge, leaving a gap on one of the seams midway between a point and a seam. Turn right side out, pad with wadding and hand stitch the gap closed.

■ To hang the star, stitch a short length of gold thread through one of the points and knot the ends.

You will need

- Small scraps of 12 toning fabrics
- Scraps of wadding or toy filling
- Matching thread
- Gold thread to hang

Crazy Christmas stocking

Use up all those leftover snippets of Christmas fabric for this stocking. It has a solid fabric cuff and back, but you could crazy-patch both sides.

Size of stocking: 43 cm (17 in.) tall x 20.5 cm (8 in.) wide at top

■ Make your template and cut the foundation fabric about 5 cm (2 in.) larger than required. Referring to the Crazy Patchwork block on page 163, work the front of the stocking. Press and trim to shape, 44.5 cm (17½ in.) tall x 22 cm (8½ in.) wide at the top. Cut the back of the stocking, remembering to turn the template over.

■ With right sides together, stitch the front and back of the stocking together. With right sides together, join the two strips for the cuff into a ring and hem one long side of the cuff. Slide the cuff over the top of the stocking, with the folded loop sandwiched in between, and stitch around the top. Turn the stocking right side out, fold the cuff down and press.

You will need

- 46- x 33-cm (18- x 13-in.) piece of foundation fabric (double if you are crazy patching both sides)
- Scraps of Christmas fabric for the patchwork
- Two 22- x 9-cm (8½- x 3½-in.) strips for the cuff
- 46- x 33-cm (18- x 13-in.) piece of fabric for the back (unless you are crazy patching both sides)
- 22- x 4-cm (8½- x 1½-in.) strip folded and topstitched for the hanging loop
- Matching thread

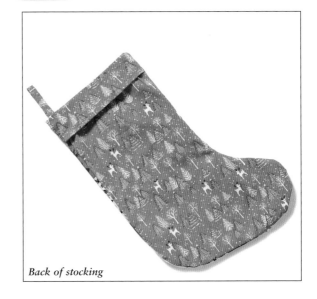

Back of stocking

Sawtooth border napkins

These elegant linen napkins have a random Sawtooth border along two sides and a binding all around the outer edge. You could use any of the border blocks on pages 58–62 for the borders.

Size of napkin: 56 cm (22 in.) square
Width of finished border: 5 cm (2 in.)

■ Referring to the Sawtooth border (see page 58), draft and make 19 triangle squares in random colours – each 5 cm (2 in.) square, plus the seam allowances. Join them edge to edge into strips of nine and ten. Press the seams in the same direction along the strips.

■ With right sides together, pin the shorter Sawtooth strip to the napkin 4.5 cm (1¾ in.) from the edge, level with the right-hand edge of the napkin. (It will not reach the whole length of the napkin.) Stitch, fold back and press flat. Turn the napkin anticlockwise and pin the other strip so that it overlaps the first border by one triangle square. Stitch, fold back and press.

■ Stitch the right side of binding to the back of the napkin, fold the binding over to the front, fold the raw edge under and topstitch. Working anticlockwise, repeat on all sides, folding in the end of the binding strips and stitching across or hand stitching to neaten.

You will need

- 19 scraps at least 8 cm (3 in.) square for the patchwork
- 56-cm (22-in.) square of linen
- Four 60- x 4-cm (23½- x 1½-in.) strips of fabric for the binding
- Matching thread

Diamond Squares napkin rings

The diamond squares on this napkin ring are just 5 cm (2 in.) square. Look for small-patterned fabrics with motifs, such as the blue and red birds, to use as centres, like tiny framed pictures. The backing fabric is folded to the front as binding.

Size of napkin rings: 7.5 x 17.5 cm (3 x 7 in.)
Size of finished block: 5 cm (2 in.) square

■ Referring to the Diamond Squares border (see page 60), draft and make three diamond squares in two different colours – each 5 cm (2 in.) square, plus the seam allowance – and piece into a strip.

■ Centre the patchwork on the backing fabric and pin it in place, sandwiching a layer of fabric or interfacing in between the patchwork and the backing to stiffen. Fold the top and bottom edges of the backing fabric to the front, folding under the raw edges, and topstitch. Repeat at the sides. With right sides together, overstitch the ends of the ring together and turn it right side out.

You will need

- Scraps of fabric in two colours and three centre motifs
- 12- x 22-cm (4¾- x 8¾-in.) piece of backing fabric
- 7.5- x 17.5-cm (3- x 7-in.) piece of interfacing or scrap of cotton fabric
- Matching thread

Gentleman's Fancy shoulder bag

The green in the patchwork panel matches the plain green of the bag's back. Blocks with a central square and radiating patches work best; Air Castle or Pin Wheel are good alternatives.

Size of bag: 47 x 50 cm (18½ x 19½ in.)
Size of finished block: 31 cm (12 in.)

■ Referring to the Gentleman's Fancy block (see page 34), draft and make a block 31-cm (12-in.) square, plus the seam allowance.

■ Cut the borders from pink striped fabric. You need two 33- x 12.5-cm (13- x 5-in.) strips for the top and bottom borders cut from the length of the fabric and two 60- x 10-cm (24- x 4-in.) strips for the side borders cut from the width. Attach the top and bottom borders to the block first, and then the side borders. Press the seams outwards.

■ Lay the front of the bag on the wadding, tack in place and quilt along all the seams.

■ Cut a 49- x 55-cm (19¼- x 21½-in.) piece of green fabric for the back of the bag. Stitch the front of the bag to the back along the lower edge.

You will need

- 43 cm (17 in.) pink striped furnishing-weight fabric for the borders, strap and patchwork
- 60 cm (24 in.) green furnishing-weight fabric for the back of bag and patchwork
- 15- x 90-cm (6- x 35½-in.) piece of cream floral furnishing-weight fabric for the patchwork
- 49- x 100-cm (19- x 40-in.) piece of lining fabric
- 50-cm (19½-in.) square of 70-g (2-oz) polyester wadding
- 61-cm (24-in.) length of elastic, 6 mm (¼ in.) wide
- Matching thread

■ Cut a 100- x 8-cm (40- x 3-in.) strip of pink striped fabric for the strap. Fold it in half, turn under the raw edges and topstitch the strap lengthways, padding it with scraps of wadding as you go.

■ With right sides together, stitch the lining to the bag along the top edges, taking a 1 cm (½ in.) seam allowance, sandwiching the strap ends in between the lining and the back about 2.5 cm (1 in.) in from the sides.

■ Stitch the side seams (lining to lining and front to back), taking a 1 cm (½ in.) seam allowance, leaving a 24-cm (9½-in.) gap in the lining; this will be stitched once the bag has been turned right side out. Pinch the bottom corners together so that the side and bottom seams are in line and stitch across about 4 cm (1½ in.) in from the corners.

■ Turn the bag right side out and push the lining into the bag by 2.5 cm (1 in.). Topstitch around the top of the bag 1 cm (½ in.) and 5 cm (2 in.) down to create a channel. Snip the seam of this channel on one side of the bag, so you can thread through the elastic, and hand stitch to secure.

Grandmother's Flower Garden cushion

This piped cushion is made in furnishing fabrics with appliquéd Flower Garden rosettes. It is a good way of using up any leftover rosettes from a quilt project or for trying out the technique.

Size of cushion: 38 cm (15 in.) square

■ Referring to the Grandmother's Flower Garden block (see page 40), draft and make two floral hexagon rosettes, and tack and press five pointed pentagons over papers for the leaves. Press the rosettes and leaves and remove the papers.

■ Cut a 40-cm (16-in.) square of checked fabric for the cushion front. For the back, cut one piece measuring 40 x 30 cm (16 x 12 in.) and another measuring 40 x 12 cm (16 x 5 in.).

■ Pin and then hand appliqué (using slipstitch) the rosettes and the green leaf shapes to the cushion front.

You will need

- 40 cm (16 in.) checked fabric for the cushion front and back
- 1.65 m (65 in.) piping cord
- 50 cm (20 in.) fabric for piping
- 20- x 40-cm (8- x 16-in.) piece of floral fabric for the rosettes and scraps for the centres and leaves
- 30-cm (12-in.) zip
- Matching thread
- 38-cm (15-in.) square cushion pad

■ Cut the piping fabric on the bias into strips 5 cm (2 in.) wide and join into a continuous length. Fold the strip over the piping and stitch close to the piping with a zipper foot. Pin around the edge of the cushion front and stitch again. Trim the piping to size, leaving 2 cm (¾ in.) fabric at one end. Fold this under to cover the raw edge of the other end where they meet.

■ With right sides together, tack the two back pieces together along one long side, taking a 1-cm (½-in.) seam. Machine stitch from each corner for 3.5 cm (1½ in.). Press the seam open and lay the zip right side down on the wrong side of the seam. Tack and then machine stitch the zip in place. Remove the tacking stitches.

■ Open the zip. With right sides together, stitch the front of the cushion to the back, stitching as close to the piping as possible. Trim the edges and zig-zag or overlock to secure and neaten. Turn right side out.

Star upon Stars cushion

The star is made of five different Liberty lawn fabrics, bordered and backed by heavier-weight furnishing fabrics, which is best for a floor cushion, as it will take more wear. The cushion pad is 56 cm (22 in.) square.

Size of cushion: 53 cm (21 in.) square
Size of finished star block: 47 cm (18½ in.) square
Length of finished diamond: 9 cm (3½ in.)

■ Referring to the Star upon Stars block (see page 45), draft and cut the fabrics. The grain line should run along the centre of the diamonds.

■ Each row is in a different fabric. Cut eight diamonds for the centre (A) and another eight for the tips (E) of the star, 16 diamonds each for the second (B) and fourth (D) rows, and 24 for the third (C) row.

■ Lay the pieces on a design board in sequence. Piece into eight strips each of ABC, BCD and CDE. Press the seams in alternate directions. Assemble into star points and then into the star.

You will need

- 55 cm (21¾ in.) furnishing-weight fabric for the back and borders
- 13 cm (5 in.) lawn fabric in each of four patterns (A, B, D, E)
- 20 cm (8 in.) lawn fabric in fifth pattern (C)
- 25 cm (10 in.) cream floral furnishing-weight fabric for the outer squares and triangles
- 55-cm (21¾-in.) square of 70-g (2-oz) polyester wadding
- 46-cm (18-in.) zip
- Matching thread
- 56-cm (22-in.) square cushion pad

■ Piece the triangles (see page 45). If the triangles and squares are heavier than the stars, press the seams towards the star; if they are all the same weight, press the seams away from the star.

■ From the length of the furnishing fabric, cut four border strips 5 cm (2 in.) wide. Attach the borders first to the side edges (trimming off any excess length), then to the top and bottom. Press the seams towards the borders.

■ Tack the cushion top to the wadding. Quilt along the seams around central star A, then around star B, and so on. This will emphasize the starburst effect.

■ Cut one backing piece 55 x 41 cm (22 x 16½ in) and another 55 x 16 cm (22 x 6½ in.). With right sides facing, tack the two pieces together along one long side, taking a 1-cm (½-in.) seam. Machine stitch from each corner for 3.5 cm (1½ in.). Press the seam open and lay the zip right side down on the wrong side of the seam. Tack and then machine stitch the zip in place. Remove the tacking stitches.

■ Pin the patchwork right side down on the cushion back, with zip open. Machine stitch all around, taking a 1 cm (½ in.) seam allowance, snip off excess fabric on corners and turn cover right side out. Topstitch around cushion edge.

Swamp Patch floor cushion

When the Swamp Patch blocks are joined edge to edge and two or more fabrics are used for the corner triangles, Broken Dishes blocks appear between the stars. To keep the star pattern prominent, use the darkest fabric on the triangles that make up the arms of each star.

Size of cushion: 75 cm (29½ in.) square
Size of finished block: 34 cm (13½ in.) square

■ From cream floral fabric, cut one back piece measuring 77 x 56 cm (30½ x 22 in.) and one measuring 77 x 21 cm (30½ x 8½ in.).

■ With right sides together, tack the two back pieces together along one long side taking a 1-cm (½-in.) seam. Machine stitch from each corner for 3.5 cm (1½ in.). Press the seam open and lay the zip right side down on the wrong side of the seam. Tack and machine stitch the zip in place. Remove the tacking stitches.

■ From plum fabric, cut four borders measuring 74 x 5 cm (29½ x 2 in.). Two of these are slightly longer than needed but it is easier to trim later.

You will need

- 80 cm (31½ in.) large-scale cream floral fabric for the back and centre squares
- 35 cm (14 in.) plum fabric for the border and stars
- 15 cm (6 in.) in each of two pink fabrics for the small inner triangles and the corner triangles
- 35 cm (14 in.) cream sprig fabric
- 15 cm (6 in.) of a second cream sprig fabric
- 80-cm (31½-in.) square of 70-g (2-oz) wadding
- 70-cm (27½-in.) zip
- Matching thread
- 79-cm (31-in.) square cushion pad

■ Referring to the Swamp Patch block on page 30, draft the templates and cut the pieces for four blocks – each 34 cm (13½ in.) square, plus the seam allowance. Use some of the cushion back fabric for the centre squares, one of the pinks for the small inner triangles and plum for the star triangles. The smallest piece of the cream sprig fabric and the second pink are for the corner triangles, and the other cream sprig fabric is for the triangles surrounding the star. Piece the blocks and press the vertical seams in the same direction across the block. Join the blocks edge to edge into two vertical strips, then join the strips together to make a square. Add the borders to top and bottom first, then to the sides. Press the seams towards the borders.

■ Lay the patchwork on the wadding; tack it in place. Quilt along every seam (see page 159), matching the thread colour to the fabric. Remove the tacking stitches.

■ Complete as for the cushion on page 108, but when topstitching around the edge of the cushion, match the thread colour to the fabric.

Lady of the Lake floor cushion

This bold, graphic design works best using strongly contrasting plain or small-scale patterned fabrics. Use furnishing-weight fabrics, as they will take more wear and tear.

Size of cushion: 66 cm (26 in.) square
Size of finished block: 28 cm (11 in.) square

■ From teal fabric, cut two back pieces measuring 70 x 56 cm (27½ x 22 in.) and 70 x 18 cm (27½ x 7½ in.) respectively.

■ With right sides together, tack the two back pieces together along one long side, taking a 1-cm (½-in.) seam. Machine stitch from each corner for 3.5 cm (1½ in.). Press the seam open and lay the zip right side down on the wrong side of the seam. Tack and then machine stitch the zip in place. Remove the tacking stitches.

■ Cut two borders in cream and two in teal, each measuring 70 x 9 cm (28 x 3¼ in.). These are larger than needed, but it is easier to trim them to size later.

■ Referring to the Lady of the Lake block (see page 22), draft the templates and cut the pieces for four blocks – each 28 cm (11 in.) square, plus the seam allowance. If

You will need

- 1 m (1 yd) teal furnishing-weight fabric
- 50 cm (20 in.) cream furnishing-weight fabric
- 63-cm (25-in.) zip
- 70-cm (27½-in.) square of 70-g (2-oz) polyester wadding
- 66-cm (26-in.) square cushion pad
- Matching thread

the fabric has a pattern or texture direction, it is best to keep this uniform across the cushion.

■ Piece the blocks and press the seams towards the darker fabric on the small triangle squares, then towards the larger triangles. Join the blocks edge to edge into two vertical strips, then join the strips together to make a square. Add the borders – teal to the teal edges first, then the cream edges. Press the seams towards the borders.

■ Lay the patchwork on the wadding and tack it in place. Quilt along every seam (see page 159), matching the thread colour to the fabric. Remove the tacking stitches. Trim the cushion front and back to 69 cm (27 in.) square.

■ Pin the patchwork right side down on the cushion back, with the zip open. Machine stitch all around, snip off excess fabric on the corners, and turn the cover right side out. Topstitch around the edge of the cushion, again matching the thread colour to the fabric.

Broken Dishes drawstring bag

The bag is made of canvas-weight checked and striped fabrics. Choosing fabrics with woven, rather than printed, designs ensures that checks and stripes follow the grain of the fabric. Tartans and old-fashioned pillow ticking in blue, brown or black are perfect.

Size of bag: 33 x 37 cm (13 x 14½ in.)
Size of finished block: 15 cm (6 in.) square

■ Referring to the Broken Dishes block (see page 11), make a block 15 cm (6 in.) square, plus the seam allowance.

■ With right sides together, pin the frame strip along the top edge of the block and machine stitch, cutting off the excess at the end of this side. Repeat along the bottom of the block, again cutting off the excess. Finally, add the checked fabric to the sides. Press the seams away from the block.

■ Cut the back of the bag 35 x 43 cm (14 x 15½ in.), 3 strips 7cm (2¾ in.) wide and one 14 cm (5½ in.) wide for the bag top from the remaining width. Add them to the patchwork as for the frame. Press seams away from the block.

■ Tack the patchwork backing fabric to the back of the patchwork, and topstitch the seams.

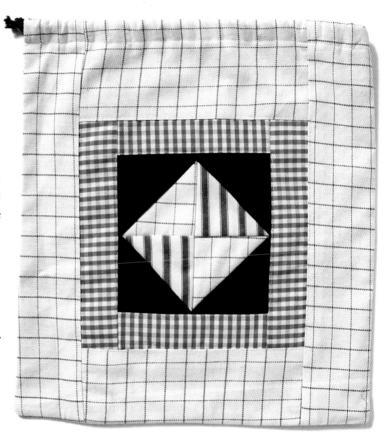

You will need

- 36 cm (14 in.) checked canvas for the back, borders and block
- 5- x 84-cm (2 x 33-in.) strip of small checked fabric for the frame
- 10-cm (4-in.) square of striped fabric and 20-cm (8-in.) square piece of navy fabric for the patchwork
- 35 x 43 cm (14 x 15½ in.) piece of fabric for the patchwork backing
- 80-cm (32-in.) length of cord
- Matching thread

■ With right sides together, stitch the front to the back, taking a 1 cm (½ in.) seam, leaving 6 cm (2½ in.) unstitched at the top of each side.

■ Press the tops of the seams open, fold the unstitched edges under and topstitch to neaten.

■ Turn the bag right side out. Fold the top of the bag down into the bag by 5 cm (2 in.), fold the raw edge under by 1 cm (½ in.) and stitch by machine. This will give a channel through which to thread the cord.

Beach duffel bag

Although it is called Nelson's Victory, this patchwork border design resembles beach huts, the blue and cream stripes and checks looking like sun and shadow on wooden boards, with a dark blue sky and gingham sea. The bag is quilted and lined in cotton. Lining it with shower-proof fabric or oilcloth would make it perfect for wet swimming costumes.

Size of bag: 45 cm (17¾ in.) tall

■ Referring to the Nelson's Victory border pattern (see page 62), draft and piece a border 16 cm (6¼ in.) deep, finished size. There will be six striped and six mirror-image checked patches in all.

You will need

- 20 x 60 cm (8 x 24 in.) each of large-checked and striped fabrics for the patchwork
- 70 cm (27½ in.) small-checked furnishing-weight fabric
- 38 cm (15 in.) navy furnishing-weight fabric or canvas
- 75 cm (29½ in.) lining fabric
- 97 x 38 cm (38¼ x 15 in.) piece of 70-g (2-oz) polyester wadding
- Matching thread

■ Cut the remaining fabric for the bag. From checked furnishing fabric, cut a 28 x 97-cm (11 x 38¼-in.) piece for the top of the bag, a 9 x 97-cm (3½ x 38¼-in.) piece for the bottom of the bag, a base circle with a radius of 15 cm (6 in.) and a 12 x 7.5-cm (5 x 3-in.) strip folded and stitched lengthways for the strap loop.

■ From across the width of the navy fabric, cut a patchwork border strip measuring 5 x 97 cm (2 x 38¼ in.). Also from across the width of the navy fabric, cut two strips for the strap 7.5 x 81-cm (3 x 32-in.), join together and press the seam open. Fold lengthways, turn under the raw edges, and topstitch the whole length.

■ From the lining fabric, cut a piece measuring 43 x 97 cm (17 x 38¼ in.) and a circle with a radius of 15 cm (6 in.).

■ Join the fabrics together in the following order along one long edge, taking a 1 cm (½ in.) seam – lining fabric, wide checked strip, patchworked strip, narrow navy strip and narrow checked strip. Press the seams away from the patchwork.

■ Pin the wadding so that it comes halfway up the top checked strip and quilt along the seams. (Note that you're only stitching through the wadding and outer bag fabric – not the lining.)

■ With right sides together, stitch the side seam, making a tube and leaving a gap of 13 cm (5 in.) in the checked fabric just above the lining. Press the seam open.

■ Pin and stitch the lining circle to the lining and the checked circle to the lower edge of the bag, taking a 1 cm (½ in.) seam, with the strap loop folded and poking out to the right side of the bag near the side seam.

■ Fold in the fabric on either side of the gap so that it's level with the side seam to neaten, then turn the bag right side out through the gap.

■ Fold the top 6.5 cm (2½ in.) of the checked fabric down into the inside of the bag, pin in place and topstitch level with the lining seam to form a channel for the strap.

■ Thread the strap through both the channel and the loop at the bottom of the bag and stitch the two ends together. (You will need to undo the fold stitching a little and restitch it when you have joined the two ends of the strap in order to make the join lie flat.)

Dog Tooth Split sunglasses case

This design is perfect for the seaside! The case is quilted and lined to protect your sunglasses from damage.

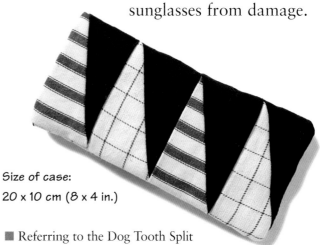

Size of case:
20 x 10 cm (8 x 4 in.)

■ Referring to the Dog Tooth Split patchwork border (see page 61), draft and piece two strips of eight triangles. The base of the triangles should be 5 cm (2 in.) and the height 10 cm (4 in.) finished size.

■ Cut the wadding in half, then pin one piece to the back of each piece of patchwork. Quilt along the seams on the right side.

■ Cut the lining fabric in half, then stitch one piece to a short end of each of the patchwork strips. With right sides together, join the two sides of the bag around the two long and one short sides, leaving a 5-cm (2-in.) gap in the lining on one side. Turn right side out and topstitch the gap closed.

You will need

- 26-cm (10-in.) square of each of navy, striped and checked furnishing-weight fabrics
- 24-cm (9-in.) square of lining fabric
- 24-cm (9-in.) square of wadding
- Matching thread

Log Cabin needle book

This pretty needle book has four felt pages for sewing needles. Foundation blocks are easy to work on a small scale – and the foundation fabric gives a stiffness to the Log Cabin cover.

Size of case: 14 cm (5½ in.) square

■ Referring to the Log Cabin block (see pages 54–55), draft and make two 14-cm (5½-in.) square blocks. Trim the foundation fabric to size and stitch the blocks together, side by side (or use a plain square of fabric for the back).

You will need

- Scraps of fabric for the patchwork
- Two 15-cm (6-in.) squares of cotton foundation fabric
- 30- x 15-cm (12- x 6-in.) piece of lining fabric
- Two 12- x 24-cm (4¾- x 9½-in.) pieces of felt
- Matching thread

■ With right sides together, stitch the patchwork to the lining, leaving a 5-cm (2-in.) gap in the lower edge. Turn right side out through the gap and hand stitch the gap closed.

■ With the inside of the book facing upwards, centre and pin the two sheets of felt in place and machine down the centre, along the 'spine' of the book.

Big Dipper pincushion

Although you could use any patchwork block, Big Dipper is easy to draft and piece on a small scale and can even be worked with every triangle in a different scrap of fabric.

Size of pincushion: 15 cm (6 in.) square

You will need

- 8 pieces of bright cottons, each 10 cm (4 in.) square
- Kapok or leftover scraps of wadding
- Matching thread

■ Referring to the Big Dipper block (see page 13), draft and make two blocks, 15 cm (6 in.) square.

■ With right sides together, stitch the two sides of the cushion together, leaving a 5-cm (2-in.) gap in one side. Turn right side out through the gap, fill with kapok or leftover wadding and hand stitch the gap closed.

Pineapple sewing box lid

Pineapple patchwork has alternating strips of pale and darker-toned fabric to make the design work. Using just two strongly contrasting fabrics gives a dramatic effect; using fabrics close in tone gives the appearance of basket weave.

Size of lid: 25 cm (9¾ in.) across

■ Referring to the Pineapple block (see page 56), draft and make a block 27 cm (10½ in.) wide. The centre square on this one measures 4 cm (1½ in.) when stitched, and there are seven dark and light strips. You won't need to fill out the dark corners as the block will be trimmed to a 27-cm (10½-in.) diameter circle.

■ Stitch the ends of the border strip together, leaving a 2.5-cm (1-in.) gap for inserting the elastic. Fold in half lengthways and stitch it to the outside edge of the trimmed patchwork.

■ With right sides together, lay the lining circle on top of the patchwork, the border strip sandwiched between, and stitch, leaving a 5-cm (2-in.) gap. Turn right side out and hand stitch the gap. Thread the elastic through the gap in the border, and hand stitch the gap closed.

You will need

- Scraps of fabric 3 cm (1⅛ in.) wide for the patchwork
- 79- x 8-cm (31- x 3-in.) piece of cream sprig fabric for the border and a 27-cm (10½-in.) diameter circle of cream sprig fabric for the lining
- 30-cm (12-in.) square of foundation fabric
- 70-cm (27½-in.) length of narrow elastic
- Matching thread

Four-patch sampler quilt

Sampler quilts can be made of any number of different quilt blocks – appliqué, or patchwork, or a combination. Keeping to the same grid blocks (four-, five-, seven- or nine-patch) gives uniformity. This quilt uses all the larger four-patch blocks, with Odd Fellow's Chain in the centre.

Size of quilt: 155 cm (61 in.) square
Size of each finished block: 30.5 cm (12 in.) square; central block 61 cm (24 in.) square
Width of border and sashing: 6.5 cm (2½ in.); frame around central block 5 cm (2 in.)

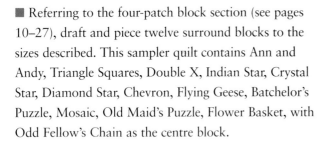
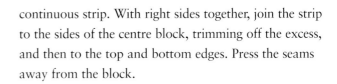

■ Referring to the four-patch block section (see pages 10–27), draft and piece twelve surround blocks to the sizes described. This sampler quilt contains Ann and Andy, Triangle Squares, Double X, Indian Star, Crystal Star, Diamond Star, Chevron, Flying Geese, Batchelor's Puzzle, Mosaic, Old Maid's Puzzle, Flower Basket, with Odd Fellow's Chain as the centre block.

■ Cut the pale yellow fabric for the centre frame into strips 4.5 cm (1¾ in.) wide and join to make a

continuous strip. With right sides together, join the strip to the sides of the centre block, trimming off the excess, and then to the top and bottom edges. Press the seams away from the block.

■ Take 1.1 m (43 in.) of the yellow striped fabric for the sashing and borders, cut it into fourteen 7.5-cm (3-in.) strips across the width of the fabric, and join into one continuous length.

■ Lay the blocks out in sequence. Join the top middle pair and the bottom middle pair horizontally edge to edge, with a length of sashing (cut from the long strip) in between each block, and press the seams towards the sashing. Stitch a sashing strip to the upper and lower edges of the centre block and join the upper and lower pairs to this. Press the seams towards the sashing.

■ Sash the left- and right-hand edges of the central piece. Join the four left- and right-hand side blocks into a vertical strip, with a length of sashing in between each block. Join these strips to the left and right of the centre block. Press the seams towards the sashing.

You will need

- 2.5 m (3 yd) in total of plain colourful fabrics for the blocks
- 20 cm (8 in.) pale yellow cotton fabric for the centre frame
- 1.5 m (59 in.) yellow striped cotton fabric for the sashing, borders and binding
- 1.7-m (67-in.) square of cotton fabric, or equivalent seamed, for the backing
- 1.7-m (67-in.) square of 70-g (2-oz) polyester wadding
- Matching thread

■ Attach lengths of the sashing to the side edges of the quilt and then to the top and bottom edges. Press the seams away from the blocks.

■ Lay the backing wrong side up and cover with the wadding. Lay the quilt top right side up on the wadding and backing, and tack through all three layers, in a vertical, horizontal and diagonal grid.

■ Quilt 'in the ditch' or just next to it, over the seam for extra strength (see page 159), in thread that matches the fabrics.

■ Trim off any excess wadding and backing fabric.

■ Cut the remaining yellow striped fabric into six strips 6 cm (2½ in.) wide and join into one length for the binding. Fold under and press 1 cm (½ in.) along one long edge. Bind the quilt from the back (see page 172), adding a little of the wadding remnants as you go.

Nine-patch framed quilt in Liberty lawns

This 25-block quilt has a repeat design of Nine Patch blocks, with alternating dark and light frames. The Nine Patch blocks and many of the inner frames are random. In all, about 50 fabrics are used; it is advisable to buy full-width fabric, not 'fat quarters' for this.

Size of quilt: 240 cm (95 in.) square
Size of each finished block: 47 cm (18½ in.) square

■ Cut 225 7-cm (2¾-in.) squares for the blocks. Piece 25 Nine Patch blocks (see page 29) in a variety of colour combinations.

■ Now cut the rest of the fabric into 6.5-cm (2½-in.) strips across the fabric width, and join together to make continuous lengths of each fabric. Lawn is very light and these fabrics are highly patterned, so seams in the strips will not detract from the design and will make the most economical use of the fabric. Put aside the four darks and pales for the borders and binding fabric for later.

■ Using the palest fabrics first, frame each block; first add the sides, cutting the strip to length as you go, and then the top and bottom. Press the seams outwards.

You will need

- 1 m (1 yd) each of two dark and two pale fabrics for the outer block frames
- 5 m (5½ yd) in total of a variety of toning fabrics for blocks
- 75 cm (30 in.) dark fabric for the binding
- 260-cm (102-in.) square of white or coloured cotton, or the equivalent seamed, for the backing
- 260-cm (102-in.) square of 70-g (2-oz) polyester wadding
- Matching thread

■ The second frame is made up of two different fabrics, which are best attached in Log Cabin style (see pages 54–55) – piecing a first and second strip clockwise around the block in one fabric and the third and fourth in a different fabric.

■ Finally, use the pales and darks for the outer frames. Lay the blocks out in five rows of five and decide whether a pale or a dark frame would work best for each one. Alternate light and dark frames across the quilt. The outer frames are not random, so keep to your chosen sequence throughout.

■ Join the blocks into five vertical strips and press the seams in alternate directions. Join these strips and press the seams in the same direction across the quilt.

■ To quilt, centre the wadding on the backing fabric and then centre the quilt top on top. Tack through all three layers, vertically, horizontally and diagonally (see page 157). Starting in the centre of the central block, machine or hand quilt over every seam, quilting the nine-patch seams first and then the frames. Leave quilting the seams that join the blocks until the end.

■ Remove the tacking thread carefully – it may be caught by machine-quilting stitches.

■ Trim off the excess wadding and backing.

■ Cut the binding fabric into strips 6 cm (2½ in.) wide across the width of the fabric. Join them together to make a continuous strip and press the seams. Fold over one long edge by about 1 cm (½ in.) and press. Bind the quilt from the back (see page 172), adding a little of the wadding remnants as you go.

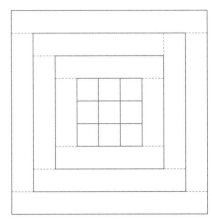

Fly block cot quilt

This is a soft and warm cot quilt in blues and greens. The plain and simple blue and green fabrics contrast with the busy design of the blue rose design fabric. The quilt is four blocks across and four down, with top and lower edge borders made up of random triangle squares.

Size of quilt: 76 x 106 cm (30 x 41½ in.)
Size of each finished block: 18 cm (7 in.)

■ Referring to the Fly block (see page 12), draft and make six blue floral/mid-blue blocks, five floral/pale blue blocks and five floral/green blocks. Piece 16 random 9-cm (3½-in.) triangle squares from the leftovers and join them into two strips.

You will need

- 75 cm (30 in.) blue floral fabric
- 50 cm (20 in.) each of mid blue and pale blue cotton fabric
- 25 cm (10 in.) green cotton
- Two contrasting strips 7.5 cm (3 in.) wide, cut across the width of the fabric, for the top and bottom sashing
- 86- x 116-cm (34- x 45½-in.) piece of cotton fabric for backing
- 86- x 116-cm (34- x 45½-in.) piece of 70-g (2-oz) polyester wadding
- 25 cm (10 in.) binding fabric
- Matching thread

■ Lay the blocks out in sequence, with four blocks across and four down, and assemble. Sash the top and bottom edges with the contrasting strips and join the strips of triangle squares to the top and bottom edges. Press the seams towards the sashing.

■ Centre the wadding on the backing fabric and then centre the quilt top on top. Tack through all three layers, vertically, horizontally and diagonally (see page 157).

■ Quilt along every seam (see page 159). Remove the tacking thread carefully – it may be caught by machine-quilting stitches.

■ Cut the fabric for the binding across the width of the fabric into four strips 6 cm (2½ in.) wide, fold one long edge over by about 1 cm (½ in.) and press the entire length.

■ Bind the quilt from the back (see page 172), adding a little of the wadding remnants as you go.

Tumbling Blocks baby quilt

This is a soft baby quilt made from printed lawns. It is a good design for using a multitude of scraps, provided they are in pale, mid and dark tones. It can be worked over papers, seamed by hand or by machine. The backing fabric is folded over to the front as the binding.

Size of quilt: 50 x 64 cm (19½ x 25 in.)
Length of each finished diamond: 9 cm (3½ in.)

■ Referring to the Tumbling Blocks block (see page 43), draft and piece 32 blocks; the diamond should be 9 cm (3½ in.) long when stitched.

■ Cut 12 extra diamonds in a pale colour to even out the top and bottom edges and, using a finished block as template, 6 half hexagons for the side edges.

■ Lay all the blocks out in sequence. For rows 1, 3, 5 and 7, you will need five whole blocks; for rows 2, 4 and 6, you will need four whole blocks. Start in a corner and join two blocks together side by side, then add a third one below them. Next, piece a block to the right of the

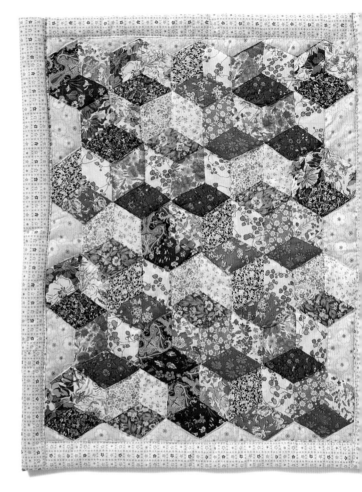

lower one and a fourth below this pair, always trying to have just two edges to stitch each time. Finally, level the edges by adding the extra diamonds and half hexagons. Press all the seams in the same direction across the quilt.

■ Centre the quilt top on the wadding and backing. Tack through all three layers vertically, horizontally and diagonally (see page 157).

■ Quilt 'in the ditch' (see page 159) of every seam.

■ Starting with top and bottom edges, fold the wadding and backing over to the front of the quilt. Fold under the edge of the backing fabric, and topstitch by machine or slipstitch by hand. Repeat on the side edges. The excess wadding will make the binding slightly puffy.

You will need

- 15 cm (6 in.) each of four pale, four mid and four dark tones of cotton fabric for the whole blocks
- 30 cm (12 in.) cotton fabric for the part blocks around the edge
- 64- x 78-cm (25- x 30½-in.) piece of cotton fabric for the backing
- 64- x 78-cm (25- x 30½-in.) piece of 70-g (2-oz) polyester wadding
- Matching thread

Double Irish Chain quilt

This is a five-patch block with two blocks to draft and piece – one mainly white, the other mainly coloured. The chain design appears when the alternating blocks are pieced edge to edge. An opaque white fabric avoids show-through.

Size of quilt: 190 x 190 cm (75 x 75 in.)
Size of each finished block: 38 cm (15 in.) square

■ A quilt needs an odd number of blocks across and down for the design to be symmetrical, so measure the bed and bed drop and divide into 3, 5, 7 or 9 to work out the size of block that you need. The blocks are best made 23–38 cm (9–15 in.) square.

■ Referring to the Double Irish Chain block on page 26, draft and make 13 blocks with a blue and green checkered pattern and 12 white blocks with blue corners. Because the checkered patches are alternated with white, you may have to trim excess dark fabric from the seams to avoid show-through.

■ Lay the blocks out in five rows of five. The first, middle and last strip should have checkered blocks top and bottom, while the second and fourth strips should

have white blocks top and bottom. Join the blocks edge to edge in five vertical strips. Press the seams in alternate directions from strip to strip.

■ Assemble the strips and press all the vertical seams in one direction across the quilt.

■ Lay the backing wrong side up on your work surface, with the wadding on top (see pages 156-159). Lay the quilt top right side up on the wadding and backing. Tack well, in a vertical, horizontal and diagonal grid. Quilt 'in the ditch' or over the seams, matching the thread to the patch colour if you are quilting by machine. If you are quilting by hand, use white thread throughout.

■ Trim off the excess wadding and backing.

■ Cut eight binding strips 5 cm (2 in.) wide across the width of the fabric and join end to end in pairs. Fold under and press 1 cm (½ in.) along one long edge.

■ Bind the quilt from the back (see page 172), adding a little of the wadding remnants as you go.

You will need

- *2 m (79 in.) blue cotton fabric for the blocks and binding*
- *90 cm (36 in.) green cotton fabric*
- *2.5 m (90 in.) white cotton fabric*
- *210-cm (83-in.) square (or equivalent seamed) of cotton fabric for the backing*
- *210-cm (83-in.) square 70-g (2-oz) polyester wadding*
- *Matching thread (or white thread, if hand quilting)*

Grandmother's Fan coverlet

This heavily padded coverlet, with vintage pink and cream toile de Jouy sashing, is four blocks across and four down, with a wide binding. The backing fabric on the blocks is a rich cream and the quarter circles are dark pink to match the toile de Jouy. The soft floral fabrics on the fan are in keeping with the vintage fabric.

Size of quilt: 158 cm (62 in.) square
Size of finished block: 28 cm (11 in.) square

You will need

- 2.5 m (90 in.) toile de Jouy
- 30 cm (12 in.) each of five different fabrics for the patches
- 20 cm (8 in.) pink fabric for the quarter circle patches
- 16 squares of cream fabric for backing the blocks, each 33 cm (13 in.) square
- 180-cm (71-in.) square of backing fabric, or equivalent seamed
- 180-cm (71-in.) square of 140-g (4-oz) polyester wadding
- Matching thread

■ Referring to the Grandmother's Fan block (see page 52), draft and make sixteen blocks. Trim to 29.5 cm (11½ in.) square.

■ The toile de Jouy has a distinct pattern direction that needs to be kept uniform across the quilt. Cut three binding strips 18 cm (7 in.) wide from the length of the toile de Jouy and join them all together to make one continuous strip. Fold one long edge over by about 1 cm (½ in.) and press the entire length.

■ Cutting across the width of the remaining fabric, cut twelve sashing strips measuring 12 x 30 cm (4¾ x 12 in.). Finally, cut three sashing strips from the length of the remaining fabric, 12 cm (4¾ in.) wide.

■ Join sets of four blocks into vertical strips, with short lengths of sashing in between. Join the strips with sashing. Press the seams towards the sashing.

■ Centre the wadding on the backing fabric and then centre the quilt top on top. Tack through all three layers, vertically, horizontally and diagonally (see page 157).

■ Quilt around the quarter circle curves and then about 6 mm (¼ in.) away from the patchwork and sashing on the cream backing fabric. Finally, quilt 6 mm (¼ in.) away from the seams on the sashing fabric.

■ Remove the tacking thread carefully – it may be caught by machine-quilting stitches.

■ Trim off the excess wadding and backing. Bind the quilt from the back (see page 172), adding strips of wadding remnants as you go.

Broken Circles quilt

This nine-block quilt has rings of varied widths, which don't match up. It is made from silk, which is easy to work with as it takes a crease well and is light to work. As long as the silk is even-weave, you can vary the direction of the grain; then the silk will seem to change colour as the light catches the different direction of weave.

Size of quilt: 143 cm (56 in.) square
Size of each finished block: 46 cm (18 in.) square

■ Referring to the Broken Circles block (see page 51), draft four quarter-block templates, each with rings of different radii as follows:
Quarter block A: 9 and 14 cm (3½ and 5½ in.)
Quarter block B: 11.5 and 19 cm (4½ and 7½ in.)
Quarter block C: 13 and 21 cm (5 and 8¼ in.)
Quarter block D: 6 and 15 cm (2½ and 6 in.)

■ When you make the card templates, add a 6-mm (¼-in.) seam allowance.

■ Cut the fabric, alternating colours for the outer and inner rings, and label each fabric piece A, B, C or D. Although the colour combinations are random, twelve quarter blocks have red on the outside, twelve cream, eight blue and four green.

■ Piece the patches and blocks as shown on page 51.

You will need

- 140 cm (1½ yards) each of red and cream silk dupion for the blocks
- 1 m (1 yd) each of blue, green and black silk dupion for the blocks
- 50 cm (½ yard) black silk dupion for the binding
- 1.5-m (60-in.) square of 135-g (4-oz) polyester wadding
- 1.6-m (64-in.) square of cotton fabric, or the equivalent seamed, for the backing
- Matching thread

■ Lay the blocks out in random sequence, piece into vertical strips and press the seams in alternate directions. Join the strips and press.

■ Centre the wadding on the backing fabric, then centre the quilt top on top. Tack through all three layers vertically, horizontally and diagonally (see page 157).

■ Machine or hand quilt 'in the ditch' (see page 159), using toning threads. First quilt the quarter circles (both the curve and the straight lines) in the centre block, and then quilt the rings (both the curve and the straight lines). Then working one block at a time, quilt the quarter circles and rings on the remaining blocks. Quilt the blocks at the top and bottom of the quilt first, then those either side of the centre one. Finally, quilt the remaining straight lines, starting from the centre seams and working outwards. Remove the tacking thread carefully; it may be caught by machine-quilting stitches.

■ Trim off the excess wadding and backing, leaving it extending about 1 cm (½ in.) beyond the quilt top.

■ Cut binding strips 9 cm (3½ in.) wide across the width of the black silk and join them together in a continuous strip. Press the seams flat, fold one long edge over by about 1 cm (½ in.) and press the entire length. Bind from the front (see page 173), adding some of the wadding remnants as you go.

Sewing order

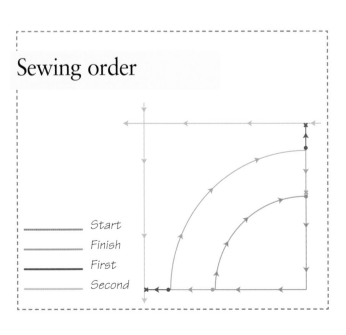

Start
Finish
First
Second

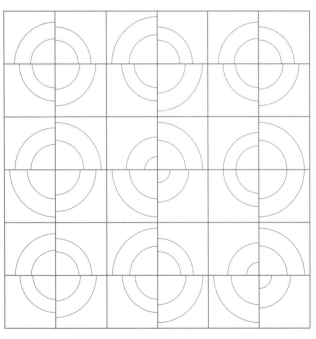

Christmas cards

Use cottons, silks, satins or even velvets for the backgrounds and appliqué. Try out metallic or rainbow threads and add beads and buttons. The Holly leaf and Dove designs (pages 66–69) would also work as Christmas-card motifs.

You will need

- Scraps of fabric for the appliqué
- 20- x 15-cm (8¼- x 6-in.) piece of light background fabric such as cotton, silk or satin
- 21- x 15-cm (8¼- x 6-in.) three-fold card with 16.5- x 10-cm (6½- x 4-in.) apertures
- Double-sided tape
- Matching thread

■ Referring to the Christmas motifs (see page 82), draft and appliqué the tree and snowman onto the background fabrics. The tree is stitched onto a satin block 9 x 12.5 cm (3½ x 5 in.) with a checked frame and has beads hand stitched on for festive sparkle, while the snowman is on a variegated wintry blues cotton rainbow fabric and is wadded and outline quilted.

■ Trim the fabric to about 1 cm (½ in.) larger all around than the aperture in the card. Open up the card blank, apply double-sided tape around the edges of the aperture, place the appliqué piece right side down on top and press down to fix the fabric in place. Apply more tape around the edges of the appliqué piece, then fold over the left-hand panel of the card and press down firmly.

Fancy Fish album cover

This removable quilted cover is designed to fit an album measuring roughly 33 x 26 cm (13 x 10 in.), but you could easily adapt it to suit other dimensions. You could also substitute other motifs to suit the occasion – entwined monograms for a wedding album, perhaps.

Size of album cover: 33 x 26 cm (13 x 10 in.)
1 cm (½ in.) seam allowance throughout

You will need

- 60 cm (24 in.) blue gingham
- 29- x 15-cm (11½- x 6-in.) piece of blue dotted cotton fabric for the wave
- Scraps of brightly coloured fabric for the fish
- 56- x 36-cm (22- x 14-in.) 70-g (2-oz) piece of polyester wadding
- Matching thread

■ From blue gingham fabric, cut one 56 x 36-cm (22 x 14-in.) piece for the lining, two 29 x 36-cm (11½ x 14-in.) pieces for the front and back and two 22 x 36-cm (8½ x 14-in.) pieces for the inside flaps. Fold and press the inside flaps to 11 x 36 cm (4¼ x 14 in.)

■ Lay the blue spot fabric on the front cover fabric about midway down. Using tailor's chalk, draw two wavy lines across the blue spot fabric, then cut out. Pin to the cover fabric and satin stitch it in place, setting the stitch width to 3.

■ Using the Fancy Fish template on page 85, cut out four fish motifs. (I used a variegated, rainbow fabric.) Appliqué the fish to the front of the cover. I varied the outline thread colour. Press from the back.

■ Stitch together the back and front covers along one long edge, taking a 1-cm (½-in.) seam, and press.

■ Lay the cover right side up on top of the wadding and baste the two layers together (see page 157).

■ Quilt around the fish, about 6 mm (¼ in.) away from the motifs and along the wave fabric, making sure you do not stitch over the fish. Vary the thread colour to match the gingham and blue spot fabric.

■ Lay the quilted piece on your work surface, right side up. Place the flaps at each side, with the folded edge towards the centre, and lay the lining on top. Pin through all layers. Machine stitch, taking a 1-cm (½-in.) seam, leaving a 10-cm (4-in.) gap at the bottom. Trim the edges and corners, turn right side out, hand stitch the gap closed, and then machine top stitch very close to the edge all the way around.

Child's counting quilt

This quilt or crawl mat has lots of colours, patterns and shapes to discover and count. Use snippets from other projects or clothing to make it more personal to the child.

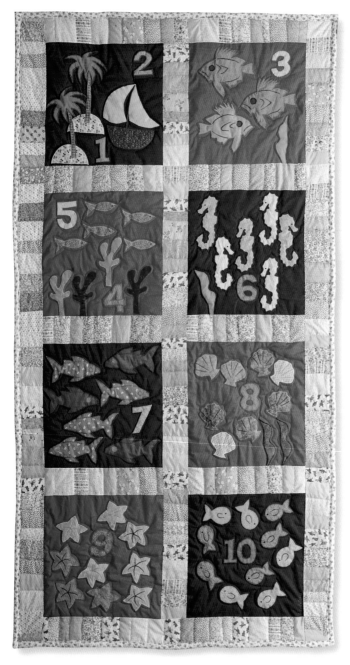

Size of quilt: 200 x 106 cm (78 x 41¾ in.)
Size of each finished block: 38 cm (15 in.) square
Border and sashing: 9 cm (3½ in.) wide
0.6 mm (¼ in.) seam allowance throughout

■ Cut four 45-cm (17½-in.) squares of each of the two block backing fabrics. These will be trimmed to size after stitching.

■ Using the templates on pages 84–85 and 96, transfer the required number of motifs onto brightly coloured scraps of fabric and cut out. Machine or hand appliqué the motifs onto the turquoise and blue backing fabrics, alternating the colour of the backing fabrics and making sure the numbers are in the right order. Press from the back and trim the backing fabrics to size and shape, to 39.5 cm (15½ in.) square.

■ To make the sashing and borders, cut widthways into strips 5–7 cm (2–2¾ in.) wide. Machine stitch the strips together in a random order into blocks of about ten strips. Press all the seams one way. With the strips running horizontally, cut these newly formed blocks of

You will need

- 1 m (1 yd) each of blue and turquoise cotton fabrics to back the blocks
- Bright scraps for the motifs
- 1.5 m (60 in.) in total of at least 10 different fabrics for the borders and sashing
- 2.2 m (2½ yd) cotton fabric for the backing
- 2.2 m (2½ yd) 70-g (2-oz) polyester wadding
- 60 cm (24 in.) cotton fabric for the binding
- Matching thread

joined strips vertically into strips 10.5 cm (4⅛ in.) wide. Piece them together to form a long strip about 11 m (12½ yd) long, making sure that all the seams are in the same direction.

■ Lay the appliquéd blocks out in sequence. Join the left-hand blocks into a vertical strip, with a length of sashing (cut from the long strip) in between each block. Repeat with the right-hand blocks. Press the seams towards the sashing. Join the two vertical block strips with a length of sashing, and press the seams towards the sashing. Attach lengths of the sashing border to the top and lower edges of the quilt, and then to the side edges. Press the seams away from the blocks.

■ Lay the backing wrong side up and cover with the wadding. Lay the quilt top right side up on the wadding and backing, and tack well, in a vertical, horizontal and diagonal grid.

■ Outline quilt the motifs (see page 159), stitching about 6 mm (¼ in.) away in thread that matches the backings, then quilt 'in the ditch' or just next to it, over the seams for extra strength.

■ Trim off any excess wadding and backing fabric.

■ Cut the binding fabric into 8-cm (3-in.) strips across the width of the fabric and join into a continuous strip. Press the seams. Fold over one long edge by about 1 cm (½ in.) and press. Bind the quilt from the back, padding with strips of wadding as you go.

Cat blanket

Perfect for cat lovers, this simple little blanket will brighten up any armchair. Make it from washable furnishing fabric that blends with your colour scheme.

Size of blanket: 81.5 cm (32 in.) square
Satin stitch width: 3

■ Referring to the Sleeping Cat block (see page 77), draft and cut out the cat motif. As the motif is large, make sure that the grain of the cat fabric matches that of the background fabric. Appliqué the cat to the background, and work the face details last.

■ Turn under a double fold of 1.5 cm (½ in.) all the way around, tack and press flat. On the right side, satin stitch all the way around, about 6 mm (¼ in.) from the edge.

You will need

- 30-cm (12-in.) square of plain-coloured furnishing-weight fabric for the cat
- 87.5-cm (34-in.) square of patterned furnishing-weight fabric for the background
- Matching thread

Farmyard quilt

With its appliquéd farmyard animals and Barn Fence border, this
makes a really colourful and cheery quilt for a child's room.

Size of quilt: 64 x 84 cm (25 x 33 in.)

Width of border: 10 cm (4 in.)

0.6 mm (¼ in.) seam allowance throughout

■ Lay background strips one above another, overlapping,
so overall length is 65 cm (25½ in.). Draw a curve on the
top edge of lowest strip (make sure the curve doesn't
extend beyond the overlap), cut the curve and pin to the
fabric above. Repeat all the way up. Satin stitch the curvy
strips. Press and trim the excess fabric away on the back.

■ Using the templates on pages 78–81, transfer the
required number of motifs onto brightly coloured scraps
of fabric and cut out. Pin and appliqué them onto the
background fabrics. Press from the back and trim to
41.5 x 61.5 cm (16⅜ x 24¼ in.).

■ Referring to the Barn Fence block (see page 36), cut
strips 4 x 11.5 cm (1½ x 4¼ in.) and piece into 24 blocks
of four different coloured strips. Press all the seams in
one direction and then piece edge to edge, rotating in
alternate directions, to make four borders six blocks
long. Press all the seams in the same direction. Attach
the side borders to the quilt top first, then add the top
and bottom borders. Press the seams outwards.

■ Lay the backing wrong side up and cover with the
wadding. Lay the quilt top right side up on the wadding
and backing, and tack well, in a vertical, horizontal and
diagonal grid.

■ Outline quilt the motifs (see page 159), stitching
about 6 mm (¼ in.) away in thread that matches the
backgrounds, then quilt over every short seam of the
border. Trim off any excess wadding and backing fabric.

■ Cut the binding fabric into three 6-cm (2½-in.) strips
across the width of the fabric and join into a continuous
strip. Press the seams. Fold over one long edge by about
1 cm (½ in.) and press. Bind from the back (see page
172), padding with strips of wadding as you go.

You will need

- Five 46- x 22-cm (18- x 8½-in.) pieces of cotton
  fabric – two in green spots for the field backgrounds,
  two in green checks and one in blue for the sky
- Bright fabric scraps for the motifs
- 20 cm (8 in.) fabric in four colours for the borders
- 70 x 90 cm (27 x 35½ in.) cotton for the backing
- 70- x 90-cm (27- x 35½-in.) piece of 70-g (2-oz)
  polyester wadding
- 20 cm (8 in.) green checked fabric for the binding
- Matching thread

Rooster hanging

This hanging is made from cottons with a furnishing-weight or linen backing panel, and is finished with a triangle squares patchwork border. Easy to wash, it is suitable for a kitchen.

Size of hanging: 46 x 51 cm (18 x 20 in.)

0.6 mm (¼ in.) seam allowance throughout

■ Draft, cut and make the Rooster block, following the instructions on pages 74–75. Trim the backing fabric to 33 x 38 cm (13 x 15 in.).

■ From scraps in random combinations, draft and make 22 triangle squares for the 6.5 cm (2½ in.) Sawtooth border (see page 58) and four 6.5 cm (2½ in.) corner squares with split triangles (see page 24).

■ Piece five triangle squares together in a strip and join to the top edge of the block. Repeat on the lower edge. Press the seams away from the block.

■ Piece the remaining triangle squares into two strips of six, and add a split triangle square to each end of each strip. Join these strips to the sides of the block. Press the seams away from the block.

You will need

- Four fabrics 20 cm (8 in.) square for the body, tails and ruff pieces, and three pieces 10 cm (4 in.) square for the leg, feet and beak, and comb
- 36- x 40-cm (14- x 16-in.) piece of furnishing-weight fabric or linen for the backing
- 50- x 55-cm (20- x 21½-in.) piece of lining fabric or calico for the back of the hanging
- 26 assorted scraps at least 9 cm (3½ in.) square for the patchwork border
- 50- x 55-cm (20- x 21½-in.) piece of 70-g (2-oz) polyester wadding
- Four 5- x 53-cm (2- x 21-in.) strips for the binding
- Matching thread

■ Place the backing fabric right side down on your work surface, with the wadding on top, and the appliqué block right side up on top of the wadding. Tack the layers together; the batting and backing should be about 3 cm (1 in.) larger than the front.

■ Outline quilt the rooster (see page 159), stitching about 6 mm (¼ in.) from the motif. Quilt the patchwork border along the diagonal and straight seams, either 'in the ditch' or on the seams.

■ Trim off the excess backing and wadding.

■ Bind the edges from the back (see page 172).

Lavender bag with hearts

This pretty little cotton bag with hand-appliquéd hearts for fresh lavender or pot pourri, can be washed and refilled when the scent evaporates.

Size of bag: 20 x 10 cm (8 x 4 in.)
1 cm (½ in.) seam allowance throughout

■ Referring to the Heart motifs (see page 68), draft and cut out two hearts – the larger one 7 cm (2¾ in.) across and the smaller one 5 cm (2 in.) across – and add a turning allowance. Hand appliqué first the larger one and then, on top and centred, the smaller one onto one piece of background fabric (see pages 166–167), using thread that matches the darkest colour of the motifs.

■ Turn under and press one long edge of the top bands by 1 cm (½ in.) and machine stitch the right side of the raw edge to the wrong side of the bag tops. Fold the fabric over to the front and topstitch.

■ With right sides together, stitch together the sides and bottom of the bag. Turn right side out.

■ To make the tie, cut a 26 x 2.5-cm (10 x 1-in.) strip of the contrasting band fabric. Fold it in half, stitch along the length and turn right side out. Turn under and hand stitch the short ends.

You will need

● Two 10-cm (4-in.) squares of cotton fabric in pale and darker colours for the hearts
● Two 18- x 12-cm (7- x 4¾-in.) pieces of background fabric
● Two 7.5- x 12-cm (3- x 4¾-in.) strips of darker-toned patterned fabric for the tops of the bags
● 26- x 2.5-cm (10- x 1-in.) strip of darker-toned patterned fabric for the tie
● Matching thread

Make-up bag with butterflies

This soft, padded zipper bag in linen and cotton has a hand-appliquéd butterfly panel on the front; you could stitch a second panel for the back with dragonflies or bees. Line it with shower-proof fabric to make a sponge bag.

Size of bag: 23 x 34 cm (9 x 13½ in.)
Size of finished block: 14 x 25 cm (5½ x 10 in.)
1 cm (½ in.) seam allowance throughout

■ Referring to the Butterfly motifs on page 65, draft, cut and appliqué the motifs onto the background fabric. Press from the back and trim to 16 x 27 cm (6¼ x 10½ in.).

■ Cut a 25 x 36-cm (9¾ x 14-in.) bag back, two strips measuring 6.5 x 25 cm (2¾ x 9¾ in.) from across the width of fabric for the side borders, and two strips measuring 6.5 x 27 cm (2¾ x 10½ in.) from the length of the fabric for the top and bottom borders. Stitch the top and bottom borders and press the seams outwards. Then add the side borders and press the seams outwards.

You will need

- Scraps of small-patterned cotton fabric for the appliqué
- 18 x 29-cm (7 x 11½-in.) piece of blue linen fabric for the background
- 27 cm (10½ in.) striped cotton fabric for the back and borders
- Two 25- x 36-cm (9¾- x 14-in.) pieces of lining fabric
- 25- x 36-cm (9¾- x 14-in.) piece of 70-g (2-oz) polyester wadding
- 30-cm (12-in.) zip
- Matching thread

■ Tack the front of the bag to the wadding. Outline quilt the motifs and quilt along the border seams, by hand or machine (see pages 158-159).

■ Tack the front and back pieces together along the top, using the seam allowance. Taking a 1-cm (½-in.) seam, machine stitch from each corner for 1 cm (½ in.). Press the seam open and lay the zip right side down on the wrong side of the seam. Tack and then machine stitch the zip in place. Remove the tacking stitches.

■ With right sides together, stitch the front of the bag to the back. Pinch the seams together at the bottom and stitch across to make a base.

■ Stitch three sides of the lining and hand sew it to the inside of the bag, just covering the zip stitching.

Dragonfly pouch

This hand-appliquéd pouch makes a beautiful nightdress case or a drawer tidy. The pouch itself is made from linen, which has a soft feel and looks good even when crumpled and creased. Use lightweight cottons or lawns for the appliqué motifs.

Size of bag: 29 cm (11½ in.) square
Size of finished block: 15 cm (6 in.) square
1 cm (½ in.) seam allowance throughout

■ Cut a 20-cm (8-in.) square of blue linen and, referring to the Dragonfly motif (see page 63), draft, cut and hand appliqué the motifs onto it. Press from the back and trim to 17 cm (6¾ in.) square.

■ Stitch the frame strip to the side edges, cutting off the excess as you go. Press the seams outwards. Stitch the frame strip to the top and bottom edges and press the seams outwards.

■ Cut the border fabric into 6-cm (2½-in.) strips, attach as for the frame strips, and press seams towards border.

You will need

- Scraps of small-patterned cottons for the appliqué
- 31 cm (12¼in.) blue linen fabric for the appliqué background and back of the pouch
- 5-cm (2-in.) strip of blue-and-white cotton fabric for the frame
- 12-cm (5-in.) strip of blue and pink stripe fabric for the border
- 31- x 81-cm (12¼- x 32-in.) piece of lining fabric
- 31- x 81-cm (12¼- x 32-in.) piece of 70-g (2-oz) polyester wadding
- Matching thread

■ Cut a 31 x 47-cm (12¼ x 18½-in.) piece of blue linen for the back of the pouch. With wrong sides together, stitch the block to the pouch back along the top edge and add a strip of border fabric to the bottom edge of the block. Press the seams away from the backing fabric.

■ Tack the top of the pouch to the wadding. Outline quilt, stitching 6 mm (¼ in.) away from the motif, and quilt either 'in the ditch' or on the seams (see page 159).

■ With right sides together, stitch the front of the bag to the lining fabric, leaving a 5-cm (2-in.) gap in one edge. Turn the bag right side out, fold the lower part up to make an envelope 19 cm (7½ in.) deep and topstitch the sides.

Tulip place mat

The wide borders on these place mats are made from the backing fabric folded over to the front. It has a strong medium-scale pattern, quite similar to the appliqué design itself. Cotton wadding inside protects the table from the heat of the plates; it can withstand a higher temperature wash and iron.

Size of place mat: 26 x 40 cm (10 x 15¾ in.)

Size of block: 18 x 23 cm (7 x 9 in.)

1 cm (½ in.) seam allowance throughout

You will need

- Scraps of cotton print fabrics in red, green and cream for the appliqué
- 22- x 28-cm (8½- x 11-in.) piece of appliqué background fabric
- Two 20- x 5-cm (8- x 2-in.) strips of border fabric
- 26- x 40-cm (10- x 15¾-in.) piece of cotton wadding
- 36- x 56-cm (14- x 22-in.) piece of backing fabric
- Matching thread

■ Referring to the Tulip Bunch motifs (see pages 64–65), draft, cut and machine appliqué the motifs onto the background fabric. Trim to 20 x 25 cm (8 x 9¾ in.).

■ With right sides together, stitch the border strips to the side edges. Press the seams outwards.

■ Centre the block on the wadding and backing fabric and tack it in place. Outline quilt the motifs and quilt along the border seams (see page 159).

■ Fold over the top and bottom edges of the backing fabric by 1 cm (½ in.) and press, then fold over to the front and topstitch to the block. Repeat with the side edges and hand stitch the corners to secure.

Dove and leaf table cloth

This square white linen tablecloth has doves along the edges and leaves and a berry on the corners. The crisp ginghams and simple floral prints lend themselves to the traditional stylized motifs, and the colours are reminiscent of old blue-and-white country crockery.

Size of tablecloth: 1 m (39 in.) square
Satin stitch width: 3

You will need

- Scraps of navy and white gingham, striped or spotted cotton fabric for the appliqué
- 1-m (39-in.) square of white linen
- Four 4- x 102-cm (1½- x 41-in.) strips of white-and-navy floral cotton fabric for the binding
- Matching thread

■ Referring to the Hearts, Dove, and Tulip motifs (see pages 68–69), draft the templates and cut out the fabric; the birds pictured are 20 cm (8 in.) long, the leaves 10 cm (4 in.) long and the berries have a radius of 3 cm (1½ in.).

■ Fold and crease the linen in four, then open it out and fold the cloth in four again from corner to corner. Use the crease lines to place the motifs symmetrically: one dove midway along each side with branch and leaf tips about 10 cm (4 in.) from the edge and a leaf and berry bunch in each corner. Stitch the motifs in place, using satin stitch width 3 and matching the thread to the darkest colour in the motif fabric. Lay the top thread along the line of stitching and stitch over it for about 3 cm (1 in.) to conceal and secure it, then trim. At the end, draw the threads to the back, thread through a needle and pass through the stitched channel and trim.

■ Fold under and press one long edge on each binding strip. Bind from the back (see page 172).

Bread basket napkin with tulip motif

Ties have been added to this linen napkin so that it can be used to line a basket and cover bread or cakes. Use thread that matches the darkest colour in the fabrics to make the motifs stand out, and place a tulip in each corner where it will be most visible.

Size of napkin: 50 cm (19½ in.) square
Satin stitch width: 3

■ Referring to the Hearts, Dove and Tulip motifs (see pages 66–67), draft the templates and cut out the fabric for four tulips; the tulips pictured are 11 cm (4¼ in.) tall. Fold and crease the linen in quarters diagonally and pin each of the four tulips on the fold lines, their points about 5 cm (2 in.) from the edges of the linen.

■ Satin stitch along the fold lines from one tulip base to another, then appliqué the tulips. Draw the threads to the front of the work, trim and conceal under the appliqué. The petals will be the last pieces to stitch; draw these threads to the back, tie and trim or thread through the satin-stitch channel.

■ Fold under one long edge of each binding strip. Pin and stitch the right side of the shortest binding strip to the back of the napkin, aligning the raw edges and stitch.

You will need

- Scraps of cotton fabric for the appliqué
- 50-cm (19½-in.) square of white linen
- One 51- x 2.5-cm (20- x 1-in.) strip, two 69- x 2.5-cm (27- x 1-in.) strips and one 87- x 2.5-cm (34- x 1-in.) strip of blue-and-white cotton for the binding and ties
- Matching thread

Fold the folded edge of the binding over to the front and topstitch.

■ Working anticlockwise, take a medium-length strip and bind the next edge in the same way, leaving the excess length at the end for the tie. Bring the binding to the front and topstitch all the way along, including the tie end (fold in the end of the strip and stitch across to neaten). Repeat on the next anticlockwise edge. The final binding strip will extend about 18 cm (7 in.) at both the beginning and end for ties.

Monogrammed cushion

This cushion makes an especially personal gift. The monogram is in small-patterned delicate Liberty lawn outlined in thread that matches one of the darker colours in the fabric and contrasts well with the larger scale patterns of the frame and border fabrics.

Size of cushion: 43 cm (17 in.) square
Size of finished block: 18 cm (7 in.) square
1 cm (½ in.) seam allowance throughout

■ Referring to the Appliqué Alphabet (see pages 89–93), draft, cut and appliqué the motif to the background fabric. Press from the back and trim to 20 cm (8 in.) square.

■ With right sides together, piece the frame strip to the side edges of the block, cutting off the excess as you go. Press the seams away from the block, and then add the frame strips to the top and bottom edges.

■ Cut four border strips measuring 10 x 45 cm (4 x 17¾ in.). Attach borders to the side edges of the block, and trim off the excess. Then attach borders to the top and bottom edges and press the seams away from the block.

You will need

- 15-cm (6-in.) square of cotton print for the appliqué motif
- 23-cm (9-in.) square of cream background fabric
- 7.5-cm x 1-m (3- x 40-in.) strip of cotton fabric for the frame
- 45 cm (18 in.) furnishing-weight fabric for the back and borders
- 43-cm (17-in.) square of 70-g (2-oz) polyester wadding
- 40-cm (16-in.) zip
- 43-cm (17-in.) square cushion pad
- Matching thread

■ Tack the cushion top to the wadding. Outline quilt the motif (see page 159), stitching about 6 mm (¼ in.) away, and then quilt over the seams.

■ Cut two 45 x 23.5-cm (17¾ x 9½-in.) pieces of backing fabric. With right sides together, tack the two back pieces together along one long side using the seam allowance. Taking a 1-cm (½-in.) seam, machine stitch from each corner for 2.5 cm (1 in.) Press the seam open and lay the zip right side down on the wrong side of the seam. Tack and then machine stitch the zip in place. Remove the tacking stitches.

■ Open the zip. With right sides together, stitch together the cushion front and back. Snip off any excess around the edges and corners, turn right side out and topstitch around the edge of the cushion.

Square cushion with leaf and berry panels

This cushion is made from furnishing fabrics, with the back and borders in a chenille-type fabric. The panels are less textured, as it is difficult to keep a smooth appliqué outline on an uneven surface.

Size of cushion: 45 cm (17¾ in.) square
Size of each finished panel: 15 cm (6 in.) square
1 cm (½ in.) seam allowout throughout

■ Draft and make four Leaf and Berry blocks, varying the number of leaves and berries. Use the middle-size leaf template on page 65 for the leaves and a coin about 2.5 cm (1 in.) across as the template for the berries. Press from the back and trim panels to 17 cm (6½ in.) square. Join the top and bottom panels together and press the seams in opposite directions. Then join the two strips and press the vertical seam either way.

■ Centre the block on the muslin square, pin it in place and quilt over the seams. The muslin square will protect the raw seam edges from fraying inside the cushion.

You will need

- 15-cm (6-in.) square of black cotton fabric for the leaves
- Scraps of red cotton fabric for the berries
- Two 20-cm (8-in.) squares each of two shades of cream
- 50 cm (19½ in.) red chenille-type fabric for the back and borders
- 50-cm (19½-in.) square of muslin or light cotton
- 40-cm (16-in.) zip
- 45-cm (18-in.) square cushion pad
- Matching thread

■ From the red chenille-type fabric, cut two 48 x 10-cm (19 x 4-in.) strips and two 32 x 10-cm (12½ x 4-in.) strips for the borders. With right sides together, stitch the short red border strips to the sides of the appliqué block (through the layer of muslin) and press the seams away from the block. Repeat with the top and bottom borders. Topstitch the red fabric around the appliqué block.

■ Cut two backing pieces measuring 48 x 25 cm (19 x 10 in.). With right sides together, tack the two back pieces together along one long side, taking a 1-cm (½-in.) seam allowance. Machine stitch from each corner for 4 cm (1½ in.) Press the seam open and lay the zip right side down on the wrong side of the seam. Tack and then machine stitch the zip in place. Remove the tacking stitches.

■ Open the zip. With right sides together, machine stitch all around the cushion cover, snip off the excess fabric on the corners, then turn the cover right side out. Topstitch around the edge of the cushion.

Butterfly and branch appliqué cushion

This cushion has a slightly textured furnishing-fabric backing with appliqué motifs in floral fabrics. Making it is a good way of using up lots of scrap-bag snippets or for recycling memory scraps from favourite clothes.

Size of cushion: 42 cm (16½ in.) square
1 cm (½ in.) seam allowance throughout

■ Using the Butterfly and middle-size Leaf templates on page 65 and 71, cut nine leaf shapes and a butterfly from a variety of fabrics. Cut a 50-cm (19½-in.) square of furnishing fabric for the cushion front. Draw a chalk curve diagonally across the front of the cushion and pin the leaves on either side of the line, with the butterfly top left.

■ Change the thread colour for each motif. The backing fabric is opaque so all the threads can be drawn to the back and tied without the risk of show-through. First stitch the leaves, then satin stitch the branch to secure all the threads of the leaves. Finally, work the butterfly – the wings first and then the body.

■ Press from the back and trim to 44 cm (17¼ in.) square, then tack to the wadding. Outline quilt 6 mm (¼ in.) away from the appliqué (see page 159) without breaking

off, but working around the contours of the design.

■ Cut two 44 x 23-cm (17¼ x 9-in.) pieces of furnishing fabric for the back of the cushion. With right sides together, tack the back pieces together along a long edge, taking a 1-cm (½-in.) seam. Machine stitch from each corner for 2.5 cm (1 in.). Press the seam open and lay the zip right side down on the wrong side of the seam. Tack and then machine stitch the zip in place. Remove the tacking stitches.

■ With right sides together, stitch the cushion front to the back. Turn right side out and topstitch the edges.

Bird and leaf ring cushion

You could use fabric off-cuts from the curtains and bed covers to create this pretty vintage-style cushion.

Size of cushion: 53 cm (21 in.) square
Size of finished block: 28 cm (11 in.) square
1 cm (½ in.) seam allowance throughout

■ Referring to the Bird and Leaf Ring appliqué blocks (see pages 66–67), draft, cut and appliqué the motifs to the background fabric. Trim to 30 cm (12 in.) square when stitched and pressed.

■ For the frames, cut one strip of each fabric across the full width, 4.5 cm (1¾ in.) deep – and then cut these into lengths 10–20 cm (4–8 in.) long and piece end to end in random order to make a long strip. Press the seams in the same direction along the length of the strip.

■ With right sides together, join the frame strip to the side edges of the block, cutting off the excess as you go. Press flat, then add the top and bottom frame strips.

■ Repeat to make a second frame around the block.

You will need

- Scraps of small-patterned cottons for the appliqué leaves and bird wing, plus a 13-cm (5-in.) square of fabric for the bird
- 33-cm (13-in.) square of background fabric
- Three different strips of furnishing-weight fabrics for the frames, 5 cm (2 in.) wide
- 55 cm (21½ in.) cream-and-pink furnishing-weight fabric for the back and borders
- 55-cm (21½-in.) square of 70-g (2-oz) wadding
- 55 x 3-cm (21½ x 1-in.) strip of Velcro
- 53-cm (21-in.) square cushion pad
- Matching thread

■ Cut four border strips from the length of fabric, 9 cm (3½ in.) wide. Attach the border strip, first to the side edges (trimming off the excess length), then to the top and bottom edges. Press the seams towards the border.

■ Tack the cushion top to the wadding. Outline quilt the motif (see page 159), stitching about 6 mm (¼ in.) away. Quilt over the long frame seams and the border seams.

■ For the back, cut two pieces measuring 55 x 32 cm (21½ x 12½ in.). Fold over one long edge of one piece to the wrong side by 1 cm (½ in.) and press. Separate the two halves of the Velcro and pin one half just below the fold to hide the raw edge of the fabric and stitch along each edge of the Velcro. On the other back piece, fold the fabric over to the right side and attach the remaining piece of Velcro in the same way.

■ Join the two halves together with the Velcro. Pin the patchwork right side down on the cushion back. Machine stitch all around, trim the edges, snip off any excess fabric on the corners, and turn the cushion cover right side out. Topstitch around the edge of the cushion, matching the thread colour to the fabric.

Fallen leaves cushion

The oak, maple and ash leaves are arranged on the linen background to look like fallen leaves, with acorns and keys strewn among them.

Size of cushion: 58 cm (23 in.) square
Size of finished block: 39 cm (15½ in.) square
1 cm (½ in.) seam allowance throughout

■ Referring to the Leaf motifs (see pages 70–71), draft, cut and appliqué the motifs to the background fabric. The oak leaf is 16 cm (6½ in.) long, the maples 14 and 7.5 cm (5½ and 3 in.) and the ash leaves 10 cm (4 in.) long. Work the leaf vein detailing last and reduce the stitch width to 1 as you stitch. Press from the back and trim to 41 cm (16 in.) square.

■ With right sides together, join the frame strips to the side edges of the block, cutting off any excess as you go. Press the seams away from the block, then add the top and bottom frame strips.

■ Cut four border strips from the length of fabric, 8 cm (3 in.) wide. Attach them first to the side edges (trimming off any excess), then to the top and bottom. Press the seams away from the block.

You will need

- *Scraps of cotton fabric for the appliqué*
- *45-cm (17¾-in.) square of linen for the block background*
- *Four 50- x 5.5-cm (20- x 2-in.) strips of furnishing-weight fabric for the frame*
- *60 cm (24 in.) furnishing-weight fabric for the back and borders*
- *60-cm (24-in.) square of 70-g (2-oz) polyester wadding*
- *50-cm (20-in.) zip*
- *58-cm (23-in.) square cushion pad*
- *Matching thread*

■ Tack the cushion top to the wadding. Outline quilt the motif (see page 159), stitching about 6 mm (¼ in.) away, then quilt over the frame and border seams.

■ Cut two 60 x 31-cm (24 x 12½-in.) pieces for the back. With right sides together, tack the back pieces together along one long side taking a 1-cm (½-in.) seam allowance. Machine stitch from each corner for 5 cm (2 in.) Press the seam open and lay the zip right side down on the wrong side of the seam. Tack and then machine stitch the zip in place. Remove the tacking stitches.

■ Open the zip. Pin the patchwork right side down on the cushion back. Machine stitch all around, snip off the excess fabric on the corners, and turn the cushion cover right side out. Topstitch around the edge of the cushion.

Hearts pillowcase

Heart shapes are often seen on old quilts and the timelessness of gingham gives a traditional rustic look. The border is folded back on itself to give more body and edged with a narrow strip of gingham that echoes the fabrics used in the appliqué. You could appliqué the same motif across the tops of sheets to create a matching set of bed linen. French seams give the pillowcase a neat finish.

Size of pillowcase: 48 x 63 cm (19 x 24¾ in.)
Size of border: 17 cm (6¾ in.) deep

■ With right sides together, stitch the binding strip across one short side of the linen, stitching 2 cm (¾ in.) from the edge. Fold the binding strip over to the other side of the piece, fold under 1 cm (½ in.) of the strip, and hand stitch it in place. Stitch and fold along the lines of the gingham to get a neat, crisp edge.

■ Referring to the Hearts motifs (see page 68), draft and appliqué the hearts along the short edge on which you machine stitched the binding.

■ Fold and hem stitch the other short side – so that the neat side is on the other side of the fabric from the appliqué.

■ Fold the appliquéd edge back to give a 17-cm (6½-in.) flap, with the appliqué showing. Now fold the case in half so that the fold line of the appliqué is level with the back edge. Stitch the side seams on the right side of the fabric, taking a 1-cm (½-in.) seam. Trim the seam to 6 mm (¼ in.) to neaten any stray threads, turn the pillowcase inside out and stitch the side seams again. Turn the pillowcase right side out.

You will need

- 52- x 145-cm (20½- x 57-in.) piece of strong white cotton or linen
- 52- x 5-cm (2- x 2½-in.) strip of gingham for the binding
- Scraps of cotton fabric for the appliqué
- Matching thread

Daisy and Checker patch bag

This simple square tote bag combines appliqué with a seven-patch Checker block. The patchwork is lined at the front and French seamed.

Size of bag: 43 cm (17 in.) square
Size of finished block: 30.5 cm (12 in.)

■ Referring to the Daisy motif (see page 67) and the Checkers block (see page 39), draft the block 33 cm (13 in.) square and cut the fabrics. Cut the gingham fabric used for the daisies diagonal to the grain, to contrast with the gingham used elsewhere on the block, which is cut on the straight of grain. Appliqué the daisies to the large checker squares.

■ Lay the patches out in sequence, placing the small squares randomly, and piece the block. Piece vertical strips 1, 4 and 7 first. Then piece the small squares in strips 2 and 3 into horizontal pairs and attach them to the large appliquéd squares; repeat for strips 5 and 6. Press the seams in alternate directions strip to strip. Finally, join all the vertical strips together and press the seams in the same direction across the block.

■ Cut four 47 x 9-cm (18½ x 3½-in.) strips of gingham for the borders. Attach the borders to the top and bottom of the block, then trim off any excess. Then attach borders to the side edges. Press the seams away from the block.

You will need

- Scraps of cotton fabric for the appliqué
- Four 10-cm (4-in.) dark blue squares for Checker centre squares
- 33 small squares in assorted blue and cream fabrics, each 5.5-cm (2¼-in.) square
- 47 cm (18½ in.) blue gingham for the borders, back and handles
- 47-cm (18½ in.) square of light cotton lining
- Matching thread

■ With right sides together, stitch the lining square to the top edge of the front of the bag and press flat. Quilt along the border seams (see page 159) to hold the lining to the patchwork.

■ Cut a 47-cm (18½-in.) square of gingham for the back. With wrong sides together, stitch the front of the bag to the back along the sides and bottom. Trim the seam and turn the bag inside out. Stitch around the same three sides and turn right side out.

■ Cut two 40 x 6-cm (15¾ x 2¼-in.) strips of gingham for handles. With right sides together, fold in half lengthways and machine stitch along the long unfolded edge. Turn right side out.

■ On both the front and back, on the inside of the bag, stitch the handle ends 11.5 cm (4½ in.) in from the sides, so that the handles hang down into the bag. Stitch in place, level with the border quilt line. Pull the handles up and stitch all round the top of the bag 1 cm (½ in.) from the top of the bag to secure the handles.

Bluebell bag

Light floral fabrics are appliquéd onto a background in furnishing-weight fabric on this bag.

Size of bag: 41 x 45 cm (16 x 17¾ in.) with a 9-cm (3½-in.) gusset
Length of handles: 56 cm (22 in.)
Size of finished block: 17 x 23 cm (6¾ x 9 in.)
1 cm (½ in.) seam allowance throughout

■ Referring to the Bluebell motifs (see page 72), draft and make one block and then trim the background fabric to 19 x 25 cm (7½ x 10 in.).

■ With right sides together, join the blue strip to the top and bottom of the appliqué block, trimming off the excess, and press the seams away from the block. Then frame the sides and press the seams away from the block.

■ With right sides together, frame the top and bottom of the appliqué block with the pink fabric, trimming off the excess as you go, and then frame the sides, each time pressing the seams away from the block. Lay the panel on the wadding and tack it in place. Outline quilt the bluebell and then quilt along the seams (see page 159).

You will need

- Scraps of cotton fabric for the appliqué
- 22- x 30-cm (8½- x 12-in.) piece of cream furnishing-weight fabric for the appliqué background
- 6 cm (2½ in.) blue furnishing-weight fabric for the frame
- Two 10-cm (4-in.) strips of pink furnishing-weight fabric for the front borders
- 60 cm (24 in.) pink spotted furnishing-weight fabric for the back, sides and handles
- Two 50-cm (20-in.) squares of lining fabric
- 50-cm (20-in.) square of 70-g (2-oz) polyester wadding
- Matching thread

■ With right sides together, stitch the two pieces of lining fabric together around three sides, leaving a 15-cm (6-in.) gap in one seam.

■ From the pink spotted fabric, cut two 8 x 57-cm (3 x 22½-in.) strips across the width for the handles. Fold in half lengthways, turn under the edges and topstitch.

■ Cut a back piece measuring 43 x 49 cm (17 x 19¼ in.) and strips 11.5 cm (4½ in.) wide for the gusset, joined together to total 142 cm (56 in.). Right sides together, stitch the gusset strip around the sides and base of the bag front, and then do the same to attach the back.

■ Pin the handles to the top of the bag 13 cm (5 in.) from the sides. With right sides together, pull the lining over the bag and stitch around the top.

■ Turn the bag right side out through the gap in the lining and hand stitch closed. Push the lining into the bag and topstitch to hold in place. Pinch the gusset seams together and topstitch all the way around, front and back.

Daisy knitting bag

Perfect for holding all your yarn and knitting needles, this little bag has an appliqué daisy framed with Liberty lawns and a floral border. The pattern scale varies for contrast.

Size of bag: 41 x 50 cm (16 x 20½ in.)
Size of finished block: 16 cm (6¼ in.) square
1 cm (½ in.) seam allowance throughout

■ Referring to the Daisy motif (see page 73), draft and make one block, then trim the background fabric to 18 cm (7 in.) square.

■ Frame the top and bottom of the block with the cream fabric strip, trimming off the excess as you go, and then frame the sides. Repeat with the pink fabric, each time pressing the seams away from the block.

■ From the aqua floral furnishing-weight fabric, cut a 43 x 60-cm (17 x 24-in.) piece for the back of bag. From the remaining fabric, cut lengthways two 9 x 60-cm (3½ x 24-in.) side borders; from the width of the fabric, cut a 9 x 29-cm (3½ x 11½-in.) strip for the bottom

border and a 26 x 29-cm (10¼ x 11½-in.) strip for the top border. Attach the top and bottom borders, and then the side borders and press the seams away from the block.

■ Lay the bag on the wadding and tack it in place. Outline quilt the daisy (see page 159) and then quilt along the seams.

■ Stitch the front of the bag to the back along the lower edge and then stitch the two lining pieces to each other along one short edge. With right sides together, stitch the lining to the bag along the top edges.

■ Stitch the side seams for the lining and the bag separately, leaving a 24 cm (9½ in.) gap at the top of each.

■ Pinch the bottom corners together so that the side and bottom seams are in line and stitch across about 4 cm (1½ in.) in from the corners.

■ Turn the bag right side out. Push the lining into the bag, fold in and stitch it to the bag along the gaps in the side seams.

■ Fold over the top of the bag to a depth of 9 cm (3½ in.), over the hoops, and hand stitch.

You will need

- *Scraps of cotton fabric for the appliqué*
- *20-cm (8-in.) square of cream fabric for the appliqué background*
- *5-cm (2-in.) strip of each of cream and pink floral fabrics for the frames, cut across the full width*
- *60 cm (24 in.) floral furnishing-weight fabric in aqua for the back and front borders*
- *43- x 60-cm (17- x 24-in.) piece of 70-g (2-oz) polyester wadding*
- *Two 43- x 60-cm (17- x 24-in.) pieces of lining fabric*
- *Ready-made plastic or cane hoop handles, 20 cm (8 in.) in diameter*
- *Matching thread*

Butterflies and Bees hanging

Rummage through your scrap bag for small-patterned fabrics in blues and greens – about twenty-five are used here. The hanging has an outline-quilted appliqué panel on a linen background and a patchwork border in Liberty lawns.

Size of hanging: 56 x 66 cm (22 x 26 in.)
6 mm (¼ in.) seam allowance throughout

■ Referring to the Butterfly and Bee motifs (see pages 65-67), draft and cut motifs. On the background fabric, draw branches in chalk or lightly in pencil. Pin pieces in place.

■ Changing the thread colour for each motif, first stitch the leaves, drawing the start and finish threads to the back, and satin stitch the branches last. This will secure all the threads of the leaves. Work the butterfly wings first, then the body. Trim the threads at the back to avoid show-through. Press from the back and trim the background fabric to 42 x 52 cm (16½ x 20½ in.).

■ From scraps in random order, piece a border strip 7.5 cm (3 in.) wide x 2.6 m (104 in.) long finished size

You will need

- *Colourful scraps of cotton fabric for the appliqué*
- *46- x 56-cm (18- x 22-in.) piece of linen for the background*
- *About 40 10-cm (4-in.) squares or strips 10 cm (4 in.) wide and up to 10 cm (4 in.) long for the patchwork border*
- *60- x 70-cm (23½- x 27½-in.) piece of lining fabric or calico for the backing*
- *60- x 70-cm (23½- x 27½-in.) piece of 70-g (2-oz) polyester wadding*
- *2.6-m x 5-cm (104- x 2-in.) strip of fabric, or equivalent seamed, for the binding*

and press all the seams in the same direction. Join the border strip to the top and bottom edges of the panel, cutting to length as you go. Press the seams away from the centre. Now attach the border to the side edges and press.

■ Place the backing fabric right side down on your work surface, with the wadding on top, and the appliqué block right side up on top of the wadding. Tack the layers together; the wadding and backing should be about 3 cm (1 in.) larger than the front.

■ Outline quilt the appliqué (see page 159), stitching about 6 mm (¼ in.) from the motifs. Quilt the patchwork border along the seams, either 'in the ditch' or on the seams.

■ Trim off the excess backing and wadding.

■ Bind the edges from the back (see page 172) and topstitch, padding it with scraps of batting as you go.

Bird and tulip ring quilt

This 16-block double-bed quilt uses the tulip, butterfly and bees motifs, with some of the tulips arranged in bunches and some appliquéd onto satin-stitch rings. The appliqué blocks are framed with randomly pieced fabric strips and the same fabrics are used in the mitred stripe borders.

Size of quilt: 244 x 270 cm (96 x 106 in.)
Size of each finished block: 23 cm (9 in.) square
Width of border: 26.5 cm (10½ in.)
6 mm (¼ in.) seam allowance throughout

■ Referring to the appliqué blocks section, plan 16 different blocks and cut the templates and fabrics. Pin the motifs in place on the background fabric; remember that the background will be trimmed later, so keep the design within a 20-cm (8-in.) window. Satin stitch or work by hand and press from the back. Trim the blocks to 25 cm (9¾ in.) square.

You will need

- 25-cm (10-in.) squares of floral cotton fabrics in two fabrics each pink, blue and green for the appliqué
- 16 x 30-cm (12-in.) squares of white cotton fabric for the block backgrounds
- 15 cm (6 in.) each of 26 floral cotton fabrics in different tones of pink, blue, cream and green for the frames
- 28 cm (11 in.) each of 15 fabrics in predominantly pink and cream tones for the borders
- 54 cm (21 in.) pink floral cotton fabric for the binding
- 260- x 290-cm (102- x 114-in.) piece of white cotton fabric, or the equivalent seamed, for the backing
- 260- x 290-cm (102- x 114-in.) piece of 70-g (2-oz) polyester wadding
- Matching thread

■ Cut the fabrics for the frames into 7.5-cm (3-in.) strips across the width of the fabric, then cut these strips into lengths 13–20 cm (5–8 in.) long. Piece about half of them end to end at random. Press the seams in the same direction and stitch to the block edges, one side after another, trimming to length as you go. Press the seams away from the blocks.

■ Lay the blocks out in sequence and join into four vertical strips. Press the seams in alternate directions from block to block. Join the strips and press all the vertical seams in the same direction across the quilt.

■ Piece more frame strips together, press and join to the outer edges of the quilt top, framing it twice. Press the seams away from the centre of the quilt.

■ Cut the fabric for the borders into 28-cm (11-in.) strips 6.5–9 cm (2½–3½ in.) wide. Piece all the border strips together long edge to long edge, at random, and press the seams in the same direction. Sew to the quilt top, mitring the corners (see page 171).

■ Piece the remainder of the frame strips and frame the entire quilt top again. Piece the remainder of the border strips to the top edge of the quilt only. Finally, frame the entire quilt again.

■ Lay the backing wrong side up with the wadding on top. Lay the quilt top right side up on the wadding and backing, and tack through all three layers vertically, horizontally and diagonally (see page 157).

■ Machine or hand-quilt about 6 mm (¼ in.) from the

block motifs, following the contours (see page 159). Now quilt the frames around the blocks, starting in the centre of the quilt and working outwards. My quilt lines are on the long edges of the frame fabrics. Then quilt between the blocks. Finally, quilt the seams on the border and the outer frames. Remove the tacking thread carefully – it may be caught by machine quilting stitches.

■ Trim away the excess wadding and backing.

■ Cut the binding fabric into nine 6-cm (2½-in.) strips across the width of the fabric, join together to make a continuous length and press the seams. Fold over one long edge by about 1 cm (½ in.) and press. Bind from the back (see page 172), padding with strips of wadding as you go.

Butterfly and tulip quilt

This 18-block quilt with appliqué borders uses the tulip, butterfly and dragonfly motifs. Two patchwork corners in Diamond Squares add extra interest. The quilt is worked on a white cotton ground, with Liberty lawn appliqué, and machine quilted.

Size of quilt: 120 x 197 cm (47 x 77 in.)
Size of each finished block: 25.5 cm
(10 in.) square
Width of border: 15 cm (6 in.)
6 mm (¼ in.) seam allowance throughout

■ First, cut the background fabric for the top and bottom borders from the width of white cotton fabric to 22 x 84 cm (8½ x 33 in.) and the side borders from the remaining length to 22 x 177 cm (8½ x 70 in.). Then cut eighteen 19-cm (7-in.) squares. (All these backing fabrics will be trimmed to size and shape once appliquéd and pressed.)

You will need

- 2.25 m (2½ yd) white cotton for background
- 10 cm (4 in.) floral lawns, in six fabrics, two tones of green, cream sprig and apricot for the appliqué and Diamond Squares corners
- 30 cm (12 in.) of fabric A for the block frames, 38 cm (15 in.) of fabrics B and C and 70 cm (28 in.) fabric D for the block and outer frames
- 40 cm (16 in.) dark apricot lawn for the binding
- 140- x 217-cm (55- x 85-in.) piece of white cotton fabric or the equivalent seamed, for backing
- 140- x 217-cm (55- x 85-in.) piece of 70-g (2-oz) polyester batting
- Matching thread

■ Referring to the appliqué block section (see pages 64–65), draft and appliqué 18 blocks with tulip and butterfly motifs. (The number of motifs and choice of fabric is random.) Press from the back and trim to 16.5 cm (6½ in.) square.

■ Cut frame strips across the width of the fabric, 6.5 cm (2½ in.) deep. From fabrics A and D cut four strips each; from fabrics B and C cut five strips each.

■ Frame the blocks – four each with fabrics A and D and five each with fabrics B and C – stitching the sides first and then the top and bottom. Press the seams away from the blocks.

■ Lay the blocks out in sequence and piece three vertical strips of six blocks each. Press the seams in alternate directions on each strip. Join the strips and press all the vertical seams in the same direction across the quilt.

■ Cut and pin motifs on the border strips. (You will need twelve tulips, about sixteen leaves, six butterflies and six dragonflies.) On the top and bottom borders draw in chalk or in pencil two tulip stems curving away from each other about 30 cm (12 in.) long, centred. Draw two pairs of stems on each of the side borders roughly 15 cm (6 in.) and 50 cm (20 in.) in from the left edges. Press the border strips and trim to 16.5 x 173 cm (6½ x 68 in.) and 16.5 x 80 cm (6½ x 31½ in.).

■ Referring to the Diamond squares border (see page 60), draft and make two 15-cm (6-in.) blocks. Join one to the top of one side border and one to the bottom of the other border.

■ Join the top and bottom borders to the quilt top and press the seams outwards. Then attach the side borders.

■ Cut six outer frame strips 6.5 cm (2½ in.) wide across the width of fabric D, join together in one continuous strip and press. Attach to the top and bottom of the quilt top, snipping off the excess, and then to the sides.

■ Lay the wadding on the backing fabric and then centre the quilt top on top. The backing and wadding should be larger all round than the quilt top; the excess will be trimmed off once the piece has been quilted. Tack through all three layers vertically, horizontally and diagonally (see page 157). Machine or hand-quilt about 6 mm (¼ in.) from the block motifs, following the contours (see page 159).

■ Now quilt the frames, starting in the centre of the quilt and working outwards. My quilt lines are on the very edge of each frame fabric. Then quilt between the blocks.

■ Finally quilt around the border motifs, the border edge and the outer frame.

■ Remove the tacking thread carefully – it may be caught by machine quilting stitches – and trim off the excess wadding and backing.

■ Cut the binding fabric across the width of the fabric into six strips 6 cm (2½ in.) wide. Join them together to make a continuous strip and press the seams. Fold over one long edge by about 1 cm (½ in.) and press. Bind from the back (see page 172), padding with strips of wadding as you go.

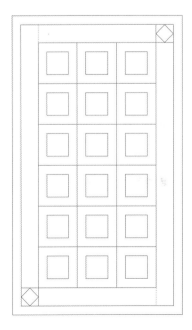

Orange Peel quilt

Hand appliquéd and quilted, this cover could be used as a cot quilt or as a throw across the width of a bed.

Size of quilt: 104 x 155 cm (41 x 61 in.)
Size of each finished block: 21 cm (8¼ in.)
Width of finished border: 16 cm (6¼ in.)
Width of finished sashing: 5 cm (2 in.)
6 mm (¼ in.) seam allowance throughout

■ Referring to the Orange Peel block (see page 88), draft and piece fifteen identical blocks from the white and the yellow patterned fabrics – each with two patches with white lozenges on yellow and two with yellow on white.

■ From the length of the plain yellow fabric, cut two border strips 19 cm (7½ in.) wide for the side borders. From the remaining width, cut two border strips 19 cm (7½ in.) wide. Next, from the remaining length cut five strips 7 cm (2¾ in.) wide for the sashing and four strips 4 cm (1½ in.) wide for the binding.

■ Lay the blocks out in sequence. Join them into three vertical strips of five blocks each, with sashing (cut from the length as required) in between, and press the seams towards the sashing. The sashing has intersection squares at each block corner. Cut ten 23-cm (9-in.) sashing lengths and eight 7-cm (2¾-in.) squares from the

remaining sashing strip and join into two alternating strips long/square/ long/square and so on. Press the seams away from the squares. Join the vertical block strips with intersecting square sashing between, and press the seams towards the sashing.

■ Add the top and bottom, and then the side, borders.

■ Lay the backing wrong side up and cover with the wadding. Lay the quilt top right side up on the wadding and backing, and tack well, in a vertical, horizontal and diagonal grid (see page 157). Press seams away from the centre of the quilt.

■ Quilt along the edge of the motifs and inside them, about 1.5 cm (½ in.) from the edge (see page 159). Quilt next to the sashing and then work the lozenges and rings. Use the appliqué template reduced to 9 cm (3½ in.) long for the lozenges. Finally, quilt the borders with 1.5-cm (½-in.) diagonal channels.

■ Fold over one long edge of each binding strip by about 1 cm (½ in.) and press. Bind from the front (see page 173), padding with strips of wadding as you go.

You will need

- 1 m (1 yd) each of white and patterned yellow fabric for patchwork
- 175 cm (69 in.) plain yellow fabric for sashing, borders and binding
- 170 cm (67 in.) cotton fabric, 115 cm (45 in.) wide, or the equivalent seamed, for the backing
- 170- x 119-cm (67- x 47-in.) piece of 70-g (2-oz.) polyester wadding
- Matching thread

TECHNIQUES

This useful section provides all the tips and advice you will need
when working by hand or machine – from choosing a fabric and
cutting motifs or patches through to setting and preparing a quilt
and finishing your work.

Fabrics

Any fabrics can be used in patchwork and appliqué, from light silks and cottons to heavy woollens. However, bear in mind that some fabrics wear faster than others, some need dry cleaning and some crease easily, which is problematic if quilted on to wadding that cannot take a hot iron. The best advice is to choose compatible fabrics, and also avoid mixing weights.

■ Fabric labels often state they have been pre-shrunk and are colourfast. If you want to test, soak a sample in very warm soapy water. When cool, wring and blot vigorously on white cotton to see if any dye transfers.

■ For quilts, 100 per cent cotton is best since it lays flat for marking, cutting and stitching, and holds a crease well. Cotton quality is measured by the number of threads to the inch. Choose either 78 square or 68 square – anything less is too loosely woven. 'Square' means there are an equal number of warp and weft threads, so the pull on these 'even weave' cottons is equal lengthways and crossways.

■ In polyester/cotton mixes, the thread count is uneven so the stretch is different, making it crease resistant. This uneven stretch can make the material pucker on seams and some poly cottons have a slight sheen (unlike most cottons), so mixing them with other fabrics can make a quilt look uneven.

■ Grain lines should be uniform across a quilt. To find the grain of a fabric, fold it and hold and stretch by the selvedges. If there are no ripples you have found the grain. If a fabric has been printed slightly off grain and the design is small or random, follow the true grain. If the pattern has an obvious repeat, then visually it is best to follow the design rather than the grain, but a big discrepancy will make piecing more difficult as the fabric will stretch.

Quilt preparation

Before your design can be quilted, it should be backed and padded. Back quilts with one of the fabrics used on the top, or seam pure cotton lengths to the desired width. Avoid poly cotton sheeting because it will stretch, gather or pucker. The layer of padding that lies between the quilt top and the backing is called wadding.

■ Synthetic wadding is light, springy, easy to stitch and washes well. It comes in different weights, known as lofts – 2 oz, 4 oz, 6 oz and upwards – and in pale or dark colours.

■ Most modern cotton wadding has been prepared to hold together well. It will have been bleached, pre-shrunk and had the seeds removed, so its texture is as uniform as that of a synthetic wadding. To achieve the wrinkled look of an old quilt, choose a cotton wadding that has been carded and bleached but not pre-shrunk. Wash the quilt when completed to shrink the wadding inside the quilt.

■ Silk wadding is costly but warm and easy to work. It needs close quilting to keep it in place.

■ Natural waddings need to be quilted at intervals of 1–3 cm (½–1¼ in.). A cotton/synthetic mix can be quilted at 5–10 cm (2–4 in.) intervals, and synthetics will stay put with much larger unquilted areas. Wadding fibres may eventually work their way through quilt tops and backings unless you use tight even-weave cottons for the top and backing.

■ The backing fabric and wadding should extend at least 10 cm (4 in.) beyond the edges of a quilt top to allow for the shrinkage that occurs during quilting. If you need to join backing fabric, it is better to make two joins that fall roughly along each side of the bed rather than down the centre.

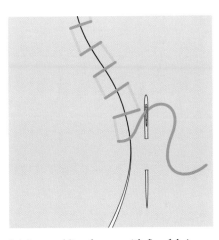
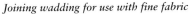

Joining wadding for use with fine fabric

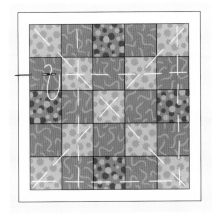

Tacking a grid through all three layers

■ To join wadding so that no ridge shows through, lay the two pieces edge to edge and ladder stitch them together. If the fabric is especially fine, overlap the two pieces by about 10 cm (4 in.) and cut a curved line along the length. Remove the excess, butt the two pieces together and ladder stitch, using matching thread to avoid show-through. Stitch across the gap, down 1 cm (½ in.) and back to the other side. Keep the stitching loose or the wadding may buckle.

■ Lay the backing fabric wrong side up on a flat surface and anchor it in place with tape or weights. Lay the wadding over it, then place the quilt top on it, right side up. Tack a grid, about 30 cm (12 in.) square, and also a cross diagonally through the centre. Use fine white tacking thread and milliner's needles to make long stitches. You could also use large safety pins, evenly spaced about every 30 cm (12 in.), or a tacking gun, which pierces the layers with plastic tabs. Long straight pins with glass heads are useful if you are working on a small area, but may come out when you are quilting a large area.

Quilting

Quilting can be done by hand or using a sewing machine. For hand quilting, use a large hoop or quilting frame because, although you can work without either of these, this risks layers becoming dislodged, even when they are well tacked. Machine quilting is much faster than hand quilting and, at its simplest, is just as unobtrusive a way of keeping the layers of a quilt together. It can also be highly decorative and intricate.

Hand quilting

For a traditional look, use white or cream thread throughout, even when quilting across dark fabrics. Alternatively, match the fabric colour or use a contrasting thread. You can reflect any patchwork or appliqué design you are using by stitching along seams

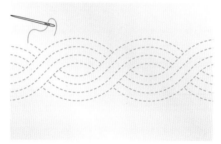

Rope design

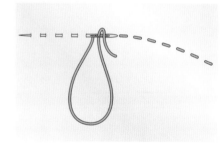

Four stitches at a time

('stitch in the ditch' quilting) or outlining motifs with stitched lines about 6 mm (¼ in.) apart ('echo' quilting). Otherwise, a diamond grid all over the quilt, diagonal or curved channels about 3 cm (1¼ in.) apart (see Orange Peel page 88), or complex plume, flower, chain or rope designs can be used.

■ To mark the design on the quilt top, use a quilter's pencil for a fine silvery line, chalk, or a pen that has 'disappearing' ink. These marks will vanish either with time or water – check that the marks stay long enough for your purposes, and that they really do disappear, on a piece of spare fabric before drawing on the quilt top. Simple curves and straight lines can be scored on the fabric with a tapestry needle. For complex patterns, either make your own templates or buy plastic ones with pattern perforations. Work on small areas and mark only as much as you need each time.

■ If you are using a hoop, start in the centre and work outwards. If you have a full-sized quilt frame, start at one end of the quilt and work your way across it.

■ Use the smallest 'sharps' needle you can manage for small and evenly spaced stitches. Quilting thread is a little sturdier than sewing thread. You can run ordinary thread though beeswax to toughen it. Use lengths of 45 cm (18 in.) at the most because the thread wears and frays at the needle's eye.

■ To start, pull the thread through the backing to the front, having tied a small knot in the end. Tug it a little so that the knot lodges in the wadding – do the same to secure at the finish. If the quilting design is large or complex, use several needles, working as far as you can reach with each one before moving the work in the hoop or frame. The running stitches should be as tiny and even as possible – about six stitches to 3 cm (1¼ in.). If the wadding is plump or the fabrics heavy, stab the needle straight down, pull the thread through, then stab stitch straight up. On lighter weight fabrics, rock the needle up and down, gathering about four stitches on the needle before pulling the thread through. A thimble on the finger underneath is essential to guide the needle point back to the quilt top.

Machine quilting

Prepare and tack your blocks carefully because the quilt top will be rolled and re-rolled, and squeezed through the sewing machine. Match the thread colour to the quilt top, or if you want the stitching to be visible, use a slightly darker or paler thread – too much contrast and the line becomes very prominent. If you need to mark quilting lines, use a quilter's pencil, as for hand quilting.

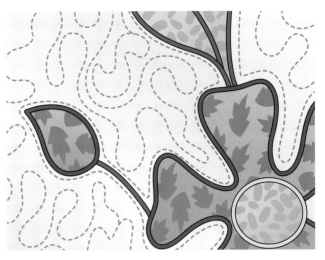

Vermicelli

■ Under the machine foot is a ridged area with sharp, pointed peaks. The foot presses the work towards these 'feed dogs' and, as they rise and fall, they pull the work along while the needle stitches. This is a problem when quilting because the wadding resists the pressure, so the lower layer of the 'quilt sandwich' moves along faster than the top and puckers. Some machines have plates to cover the feed dogs, or they can be lowered, while some have variable pressure settings.

■ A 'walking foot' locks into the feed dogs to hold the layers tight and keep them moving at the same speed. However, it is only really useful for stitching straight lines, not curves. A 'free-embroidery foot' with the machine set on 'darning' allows you to stitch in any direction. This foot generally has a small ring that the needle passes through, and the trunk of the foot is springy, so you can stitch through thick layers without downward pressure. You have to push and pull the work manually as you stitch – it will not move along otherwise. Place your hands flat on the work, either side of the needle. If working on very small areas, a 20 cm (8 in.) hoop will hold the work taut and flat and you can push the hoop without the danger of your hands getting too close to the needle. Be careful not to tug at the work because, if the needle is pulled, it may bend enough to miss the hole in the needle plate and snap.

■ Roll the quilt top from one side towards the centre so it fits under the machine. Always start quilting in the middle of the work and move outwards to the edges. To start, stitch a few reverse stitches. Do the same to finish or, for a neater look, draw the threads to the back and

thread through the fabric with a needle. You may need to slacken the tension of the top thread.

■ If the quilt has continuous lines, start at the top, work downwards and then move to the right to continue. When you have reached the right-hand edge, re-roll the quilt, and work from bottom upwards, again starting from the centre. Work methodically, and never leave unquilted islands in heavily quilted areas because these isolated patches will puff up while the surrounding area becomes tightened with the quilting and will never lie flat.

■ If you have pressed the seams open, you can quilt right in the seam. Use a ballpoint needle so as not to split the seam stitches. The quilting will not show at all as the stitching will disappear between the joined fabrics. If the seams have been pressed to one side, you can 'stitch in the ditch', right next to the seam. To give greater strength, stitch on the seam allowance.

■ On appliqué work it is essential to use an embroidery foot so you can manoeuvre around shapes. Quilt either right next to the edge of the motif or outline it by stitching about 6 mm (¼ in.) away – called 'outline' quilting. 'Vermicelli', or meandering, can be used to give texture to a background. First outline the motif, then stitch random curves and loops. As you are pushing and pulling the work yourself, you can even draw shapes or letters with the thread.

Patchwork techniques

Patchwork quilts can be put together in two main ways – with blocks or with 'all-over', or mosaic, designs. The blocks, which comprise pieced squares of patchwork, are stitched together across a quilt top, either edge to edge, alternating with plain blocks or separated from each other with sashing strips (see page 170). All-over designs have one or more geometric shapes – hexagons, for instance – pieced together without any separation or sashing. Block patchwork can be worked by hand or machine, while all-over patchwork is traditionally worked by hand over papers.

Block patchwork

Blocks can be drafted in any size, although it can be fiddly working in sizes that are much smaller than those described in the block section. When your block is complete, it will be 1.2 cm (½ in.) larger than your paper draft because it will have a 6 mm (¼ in.) seam allowance along all four edges.

■ On graph paper, draw a square the size of the finished block. In the square, mark out the grid (four-patch, five-patch or whatever you wish) and divide it into individual patches, marking the grain lines. These should run parallel with the sides of the block (fans and the eight-point star are exceptions), so when piecing two patches together, the grain matches – if it doesn't, the edge of one patch will stretch more than the edge of the other and the two won't fit together. Most blocks have repeating patches, so draft only the dark-coloured section on the block diagrams, and make templates for each different size and direction shape – for example, Odd Fellow's Chain needs just one triangle and one square template whereas Old Maid's Puzzle needs two different-sized triangles and one square template.

■ Draw a sketch of the entire block with grain lines and fabric choices marked to keep as reference because it's very easy to get in a muddle – if you put the work away for any length of time, it's easy to forget the piecing sequence entirely.

■ Cut out the graph paper templates and glue them to cardboard. Add a seam allowance of 6 mm (¼ in.) all around each shape and cut out the finished templates. Make sure there is a grain line on each template.

Cutting

Selvedges stretch less than the body of the fabric because the thread count is double, so always trim them off. Cutting accurately is important – a minor discrepancy will multiply itself across a quilt.

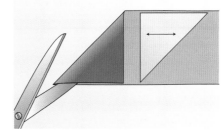

Grain along a short side

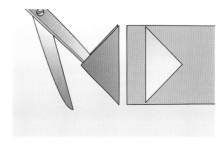

Grain along the long edge

■ Draw around the templates lightly in pencil on the wrong side of the fabric and scissor cut just a couple of thicknesses at a time. You can cut through several layers at a time with a rotary cutter. A non-slip design board is useful for keeping cut pieces in sequence. A piece of cardboard 10 cm (4 in.) larger than the block and covered with cotton wadding, felt or towelling is ideal.

■ There is a quick way to cut several same-size triangles from the same fabric. For triangles with the grain along a short side, use the template to cut strips the width of a short side, fold the strip diagonally and cut along the fold. For those with the grain running along the long edge, cut strips the width of the long side, fold the strip diagonally into quarters and cut along the fold lines. Check the block instructions to see if shapes need to be identical or mirror image – 'quick cut' triangles will be mirror image. The method is not suitable if the fabric has a directional pattern or noticeable weave direction, or is striped.

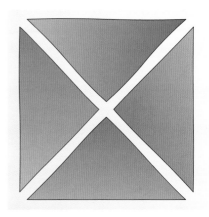

Quick-cut triangles

Piecing and pressing

Use thread matching the darker fabric and take a 6 mm (¼ in.) seam allowance.

■ **Hand piecing** Secure the start and finish with a few overstitches – knots can come undone or show through as bumps. Work about five running stitches then a backstitch before another set of running stitches. The backstitches stop the running stitches from gathering, and also, should the thread break, keep the seam secure.

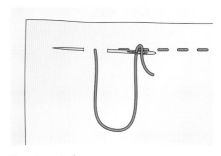

Running stitch

■ **Machine piecing** Patches can be joined one at a time using reverse stitching at the start and finish, but it is much faster to 'chain piece' and just as secure if you use a very small stitch (15 to the inch). Piece two pieces together and stitch right on to the next pair and so on. Snip the thread between the banner of patches to separate them.

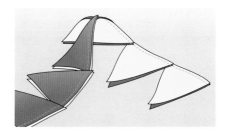

Banner of patches

■ Press the seams on each block as you go along, towards the darkest fabric, away from central squares. When piecing patches together, alternate up and down on the horizontal seams, so on one strip they lie one way and on the next strip they lie the other way. Then press vertical seams in the same direction across the block and across the quilt top. It is sometimes impossible to follow all the rules but the aim is to avoid bulk at the seams and, whenever possible, to avoid show-through of dark colours. If there is show-through, trim away the dark fabric on the seams and on the corners.

■ If you are going to hand quilt, avoiding bulk is even more important and it may be best to open seams out. This puts more strain on the seams but it will be compensated for by the quilting.

■ While you work, gently run your finger along a fold before joining to the next piece. Fabric stretches more along the bias than along the grain, so be very careful when pressing diagonals not to pull and distort the pieces. If you decide to iron each patch as you go, use pressure rather than push. Set a crease using steam and let the fabric cool before moving it because it can stretch when hot. Ironing through a layer of cloth on to a well-padded board will minimize the risk of the seam layers imprinting onto the right side of the work. Iron well once the block is finished, and again press rather than push.

■ When piecing two strips together, pin either side of the horizontal seams with the pin heads outwards, so they are easy to remove as you stitch towards them. The seams will sit well together, one slotting into the dip of the other, as long as the horizontal seams are pressed in different directions. If they don't fit exactly, tug them a little so they do. If you have pressed the seams open, put a pin right through the horizontal seams to keep them level.

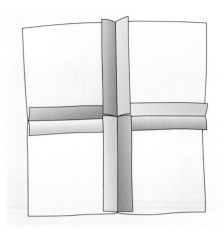

Pressing seams open

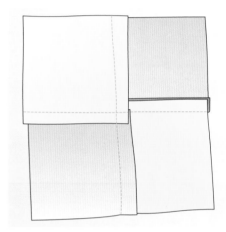

Pressing seams in alternate directions

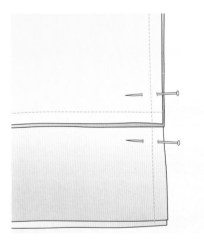

Piecing strips

Assembling a block

Some blocks, such as Ohio Star, are pieced in equal-width, vertical strips while others are pieced in square (Bear Paw) or triangular (Lady of the Lake) units before assembly. Follow the directions given for each block.

■ Place the patches in sequence on a non-slip board. Piece and press the smallest shapes first.

■ Piece these patches into strips, pressing seams in alternate directions.

■ Piece the vertical strips, pinning either side of the cross seams to keep the intersection true. Press the seams in the same direction across the block.

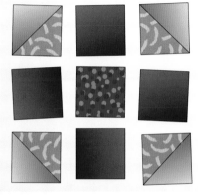
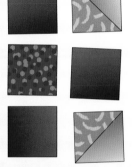

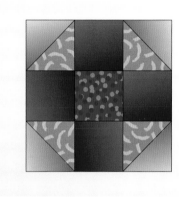

Assemble the patches in sequence   *Joining in strips*   *Block assembled*

Foundation blocks

These are generally worked from the centre outwards, with strips pieced one by one around the edges of a central square onto a backing fabric. Log Cabin is a good example, but for a more random use of odd-shaped snippets of fabric, Crazy Patchwork is hard to beat.

Crazy patchwork

Size of finished block: 33 cm (13 in.) square

■ The first piece pinned to the backing and worked around on this block was the four-sided dark turquoise shape in the centre. This was framed with strips, and then further strips were added at odd angles. It is sometimes easiest to piece a couple of snippets together and stitch these in place. Always work from the centre of the block outwards. Press and trim to shape.

Blocks with curves

These may look daunting but are not difficult. Make templates for a square with a cut-out curve and for a quarter circle, adding a seam allowance of 6 mm (¼ in.) along every edge. The cut-out curve in the square will appear too small for the quarter circle curve due to the seam allowance. If there are several curves on a block, you will need to make several templates in the relevant sizes. Always work the smallest first.

■ Fold each square and quarter circle in half and crease mid curve as a matching guide. Place a quarter circle on a square, right sides together, and pin where the creases match on the curve. Fold over and pull the straight edges at each the end of the curve so that they are level. Turn the work over, because it is easier to stitch the stretchy concave curve to the quarter-circle curve, and pin with the pin heads outwards so you can remove them easily as you go.

■ As you stitch, tug gently at the top fabric to keep the fabric edges level and make the curves fit. Press, gently ironing the quarter circle flat. If necessary, nudge the curve into shape with the tip of the iron from the front.

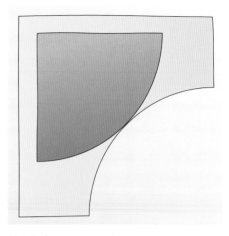

Match the creases on the curves

Pin before you stitch

All-over designs

The technique for joining geometrical shapes into a mosaic pattern is called paper piecing. Each patch is folded over a paper template and then the patches are joined edge to edge. The method is slow and painstaking, both in preparation and making-up time, but any all-over mosaic design can be worked in this way, and the shapes can vary from squares and triangles to diamonds, octagons and hexagons, as in this example.

■ Draft the template (see page 160). Cut an equal number of lightweight paper hexagons (without seam allowance added), enough to make up the finished quilt, and the same number of fabric pieces, adding a 6 mm (¼ in.) turning allowance. Two edges should be aligned on the straight grain. Pin the papers to the back of the patches, fold the edges over and tack. The securing knot should be on the right side to make it easier to remove.

■ Place two hexagons right sides together and overstitch along one edge, right on the fold line. The stitches should be tiny, the thread matching the darker fabric. Place a third hexagon face to face on one of the joined hexagons and stitch from the centre out. Pinch together to bring the next edges level and stitch. Any tenting will disappear once the rosette is complete.

■ Join the rosettes together to make the entire quilt top, press flat, then remove the tacking stitches – the papers will come away easily.

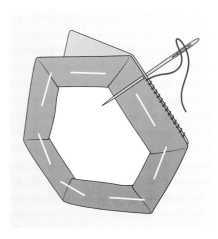

Overstitch two shapes together along one straight side

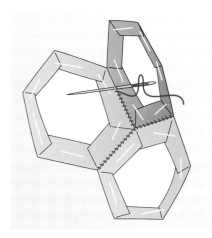

Join a third shape, starting at the centre

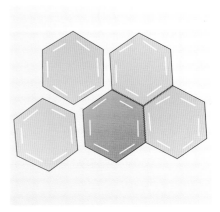

Continue joining shapes until the rosette is complete

Appliqué

Appliqué is the stitching of one fabric to another. Snippets of expensive cloth can go a long way when attached to a less expensive background fabric. The background should be the same weight or heavier than the appliqué to avoid the fabric tearing or the stitching wearing.

Hand appliqué

The grain line should run along the line of symmetry of a motif, to give equal stretch around it. Match the grain of the motif to that of the background fabric if the motif is large, so that if the finished work is stretched, the motif will stretch as much as the background and there won't be any extra strain put on the stitching or fabrics. If the motifs are tiny, discrepancy of stretch will be minimal.

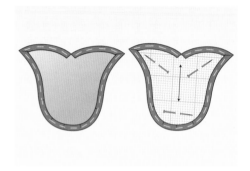

Use a paper template for a crisp edge

■ Trace or enlarge a motif on paper and mark the grain line. Cut out, adding a 6 mm (¼ in.) turning allowance along every edge. Stick the paper shape to thin card (or place on sandpaper, which won't slip). On the wrong side of the motif fabric, draw around the template lightly, using a pencil, chalk or a quilter's pen, and then cut out the motif.

■ Fold the turning allowance to the back and tack, making sure the securing knot is on the right side of the fabric, so the thread is easy to remove later. Snip into acute angles. On points, first fold the point in, then fold the two sides inwards.

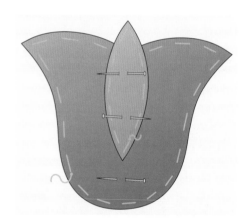

Pinning and tacking

■ For really crisp edges, cut another paper template without the seam allowance and pin it to the wrong side of the fabric motif (which has the allowance). Fold the turning allowance over the paper template and tack the edges. Press on the wrong side and remove the tacking and paper.

■ Pin or tack the motif, or layers of motifs, to the background fabric. On intricate shapes, such as Hawaiian appliqué, pin or tack the motif firmly to the background – not around the edges of the shape but through the middle. Fold the turning allowance in with the point of the needle as you stitch, snipping into angles as you reach them.

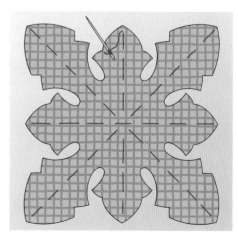

Tacking Hawaiian appliqué

Stitching

If motifs overlap, stitch the one closest to the background fabric first, starting and finishing under an overlap for neatness. Secure with overstitching rather than a knot, which could make a bump or come undone. Slipstitch hardly shows but if the piece is going to have a lot of wear – children's clothes, for example – Paris stitch is far more secure. You can pad motifs with a little wadding as you go.

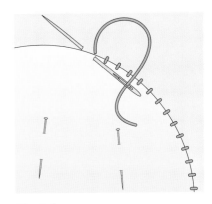

Slipstitch

■ **Slipstitch** should be worked in small, regular stitches – close to invisible. Match the thread to the darkest colour in the appliqué fabric and use the smallest 'sharps' needle you can work with – short with a tiny eye. Start stitching on a straight or smooth part of the motif, not a point or corner, and work anticlockwise with the motif towards you. Pick up 3 mm (⅛ in.) of motif fabric along the fold, insert the needle into the background fabric and pick up 3 mm (⅛ in.) parallel to the edge of the motif. Make extra stitches on points to secure well and finish with a few overstitches.

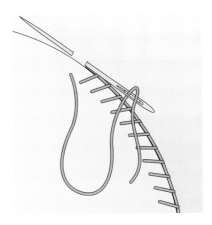

Paris stitch 1

■ **Paris stitch** is very strong. Although worked over the motif and not along the turning-allowance fold, if the stitches are kept small and regularly spaced and are in thread matching the appliqué, they should not be too noticeable. Working anticlockwise with the motif towards you, bring the needle through to the front of the motif, 3 mm (⅛ in.) from its edge. Insert the needle into the backing 3 mm (⅛ in.) diagonally right, and travel the needle horizontally left to reappear above the motif. Backstitch and travel diagonally down and left to reappear through the motif, 3 mm (⅛ in.) from its edge.

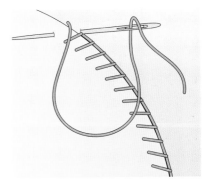

Paris stitch 2

■ **Blanket stitch** is a decorative stitch worked in contrasting colour thread. Stranded embroidery silks are a good choice. Use crewel needles, which have long eyes. Working anticlockwise, with the motif away from you, bring the needle through the background fabric just next to the motif. Insert the needle through the motif, diagonally up and right, and up to 6 mm (¼ in.) away. Travel the needle vertically down and through the background, just next to the motif, looping the thread around the needle as shown.

Blanket stitch

■ **Detail running stitching** is quick to do. Gather about four running stitches on a needle before pulling the thread through.

■ **Stem stitch** gives a solid stitched line. Working from left to right, insert the needle from the front to the back 6 mm (¼ in.) right. Travel the needle left and reappear 3 mm (⅛ in.) right of where you first started. Repeat, always keeping the thread below the line of stitching.

■ **Chain stitch** is very decorative and about 3 mm (⅛ in.) wide. Working from right to left, take a 6 mm (¼ in.) stitch and loop the thread around the needle before pulling through. Reinsert the needle in the same hole and take another 6 mm (¼ in.) stitch.

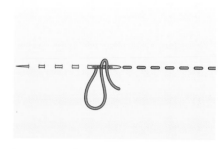

Running stitch

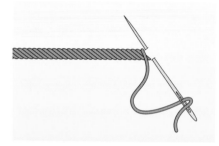

Stem stitch

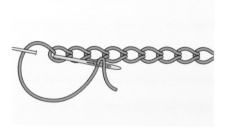

Chain stitch

The grapes here are detailed with stem stitch

Machine appliqué

Just as with hand appliqué, the grain of the motif and background should match if the motif is large. Both hand and machine appliqué can distort the background fabric, so always cut the background about 10 per cent larger than required and trim to size once stitched and pressed. Press finished work from the back on a padded surface.

■ Make the template as for hand appliqué but without the turning allowance – the satin stitch will cover the edge of the fabric and stop it from fraying.

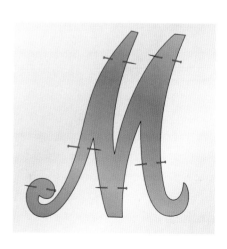

Pinning motif to the background

■ If you want to use loose-weave or stretchy fabrics, or material that frays easily, iron fusible web or interfacing to the back of the fabric before cutting out the motif. However, bear in mind that even the lightest weight interfacing can make flimsy material look flat and a little papery and, eventually, the glues will discolour the fabric.

■ Pin or tack the motif on to the background fabric, with the pins across the line of stitching to make them easy to remove as you go. If the design has several layers, pin them all at the start.

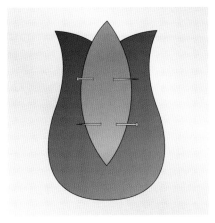

Pinning two layers to the background

Stitching

As the satin stitch is visible and outlines the motif, choose thread in colours either matching or slightly darker than the fabric – on patterned fabric you could vary the thread colour from one motif to another.

Use the same brand and weight of thread for the top of the machine and the bobbin. If your machine doesn't auto-select thread tension, you may need to loosen the tension of the top thread a little to avoid the bobbin thread being pulled to the front. If the background fabric is pale or see through, use a pale bobbin thread. Otherwise match the topstitch colour.

■ Set the machine to a close satin stitch, width 3 or 4, and stitch clockwise around the motif, right along the edge. The motif will be to the left of the needle. Start on an inside curve or point, lay the top thread along the line to be stitched and stitch over it for about 3 cm (1¼ in.) to conceal and secure it, then trim it close.

■ Turn the work gently as you stitch to manoeuvre around curves. When you reach a point or deep curve, keep the needle in the fabric, lift the presser foot and turn the work around the needle. Lower the foot and continue.

■ At the end, draw the threads to the back, tie them together and trim the ends close. If there is a risk of show-through, draw the threads to the back and, using a needle, pass them through the satin-stitch channel. Then trim the ends close.

■ If the design has overlapping motifs, stitch the one closest to the background fabric first, starting and finishing just under an overlap. If there is no risk of show-through, draw the threads to the front, trim and tuck them under the next layer.

■ On a design such as leaves on a satin-stitch stem, stitch the leaves first, then the stem. Just covering the leaf tips will keep the top threads secure and the bobbin threads can be trimmed later. You could draw the leaf threads to the front and conceal them under the stem.

■ Narrow the stitch width to make points. Always add detail last, once the motif has been stitched in place, and, again, narrow the stitch width.

Satin stitch is used here for the leaves and stem

Sashing and borders

Blocks can be joined edge to edge or alternated with plain ones, or sashing – strips of another fabric – can be inserted between them. Adding differently patterned squares at junctions can add interest to a simple design. Press seams towards the sashing.

■ **Plain sashing** Join blocks together in vertical strips, using sashing between each block. Then stitch a length of sashing to one vertical edge and piece a second vertical block strip to it. The four-patch sampler quilt on page 116 is a good example.

■ **Intersecting squares** Cut sashing strips the same lengths as the blocks, and make some small squares, equal in width to the sashing strips but in differently patterned fabric. Join blocks together in vertical strips,

using sashing between each block. Piece sashing strips to the squares to make a long strip, and stitch this to one vertical edge of a strip of blocks. Then piece a second vertical strip of blocks to the sashing strip.

■ **Tiny squares** As a variation, sashing strips can be made of tiny squares, as in Counting Fish, or of a border design, such as Sawtooth or Flying Geese. Make lengths of sashing from squares, or based on a border strip, and join as for plain sashing.

Borders

Frame a quilt top or hanging by giving it a border before binding. The border can be a patchwork or appliqué strip, or simply a narrow length of material around the quilt top in the same, or contrasting, fabric as the sashing. Cut the border fabric into strips across the fabric width, and make one long strip by stitching them together, end to end, and pressing the seams all in the same direction. Cut lengths as needed.

Lapped border

■ Cut two border strips the same length as the quilt top. With right sides together, pin the strips to two opposite edges of the work and stitch them 6 mm (¼ in.) from the edge. Flap back the strips and press flat. Cut two more border strips that measure the length of the remaining sides of the quilt plus the attached border strips. Pin, stitch and flap back as before, and press flat.

■ Using contrasting fabric on the corners, like intersecting squares on sashing, adds interest. To do this, stitch border

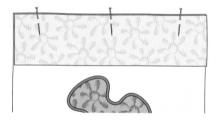

Pin the border strip to the work

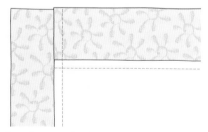

Cut the side strips the length of the sides plus the borders

strips along top and bottom edges and press, as before. Cut two more border strips the length of the sides and add squares at each end, so that the whole of each strip is equal in length to the work plus the already attached borders. Then piece these strips to the two remaining edges.

Mitred corners

■ These are fiddlier to work but give a neat appearance to a quilt top, like a picture frame. Cut a border strip for the top edge, so that it extends by a length equal to its width at both ends. Do this for all four sides. Then, right sides together, pin the first strip to the top of the quilt, top edges aligning. Fold the strip ends down at a 45° angle and cut along the fold.

■ Stitch the border strip to the quilt top, starting and stopping 6 mm (¼ in.) from each end and flap back so that the right side is now uppermost. Then pin a border strip to the side of the quilt. This should reach the top edge of the top strip.

■ Stitch this in place, starting and stopping 6 mm (¼ in.) from the end of the quilt so as not to stitch over the already attached border. Fold the strip end down at a 45° angle and cut along the fold.

■ Do not flap back the side border but align the diagonals, right sides together – which will entail folding in the top strip – pin and stitch from the quilt to the outside corner.

■ Flap back, press open the seam and press the borders flat.

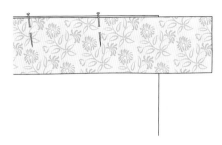

Mitred corners 1

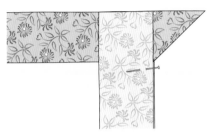

Mitred corners 2

Mitred corners 3

Mitred corners 4

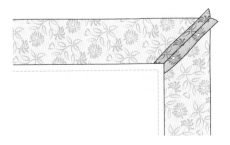

Mitred corners 5

Binding a quilt

Binding strips can be cut on the straight grain of the fabric or on the bias. They can be attached to the back of the work, folded over and machine topstitched on the front, or attached to the front of the work, folded over and hand stitched on the back. Bias strips allow you to bind around the corners of a quilt because they stretch; otherwise you need to bind one edge at a time. Alternatively, you can 'self bind' either by folding the backing fabric to the front and topstitching, or folding the quilt top to the back of the quilt and hand stitching in place.

Binding from the back

■ Cut the fabric for the binding into straight-cut strips about 6 cm (2½ in.) wide and join into one length. Fold under and press 1 cm (½ in.) along one long edge.

■ Pin the raw edge of the right side of the binding to the back of the quilt and then stitch 1 cm (½ in.) from the edge. Snip off the excess binding. Fold the other (folded) edge of the binding over to the front of the quilt, pin and topstitch, adding a little of the wadding remnants as you go.

■ Working clockwise around the quilt, pin and stitch the next length of binding in place, leaving about 1.5 cm (½ in.) extra at the start to be folded in and secured by hand later. On the last side, leave extra at both the start and the finish for turnings.

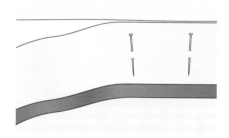

Binding from the back 1

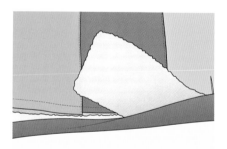

Binding from the back 2

Binding from the front

■ With right sides together, pin and stitch the raw edge of the straight-cut binding along one side of the quilt. Snip off the excess binding. Fold the folded edge of the binding over to the back of the quilt, pin and hem, adding wadding if desired.

■ Working clockwise around the quilt, pin and stitch the next length of binding, leaving about 1.5 cm (½ in.) extra at the start to be folded in and secured by hand later, when you hand stitch the back. On the last side, leave extra at both the start and the finish for turnings.

■ **Bias-cut binding** If you are using bias-cut binding strips, cut the strips diagonally across the fabric and sew them together along their diagonal edges – the strips will be at right angles as you stitch. Make a continuous strip long enough to bind the entire quilt.

Self binding

■ Trim the backing fabric of the quilt to within 5 cm (2 in.) of the quilt top, and the wadding to about 2.5 cm (1 in.) of the quilt top. Position the layers (see below), then fold the backing fabric to the front of the quilt on opposite edges, folding under by 1 cm (½ in.). Hem by hand or machine topstitch. Fold over and stitch the remaining two edges as before, and hand stitch the corners to neaten. To self bind from the front, fold the quilt top over to the back of the work and hand stitch.

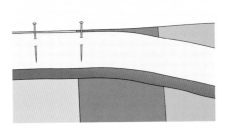

Binding from the front 1

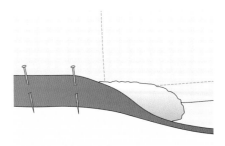

Binding from the front 2

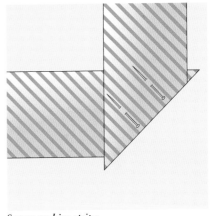

Seams on bias strips

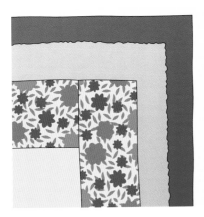

Lay the quilt top on the wadding and backing

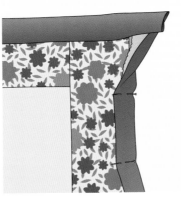

Fold the backing and wadding to the front, pin and stitch

Neaten corners by hand

Suppliers

Butterfly Quilters
Marvic House
Kilkhampton
Bude
Cornwall
EX23 9RF
Tel: 01288 321480
Web: www.butterflyquilters.co.uk

The Cotton Patch
1283-1285 Stratford Road
Hall Green
Birmingham
B28 9AJ
Tel: 0121 702 2840
Fax: 0121 778 5924
Web: www.cottonpatch.co.uk

Creative Quilting
32 Bridge Road
East Molesey
Surrey
KT8 9HA
Tel: 020 8941 7075
Fax: 020 8979 3381
Web: www.creativequilting.co.uk

Dreamcatcher Quilts
5a Beulah Road
Rhiwbina
Cardiff
CF14 6LT
Tel: 029 2047 3126
Web: www.dreamcatcherquilts.co.uk

Lady Sew and Sew
Moy House
57 Institute Road
Marlow
Buckinghamshire
SL7 1BN
Tel: 01628 890532/01491 575788
Fax: 01491 577585
Web: www.ladysewandsew.com

Liberty of London
Regent Street
London
W1B 5AH
Tel: 0207 734 1234
Web: www.liberty.co.uk

Midsomer Quilting
Norton Green Garden Centre
Chilcompton
Bath
BA3 4RR
Tel: 01761 239333/232509
Fax: 01761 233649
Web: www.midsomerq.com

Pauline's Patchwork
Brewers Quay
Hope Square
Weymouth
Dorset
DT4 8TR
England
Tel: 01305 766543

Patchwork Direct
Wesleyan House
Darley Dale
Derbyshire
DE4 2HX
Tel: 01629 734100
Web: www.patchworkdirect.com

The Quilting Bee
14 Enfield Road
Enfield
Middlesex
EN2 7HW
Tel: 020 8364 5237
Web: www.quiltingbee.co.uk

The Quilt Room
20 West Street
Dorking
Surrey
RH4 1BL
England
Tel: 01306 877307

Quilt Studio
Unit 26 Zan Industrial Park
Crewe Road
Wheelock
Sandbach
Cheshire
CW11 4QH
Tel: 07870 648156
Web: www.quiltstudio.co.uk

Seattle Quilt Company
First Floor
Berryden Retail Park
Berryden Road
Aberdeen
AB25 3SA
Tel: 01224 646074
Fax: 01224 644967
Web: www.seattlequiltcompany.com

Shaukat & Company,
170-172 Old Brompton Road
London
SW5 0BA
Tel: 0207 373 6927/8936
Web: www.shaukat.co.uk

Sunflower Fabrics
66 Phillpotts Avenue
Bedford
MK40 3UD
Tel: 01234 273819
Web: www.sunflowerfabrics.com

Strawberry Fayre
Dept. W
Chagford
Devon
TQ13 8EN
Tel: 01647 433250
Web: www.strawberryfayre.co.uk

Tikki Limited
293 Sandycombe Road
Kew Gardens
Greater London
Surrey
TW9 3LU
Tel: 0208 948 8462
Web: www.tikkilondon.com

Whaleys (Bradford) Ltd.
Tel: 01274 576718
Web: www.whaleys-bradford.ltd.uk

Index